CADOGAN

Dana Facaros and Michael Pauls

Granada Seville Cordoba

D1113735

Cadogan Guides
West End House, 11 Hills Place,
London W1R 1AH, UK

The Globe Pequot Press
6 Business Park Road, PO Box 833, Old Saybrook,
Connecticut 06475–0833

Book and cover design by Animage
Cover photographs by Spanish National Tourist Office
Inside back cover photograph by Catherine Charles
Maps © Cadogan Guides, drawn by RJS Associates and Map Creation Ltd

Editorial Director: Vicki Ingle
Series Editor: Linda McQueen

Editing: Linda McQueen
Indexing: Dorothy Frame
Production: Book Production Services

A catalogue record for this book is available from the British Library
ISBN 1–86011–937–9

Reprinted 1999

Printed and bound by Cambridge University Press

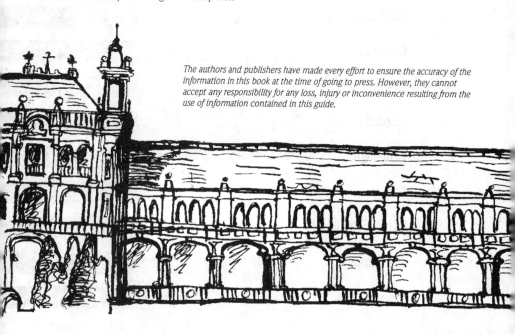

*The authors and publishers have made every effort to ensure the accuracy of the
information in this book at the time of going to press. However, they cannot
accept any responsibility for any loss, injury or inconvenience resulting from the
use of information contained in this guide.*

About the Authors

Dana Facaros and **Michael Pauls** have written over 20 books for Cadogan, including a series on Italy and another on Spain. They have lived all over Europe, but recently hung up their castanets in a shoreside cottage in southwest Ireland.

About the Updater

Alex Robinson studied religion with literature at Bristol and divinity at Cambridge. He is now a freelance travel writer, photographer and television producer based in London. He has visited 42 different countries and spent much time in Spain and Latin America.

Acknowledgements

The updater, Alex Robinson, would like to thank Alé and Alvaro in Madrid, Dr Elizabeth Robinson, Mary-Ann Gallagher and, above all, his wife Gardênia.

Please help us to keep this guide up to date

We have done our best to ensure that the information in this guide is correct at the time of going to press. But places and facilities are constantly changing, and standards and prices in hotels and restaurants fluctuate. We would be delighted and grateful to receive any comments concerning existing entries or omissions, as well as suggestions for new features.

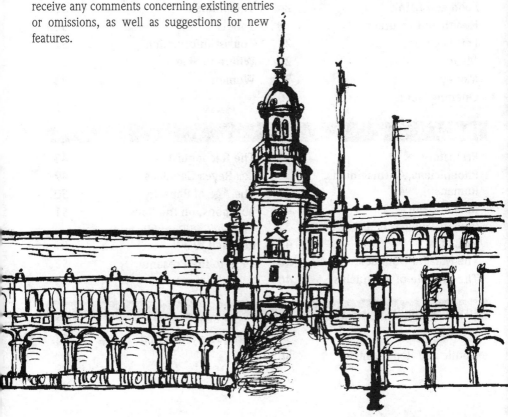

Contents

You don't often see Andalucíans going off on picnics in the country. The ground is dry, vegetation sparse, and the sun can seem like a death-ray even in winter. Climate has always forced people here to seek their pleasure elsewhere; it is the impetus behind their exquisite gardens, and it has made of them the most resolutely urban people in Europe. In city centres the air is electric, a cocktail of motion, colour, and fragrances that goes to your head like the best *manzanilla*. But the cities of the south didn't get this way overnight.

Introduction

Nearly everything that is special about modern Andalucía got its start in the charmed lost world of al-Andalus. When the Arab raiders settled in these towns after their conquest, they rather quickly went mad for gardens and poetry, for fountains and fairytales. A thousand years ago, when the Christian kings of Europe were sleeping on rushes and learning to write their names, a Caliph of Cordoba was holding court in a garden pavilion with walls made of falling water, around a reflecting pool of liquid mercury. The Moors brought the first oranges, and the first roses (both from Persia). They brought Ziryab, the Blackbird, greatest musician of his day, from Baghdad, and he added a fifth string to the local version of the lute to create the Spanish guitar—when he played it, the audience would cry 'Allah!', which their modern counterparts have turned into 'Olé!'

And as a special gift to these three cities, the Moors left each one a magic building, something unique in all the world, to serve as the city's symbol and mould its destiny through the centuries to come.

Seville got La Giralda, still the tallest tower in Spain and by far the showiest. To live up to this symbol Seville after the Moors became the capital of all the finest Spanish stereotypes: the home of roses and passion, mantillas and bulls and Flamenco. Aristocrat Seville is the compulsive exhibitionist among these three cities, and she keeps herself on permanent display even when she is not putting on another World's Fair.

Cordoba got the Great Mosque. This city is strong for *los toros* too, and all the rest of the Andalucían shibboleths, but, being home to such a magnificently subtle and philosophical monument, Cordoba has become a much more quiet and introspective city than its neighbour down the Guadalquivir. Besides the mosque, Cordoba's beauties are the flower-strewn patios hidden behind the walls of its houses. They leave the gates open so you can have just a peek.

Granada's gift was the Alhambra, by common consent the loveliest palace in the world, in the loveliest setting, underneath the snowcapped Sierra Nevada. Such a past, combined with the rather gloomy history that followed, makes Granada the most wistful and melancholy of these cities; how you see it may depend on the mood you're in when you come.

Even on a rare cloudy day, though, melancholy will never set in too deeply. You'll find that all three of these towns have thrived in the 'New Spain' of the last twenty years. And they all seem to be full of noisy, happy folk who care only to remember the fun parts of their past, while getting along with the important things of life—seafood and sherry, music and dancing. You won't be bored.

A Guide to the Guide

For many Hispanophiles with little time to spare, combining visits to two or three cities is the best option; indeed many tour operators (including those listed on pp.11–13) offer such holidays tailor-made. If you prefer to draw up your own itinerary and choose your own accommodation, the **Travel** and **Practical A–Z** chapters are packed with information to help you plan your journey, travel between cities, and select a place to stay.

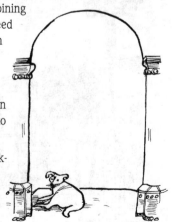

The next three chapters offer an anthropological background. **History** begins in the caves around Gibraltar, and then develops over 50,000 years to rest awhile in the pavilions of Seville. **Art and Architecture**

follows through the design of Spanish buildings. **Snapshots of Andalucía** provides a random glimpse of the region's culture in a potpourri of short essays.

The three dazzling cities of **Granada, Seville** (Sevilla) and **Cordoba** (Córdoba) are then covered in detail, each with its own background of history and art, and all the sights you might choose to visit: museums, art galleries, mosques and cathedrals, marketplaces, squares, or simply those atmoospheric streets that are a pleasure just to wander around. Each chapter follows with a practical guide to where to stay and eating out, shopping and nightlife, flamenco and tapas bars. Finally there are suggestions for day trips out of each city that can be made by car, or by local bus or train.

The book concludes with **Language** (including a helpful menu reader), a Glossary of artistic and architectural terms used in the guide, suggestions for **Further Reading** that might enlighten you, and a **Chronology.**

Geography of the Region

Andalucía covers the southern fifth of the Iberian peninsula, occupying an expanse equivalent to slightly more than half the area of Portugal. Its natural border to the north is the rugged Sierra Morena mountain chain; the wild Atlantic batters its western shores and the timid Mediterranean laps its southern coast. The Sierra Morena mountains, although reaching barely 4000ft, were for a long time a deterrent to northern invaders. The only natural interruption is the Pass of Despeñaperros, or the 'gateway to Andalucía'. Numerous early travellers spoke with awe of the first time they traversed this pine-clad gorge; the frontier that separated 'the land of men from the land of gods'. Arriving in Andalucía at this point provides a strong contrast indeed from the barren plains of La Mancha to the north. These peaks, rich in minerals, sweep down to the fertile Guadalquivir plain, widening towards the western coast to form broad salt marshes and mud flats—including the Coto Doñana National Park, one of the largest bird sanctuaries in Europe. From here, the coast as far as the Portuguese border is virtually one long sandy beach, with a hinterland of undulating farming terrain and the gentle mountains of Huelva province.

South of the Guadalquivir valley the land rises again to form the craggy, spectacular Serranía de Ronda mountain range, home to bandits and smugglers for centuries; the terrain then descends sharply to meet the balmy palm-lined shores of the Mediterranean, with Tarifa, the furthest south you can go on mainland Europe, and a mere 12km from the African coast, and Gibraltar, that geological oddity of a rock, whose outline resembles one of the sentinel lions on guard at the foot of Nelson's column. From the Serranía de Ronda the land dips and rises as it goes east till it joins the heights of the snow-capped Sierra Nevada, the highest peaks on mainland Spain, below which lie long beaches, tiny coves and crystal-clear water.

Dry as it is, Andalucía when properly tended has been the garden of Spain. The soil in most areas, *argiles de montmorillionite*, holds water like a sponge. The Romans first discovered how to irrigate it; the Moors perfected the system, and also introduced the palm and such crops as cotton, rice, oranges and sugar. Today most of the inhabitants of the region live in cities—it's traditionally one of the most urbanized regions in Europe—but its farmers have discovered the modern delights of tractors and of owning their own land. Unless the Habsburgs or the Francoists come back, the region will have no excuse for not making a good living. Between the towns, spaces seem vast and empty, endless hillsides of olives, vineyards, wheat and sunflowers. Come in the spring, when the almond trees are in blossom, the oranges turn orange and wild flowers surge up along the road-sides—the unforgettable splash of colour that characterizes cheerful Andalucía and its warm, vibrant people.

Animal Magic: Wildlife Reserves

There are over 20 important wildlife reserves in Andalucía—the coast, the wetlands behind it, the scrub deserts of Almería and the mountain slopes of the Sierra Nevada, and many of them are accessible as day trips from Granada, Seville and Cordoba. They are given different names, depending on their importance. **Reservas Naturales** are usually small sites of specific scientific interest such as lagoons or copses. **Parques Naturales** are larger and permit traditional land use within their borders. **Parques Nacionales** are of international importance with restricted access and close control of human activities.

LYNX -
LAS MARISMAS

The Coast West of Seville

Most famous and most spectacular of all is the **Coto Doñana**, on the Cadiz coast west of Seville, southern Spain's only Parque Nacional. Though the terrain may appear flat and monotonous at first sight, it consists of a range of different and distinct habitats including cork oak forest, scrubland, swamp, raised flooded areas and reedy channels filled by the Guadalquivir as it reaches the coast. These are a haven for hundreds of species of native and migratory birds including the largest population of Spanish imperial eagles in the world. These share the wetlands with pardel lynx, wild boar and 50 other species of mammals, reptiles and amphibians. Disaster struck the Doñana in 1998 when a tank holding thousands of gallons of sluice ruptured at a chemical plant near the park. Heavy metals leaked into marshes, killing thousands of animals. The clean-up operation was still going on in 1999 and as yet it is too early to assess the damage to Europe's most important wetlands.

The Sierra Nevada South of Granada

The **Sierra Nevada Parque Natural** which peaks at 3482m is famous for its alpine flowers, which include 70 endemic species and its butterflies. Spanish Ibex, rescued from the brink of extinction in the 1940s, also live here. They are seen most easily in the evening on the lower peaks. The lower slopes, known locally as '*zona erizo*' (hedgehog zone) are shrouded in prickly scrub, and below them the valleys of the Alpujarras are filled with birdsong, butterflies and semi-tropical fruits—even custard apples grow here.

Travel

Getting There from the UK and Europe

By Air

From the UK, **British Airways** operates direct services between Heathrow, Gatwick, Manchester and Birmingham, and Madrid, Malaga and Seville (only Gatwick).

The Spanish airline, **Iberia**, operates on many of the same routes, and also offers direct services from the UK to Jerez de la Frontera and Seville.

Monarch Airlines (✆ 01582 398333) flies from Luton to Malaga, with increased frequency in summer. Malaga is also served by **British Midland Airways** (✆ 0345 554554) with a weekly service from East Midlands Airport.

APEX and other discounted fares carry various restrictions, such as minimum and maximum stays, and no change of reservation is allowed. They do, however, represent substantial savings on standard published fares. Most companies offer promotional fares from time to time outside the peak seasons of mid-summer, Christmas and Easter, although a degree of flexibility over travel dates may be necessary to secure them.

British Airways Information and Reservation Lines

Spain	(Malaga airport) ✆ 95 223 06 23. Madrid ✆ 901 111 33.
UK	from London and abroad, ✆ (0181) 897 4000; from UK outside London, ✆ (0345) 222 111.

Iberia Offices in Europe

France	1 Rue Scribe, 75009 Paris, ✆ 01 47 42 15 06.
Germany	Kurfürstendamm 207–D, 10719 Berlin, ✆ (30) 88 09 71 20.
Ireland	54 Dawson Street, Dublin 2, ✆ (1) 407 3017.
Italy	Via Bertoloni 3D (Angolo Piazza Pitagora), Rome 00197, ✆ 06 808 3105.
Netherlands	Aurora Building, Stadhouderskade 2, 1054 ES Amsterdam, ✆ (20) 685 0401.
UK	Venture House, 27–29 Glasshouse Street, London W1R 6JU, ✆ (0171) 830 0011.

Other Airlines with Direct Routes to Spain

Air France	Paris, ✆ 01 44 08 22 22.
Alitalia	Rome, ✆ 06-65642/3.
KLM	Amsterdam, ✆ (20) 474 7747.
Lufthansa	Frankfurt, ✆ (69) 255 255; Düsseldorf, ✆ (211) 868 686.

These can be incredibly cheap, and offer the added advantage of departing from local airports. Companies such as **Thomson, Airtours** and **Unijet** offer return flights from as little as £80. This theoretically includes basic accommodation, but nobody expects you to make use of this facility. Some of the best deals have return dates limited strictly to one week or two, sometimes four, the maximum allowed under the regulations. In many cases a return charter ticket is a big saving over a one-way regular fare, even if your itinerary means you have to let the return half lapse. Check it out at your local economy travel agent, bucket shop, in your local paper, or in the Sunday papers. In London, look in the *Evening Standard* and in *Time Out.* TV Teletext is also a good source of information on cheap charter flights to Spain, with some remarkable last-minute deals often available.

Get your ticket as early as possible, but try to be sure of your plans, as there are no refunds for missed flights—most travel agencies sell insurance and indeed, most charter companies now insist upon it, so that you don't lose all your money if you become ill. Students and people under 26 have the additional option of special discount charters, departing from the UK, but make sure you have proof of student status. An STA Youth card costs £4; an STA Academic card is available for £6 to those who teach at a recognized educational institution.

Discount and Youth Travel Specialists

Campus Travel: 52 Grosvenor Gardens, London SW1, ✆ (0171) 730 3402.

STA Travel: 117 Euston Road NW1 and 86 Old Brompton Road SW7 are the main London centres, ✆ (0171) 361 6161.

By Sea

Sea links between the UK and Spain are operated by **Brittany Ferries** and **P&O European Ferries**. This is a good way to go if you mean to bring your car or bicycle. **Brittany Ferries** operates between Plymouth and Santander (Portsmouth and Santander between November and March), and prices for foot passengers are roughly equivalent to a charter flight; children of 4–13 go for half-price, under-4s free. Prices for vehicles vary according to size and season: high season is from late June until early September, when the return fare for a driver and three passengers travelling in an average-length vehicle is £750, going down to £500 in low season. An adult foot passenger pays £149 return in high season. These fares do not include on-board accommodation, which is strongly recommended; in the high season, this costs from £6 for a simple Pullman seat, and £23 per person based upon four people sharing a four-berth cabin, to £120+ for a deluxe twin-berth cabin. There are also cheaper 8-day return specials, and two-night mini-cruises. The 24–27-hour crossing is made twice a week and can be rough.

P&O European Ferries operates the Portsmouth–Bilbao route with crossings twice weekly. Peak season runs from mid-July to mid-August when the return fare for an average-length car and four adults is £945, including accommodation in a four-berth cabin. This drops down to £585 in the winter months. Return fare for an adult foot passenger in peak season is £330, including accommodation in a two-berth cabin. Note that P&O fares include accommodation on all crossings. Children between 4 and 14 travel for half-price and under-4s go free. Good value 5- and 8-day mini-breaks are also available.

Brittany Ferries: Millbay Docks, Plymouth PL1 3EW, ℰ (0990) 360360. In Santander the address is the Estación Marítima, ℰ (94) 221 4500.

P&O European Ferries Ltd: Channel House, Channel View Rd, Dover, CT17 9TJ, ℰ (0990) 980980. In Bilbao, Cosmé Echevarría 1, 48009 Bilbao, ℰ (94) 423 4477.

By Rail

From London to Andalucía takes at least a day and a half and requires a change of trains in Paris and Madrid or Barcelona. A two-month return London–Seville costs £212. Students, those under 26 and holders of a Senior Citizen's Railcard can get reductions. Time can be saved by taking the Eurostar (ℰ (0990) 186186) rail service, which runs very frequently and take three hours from London (Waterloo) to Paris (Gare du Nord). Fares are lower if booked at least 14 days in advance.

If you've been a resident in Europe for the past 6 months and are under 26, you can take advantage of the two-zone **InterRail Pass**, available at British Rail or any travel agents, giving you a month's rail travel for £220, as well as half-price discounts on Channel crossings and ferries to Morocco, where the pass is also valid. The full InterRail Pass, covering all of Europe, costs £275 for one month. **Bookings**: rail tickets to Spain from England, or vice versa, can be obtained from British Rail International, Ticket and Information Office, Platform 2, Victoria Station, London SW1V 1JX (take your passport), or booked and paid for over the telephone, ℰ (0990) 848848. Tickets for local Spanish services can be obtained from certain UK travel agents, but bookings must be made weeks in advance. For *couchette* and sleeper reservations in France, contact French Railways, 179 Piccadilly, London W1, ℰ (0171) 495 4433.

By Bus or Coach

One major company, Eurolines, offers departures several times a week in the summer (once a week out of season) from London to Spain, to Algeciras via Cordoba, Granada and Malaga. Journey time is 33 hours from London to Granada. The fare to any destination south of Madrid, which includes Granada, Seville and Cordoba, is from £79 single, £143 return. Peak season fares between 22 July and 4 September are slightly higher. There are discounts for anyone under 26, senior citizens and children under 12. The national coach companies operate services that connect with the continental bus system. In the summer, the coach is the best bargain for anyone over 26; off-season you'll probably find a cheaper charter flight. **Information and booking**: Eurolines, 52 Grosvenor Gardens, London SW1, ℰ (0171) 730 8235; National Express, ℰ (0990) 808080. Details of all UK–Spain bus services can be obtained from the Spanish Tourist Office in London.

From the UK via France you have a choice of routes. Ferries from Portsmouth cross to Cherbourg, Caen, Le Havre and St-Malo. From any of these ports the most direct route takes you to Bordeaux, down the western coast of France to the border at Irún, and on to San Sebastián, Burgos and Madrid, from where you can choose your entry point into Andalucía. An alternative route is Paris to Perpignan, crossing the border at the Mediterranean side of the Pyrenees, then along the coast to Barcelona, where the E15 will take you south. Both routes take an average of two days' steady driving.

You may find it more convenient and less tiring to try the ferry from Plymouth to Bilbao or Santander, which cuts out driving through France and saves expensive *autoroute* tolls. For the scenery, opt for one of the routes over the Pyrenees, through Puigcerdá, Somport-Canfranc or Andorra, but expect heavy traffic; if you're not in a hurry, take the classic route through Roncesvalles, Vall d'Arán, or through Tarbes and Aragnouet through the tunnel to Parzán.

Getting There from the USA and Canada

By Air

There are numerous carriers that serve Spain. Most regular flights from the USA or Canada are to Madrid or Barcelona. **Iberia**, the national airline, offers fly-drive deals and discounts: enquire about the 'Visit Spain' offer. From anywhere in the USA, you can use Iberia's toll-free number, ✆ (800) 772 4642.

Iberia Offices in the USA and Canada

Florida	6100 Blue Lagoon Drive, Miami FLA 33126, ✆ (305) 358 8800.
Illinois	500 North Michigan Ave, Chicago, IL 60601, ✆ (312) 819 2900.
New York	655 Madison Ave, NY 10022, ✆ (212) 644 8797.
California	4227 Wilshire Blvd., 3209 Los Angeles, ✆ (323) 692 2965.
Washington	1725 K St NW, Washington DC 20006, ✆ (202) 293 6970.
Ontario	102 Bloor St West, Toronto M5S IM8, ✆ (416) 964 6625.
Québec	2020 University St, Montreal H3A 2A5, ✆ (514) 849 3352.

Other Airlines with Direct Routes to Spain

American Airlines	toll free ✆ (800) 433 7300.
Continental Airlines	toll free ✆ (800) 231 0856.

Delta	toll free ✆ (800) 241 4141.
TWA	toll free ✆ (800) 892 4141.
United Airlines	toll free ✆ (800) 538 2929.
Air Canada	toll free ✆ (800) 268 7240.

Other Airlines with Routes via Europe

British Airways	toll free ✆ (800) AIRWAYS.
KLM	toll free ✆ (800) 447 4747.
Lufthansa	toll free ✆ (800) 645 3880.
TAP	toll free ✆ (800) 221 7370.
Virgin Atlantic	toll free ✆ (800) 862 8621.

charter flights

These require a bit more perseverance to find, though you can save considerably on the cost of a regular or even APEX flight—currently a charter from New York to Madrid varies between $400–700 depending on the season, with winter charters from New York to Malaga at around $350. You may want to weigh this against the current transatlantic fares to London, where in most cases you can get a low-cost flight to Spain departing within a day or two of your arrival. This is an especially cheap way to go in the off season. The Sunday *New York Times* has the most listings.

Some Major Charter Companies and Consolidators

Council Charters	205 East 42nd St, New York, NY 10017, toll free ✆ (800) 800 8222; uses Air Europa.
DER	toll free ✆ (800) 782 2424.
Spanish Heritage	116–47 Queens Blvd, Forest Hills, NY 11375.
TFI	34 West 32nd Street, New York, NY 10001, ✆ (212) 736 1140, toll free ✆ (800) 745 8000.
Tours	✆ (718) 520 1300; uses Air Europa.

By Rail

The American **EurRail Pass**, which must be purchased before you leave the States, is a good deal only if you plan to use the trains every day in Spain and elsewhere—and it's not valid in the UK, Morocco or countries outside the European Union. A month of travel is around $598 for those under 26; those over 26 can get a 15-day pass for $522, a 21-day pass for $678 or one for a month for $838. In Spain you'll have to pay supplements for any kind of express train and the EurRail pass is not valid on Spain's numerous narrow-gauge (FEVE) lines.

Contact: CIT Tours, 342 Madison Avenue, Suite 207, New York 10173, ✆ (212) 697 2100, or toll free ✆ (800) 248 7245.

Andaluz cuisine

The region's centre for culinary research is housed in a charming renovated old mill on a river near Granada. There is a restaurant offering a delicious range of Andaluz, Moorish and Sephardic dishes, besides the cookery training centre and workshops, conducted in a very practical way. **Contact:** Centro Andaluz de Investigaciones Gastronómicas, Plaza del Carmen 2, 18009 Granada, ✆ 95 822 7123.

flamenco

Athough 'flamenco players are not born, they are made in heaven', you may nevertheless consider a course from the protégés of the *maestro* himself, Paco Peña. Peña now lives in London, and teaches Tony Blair among others. His Spanish school is in the Plaza del Potro, in the historic and picturesque centre of Cordoba. Students from around the world come here for the lectures in classical or flamenco guitar, and flamenco dancing. **Contact:** Centro Flamenco Paco Peña, Plaza del Potro 15, 14002 Cordoba.

language and arts

Courses generally last from 2–12 weeks, beginners to advanced. Course fees average 30,000 pts for 2 weeks; private tuition costs around 2500 pts per hour. Accommodation can be arranged, whether boarding with families (50–70,000 pts per week) or sharing an apartment (20–26,000 pts per week). **Contact:** the Instituto Cervantes, 102 Eaton Square, London, ✆ (0171) 235 0353, for information and complete listings.

Some Specialist Centres

Granada	Espalengua, C/ Nueva de Cartuja 24, 18012 Granada, ✆ 95 820 7782; Escuela de Español de las Alpujarras, C/ Natalio Rivas 1, 18001 Granada. Language courses integrated with activities in the Alpujarras area, including cycling, hiking, horseriding, cooking and flamenco-dancing.
Seville	Hispalis Center, Instituto de Lenguas y Cultura Española, Amor de Dios 31–2, 41002 Seville.

spas

In Andalucía there's a spa to cater for every complaint, from allergies to rheumatism.

Granada	Balnearios Alhama de Granada, 18120 Alhama de Granada, ✆ 95 835 0011.

Specialist Operators

Abercrombie & Kent International, 1520 Kensington Road, Oak Brook, Illinois, IL 60521, toll free ✆ (800) 323 7308, and in the UK, Sloane Square House, Holbein Place, London SW1W 8NS, ✆ (0171) 730 9600, tailor-made breaks in Granada, Seville and Cordoba.

ACE Study Tours, Sawston Road, Babraham, Cambridge CB2 4AP, ✆ (01223) 835055, ⊜ 837394, focusing on Moorish art, history and architecture in Cordoba, Granada, Seville and Ronda; all inclusive ten-day tours from £975, staying in 3 and 4 star hotels.

Al-Andalus Expreso, C/ Capitán Haya 55, 28020 Madrid, ✆ 91 571 5750, ⊜ 91 571 7482, luxury train tours across Andalucía.

Alternative Travel Group, 69–71 Banbury Road, Oxford OX2 6PE, ✆ (01865) 315665, escorted walking tours emphasising food, drink, history, art and relaxation; in the Granada area, accommodation in 3 or 4 star hostels and hotels.

Andante Travel, Grange Cottage, Winterbourne Dauntsey, Salisbury SP4 6ER, ✆ (01980) 610555, archaeological and historical study tours of Roman and Moorish Seville and Cordoba; 9-day tours from £1150 including flights, accommodation, meals and luxury picnics.

Andrew Brock Travel, 54 High Street East, Uppingham, Rutland LE15 9PZ, ✆ (01572) 821330, walking holidays through hill-top Moorish villages, accommodation in hotels and luxury tented camps. All inclusive 8-day trips from £1280.

BA Holidays, 156 Regent Street, London W1R 6LB ✆ (0171) 434 4700, city breaks in Granada and Seville.

Bird Holidays, Mantra WGT Ltd, Oxford House, Oxford Road, Guiseley, Leeds LS20 9AA, ✆ (01943) 882800, bird-watching holidays near Almería, from £819 per week including flights, accommodation and meals.

Cabalgar-Rutas Alternativas, 18412 Bubión (Granada), ✆/⊜ 95 876 3135, horse riding and 4x4 trips in the sierras of Granada and to the coast of Almería.

Cadogan Holidays, 9–10 Portland Street, Southampton SO14 7EB, ✆ (01703) 828300, 3 and 4 star hotel city breaks in Granada, starting from £285 per weekend.

Charlotte Scott, Trasierra, 41370 Cazalla de la Sierra (Seville), ✆ 95 488 4324, ⊜ 95 488 3305, organizes painting holidays and private parties.

Club Nautique, Puerto Deportivo Marina del Este, Punta de la Mona, 18690 Almuñécar, (Granada), is an excellent scuba diving centre.

Cox & King's Travel Ltd, Gordon House, 10 Greencoat Place, London SW1P 1PH, ✆ (0171) 873 5000, all-inclusive 4-day tours of 'Islamic Spain': gardens in Seville, Roman ruins in Cordoba and the Alhambra in Granada.

CV Travel, 43 Cadogan Street, London SW3 2PR, ✆ (0171) 581 0851, ⊜ (0171) 584 5229. Fou-r and five-star luxury hotels and villages in Seville and Ronda.

Exodus Travel, 9 Weir Road, London SW12 0LT, ✆ (0181) 675 5550, walking, trekking, mountain biking and cultural tours in and around Granada, Seville and Cordoba, from £500 for 8 days (all-inclusive, flights included).

Explore Worldwide, 1 Frederick Street, Aldershot, Hants GU11 1LQ, ✆ (01252) 344161; small escorted 15-day cultural and walking tours focusing on Moorish Andalucía, foothills of the Sierra Nevada and Cazorla National Park; from £465 and including day trips to Seville, Cordoba and Granada.

Kirker Holidays, 3 New Concordia Wharf, Mill Street, London SE1 2BB, ✆ (0171) 231 3333, highly reliable expert specialists in tailor-made packages to Seville, Granada, Cordoba, rural Andalucía and the *paradores*.

Learning for Pleasure, Apartado 25, Las Limas, 11330 Jimena de la Frontera (Cadiz), ✆/✉ 95 664 0102, courses in painting, creative writing, cooking, herbal medicine and gardening, and riding and walking tours.

Magic Travel Group, 227 Shepherd's Bush Road, London W6 7AS, ✆ (0181) 748 4220, ✉ (0181) 748 3731, tailor-made city breaks in Granada, Cordoba and Seville.

Marketing Ahead Inc., 433 Fifth Avenue, New York, NY 10016, ✆ (212) 686 9213, ✉ (212) 686 0271, the leading hotel and *parador* agents in the USA.

Martin Randall, 10 Barley Mow Passage, London W4 4PH ✆ (0181) 742 3355, lecture tours in Granada and Cordoba, focusing on art history and architecture.

Mundicolor Holidays, 276 Vauxhall Bridge Road, London SW1V 1BE, ✆ (0171) 828 6021, specializes in tailor-made tours in Granada, Seville and Cordoba; also offers a luxury train tour of Andalucía and gastronomy and wine tours.

Page & Moy Ltd, 136–140 London Road, Leicester LE2 1EN, ✆ (0116) 250 7000, escorted historical and scenic guided tours of Cordoba, Granada and Seville: from £529 for 9 days.

Prospect Music & Art Tours, 36 Manchester Street, London W1M 5PE, ✆ (0171) 486 5704, ✉ (0171) 486 5868, art, architecture and history tours of Granada, Seville and Cordoba, from £900 for 7–8 days.

Ramblers Holidays, Box 43, Welwyn Garden City, Herts AL8 6PQ, ✆ (01707) 331133, easy-going 1–week walking holidays in Granada and Seville; 2 star hotels and hostels.

Spanish Chapters, 102 St John's Road Terrace, London NW8 6PL, ✆ (0171) 722 9560, luxury self-catering villas in Seville, with swimming pools.

The Spirit of Andalucía, c/o Sally von Meister, Apartado 20, El Nobo, 29480 Gaucín, (Malaga), ✆ 95 215 1303; and at 22 Hans Place, London SW1X 0EP, ✆ (0171) 589 2425, offers courses in cooking, painting and decorative arts.

Thomson Breakaways, Centenary House, 3 Water Lane, Richmond, Surrey, ✆ (0181) 210 4500, city breaks in 2, 3 and 4 star hotels in Granada, Seville and Cordoba.

Thomas Cook, Units 1–3, Coningsby Road, Peterborough TE3 8BX ✆ (0990) 666222, city breaks in Seville, minimum stay 2 nights.

Time Off, 1 Elmfield Park, Bromley, Kent BR1 1OU ✆ (0990) 846363, city breaks in 2, 4 and 5 star hotels in Seville.

Unicorn Holidays, 2 Place Farm, Wheathampstead, Herts AL4 8SB, ✆ (01582) 834400, specializes in tailor-made holidays, focusing on high-quality character hotels and *parador* accommodation.

Waymark Holidays, 44 Windsor Road, Slough SL1 2EJ, ✆ (01753) 516477, ✉ (01753) 517016, walking holidays in Las Alpujarras with day excursions to Granada.

Passports and Visas

There are no formal entry requirements for EU passport holders travelling to Spain, regardless of the purpose or duration of the visit. In fact, nationals of the EU countries that are signatories to the *Schengen* agreement no longer require even a passport. However, the UK is *not* a signatory and passengers arriving at Spanish airports from Britain must still present a valid passport.

Holders of US or Canadian passports can enter Spain for up to 90 days without a visa; holders of Australian or New Zealand passports need a visa, available from any Spanish consulate.

Spanish Consulates

Canada	1 West Mount Square, Montreal H3Z 2P9, ✆ (514) 935 5235. 1200 Bay Street, Toronto, Ontario M5R 2A5, ✆ (416) 967 4949.
Ireland	17a Merlyn Park, Ballsbridge, Dublin 4, ✆ (1) 691 640.
UK	20 Draycott Place, London SW3 2RZ, ✆ (0171) 581 8989. 1a Brooks House, 70 Spring Gardens, Manchester M22 2BQ, ✆ (061) 236 1233. 63 North Castle Street, Edinburgh EH2 3LJ, ✆ (0131) 220 1483.
USA	545 Boylston Street, Boston, MA 02116, ✆ (617) 536 2506. 180 North Michigan Avenue, Chicago, IL 60601, ✆ (312) 782 4588. 6300 Wilshire Blvd, Los Angeles, CA 90048, ✆ (305) 446 5511. 150 East 58th Street, New York, NY 10155, ✆ (212) 355 4090. 2700 15th Street NW, Washington, DC 20009, ✆ (206) 265 0190.

Customs

Customs are usually polite and easy to get through—unless you come in via Morocco, when they'll search everything you own. EU limits of duty free are: 1 litre of spirits or 2 litres of liquors (port, sherry or champagne) plus 2 litres of wine and 200 cigarettes. Much larger quantities (up to 10 litres of spirits, 90 litres of wine, 110 litres of beer) can be taken through Customs if they have been bought locally, you are travelling between EU countries, and you can prove that they are for private consumption only.

If coming from the UK or USA, don't bother to pick up any duty-free alcohol—it's cheaper on the supermarket shelves in Spain.

By Air

Internal flights in Spain are primarily on Iberia, Aviaco, Binter and Air Europa. However, there are several other carriers on national routes, such as the Alitalia service between Malaga and Barcelona. In Andalucía you'll find airports in Cordoba, Granada, Jerez, Malaga and Seville. Prices are less of a bargain than they used to be, compared to most of Europe, although if you shop around and are willing to travel at night on slow days you can pick up some cheap deals, especially if you're going on a round trip. Also, check out the national charters in Spanish travel agencies.

Iberia Offices

Cordoba	Ronda de los Tejares 3, ✆ 95 747 1227.
Granada	Pza. Isabel la Católica 2, ✆ 95 822 7592.
Seville	Almirante Lobo 2, ✆ 95 422 8901.

Or throughout Spain on the central number in Madrid ✆ 902 400 500 (Mon–Sun 24 hours) to connect with Iberia reservations at local rates.

By Sea

The *Transmediterránea* line operates services from the Spanish mainland to the Balearic Islands, North Africa and the Canary Islands. In **Malaga**, Estación Marítima, 29016, ✆ 95 222 4393, ✉ 95 222 4883. **UK Agents:** Southern Ferries, 179 Piccadilly, London W1V 9DB, ✆ (0171) 491 4968.

By Rail

Mister Traveler, take the Spanish Train!

RENFE brochure

Democracy in Spain has made the trains run on time, but Western Europe's most eccentric railway company, **RENFE**, still has a way to go. The problem isn't the trains themselves; they're almost always clean and comfortable, and do their best to keep to the schedules, but the new efficient RENFE remains so complex it will foul up your plans at least once if you spend much time in Spain. To start with, there are no fewer than 13 varieties of train, from the luxury **TEE** (Trans-Europe Express) to the excruciating *semi-directo* and *ferrobús*. Watch out for these; they stop at every conceivable hamlet to deliver mail.

The best for getting between the big cities are the **Talgo** trains, speedy and stylish beasts in gleaming stainless steel, designed and built entirely in Spain; the Spaniards are very proud of them. **TER** trains are almost as good. Note that a majority of lines are still, incredibly, single-track, so whatever train you take, you'll still have to endure delays for trains coming the other way. This said, there has been one great leap forward in Spanish rail transport in the last few years, and that is the introduction of **AVE** services—high-speed rail links—originally developed for the Seville Expo in 1992.

Every variety of train has different services and a different price. RENFE ticket people and conductors can't always get them straight, and confusion is rampant, except again on Talgo and AVE routes where the published prices are straightforward and easy to read There are discounts for children (under 4 years old, free; 4–12 half-price), large families, senior citizens (half-price) and regular travellers, and 25 per cent discounts on *Días Azules* ('blue days') for *round-trip tickets only*. 'Blue days' are posted in the RENFE calendars in every station—really almost every day is a 'blue day'. Interpretations of the rules for these discounts differ from one ticket-window to the next, and you may care to undertake protracted negotiations over them as the Spaniards do. There is a discount pass for people under 26, the *tarjeta joven*, and BIGE or BIJ youth fares are available from TIVE offices in the large cities.

Every city has a **RENFE travel office** in the centre (*see list below*), and you can make good use of these for information and tickets. Always buy tickets in advance if you can; one of RENFE's little tricks is to close station ticket-windows 10 minutes before your train arrives. Other stations don't open the ticket-windows until the train is a couple of minutes away, causing panic and confusion. Don't rely on the list of trains posted; always ask at the station or travel office. **Fares** average 500 pts for every 100km (63 miles)—750 pts first class—but there are supplements on the faster trains that can put another 80 per cent on top of the basic price. If you plan to do a lot of riding on the rails, buy the *Guía RENFE*, an indispensable government publication with all the schedules and tariffs, available from any station newsagent.

rail excursions

Southern Spain's answer to the famous *Transcantábrica* which operates in northwest Spain is the *Al-Andalus Expreso*, a luxury tour taking passengers from Seville to Cordoba, Granada, Malaga and Jerez. Although expensive, the trip is a memorable experience—the carriages are done out in fancy period décor and the cuisine is superb. The trip takes 4–5 days, depending on which 'cruise' you take, but a common complaint we have heard is that the train spends an excessive amount of time in a railway siding!

Contacts for Al-Andalus Expreso

Spain Al-Andalus Iberrail, C/Capitán Haya 55, Madrid 28020,
Ⓣ 91 571 58 15.

UK Cox & King's Travel Ltd, Gordon House, 10 Green Coat Place,
London SW1P 1PH, Ⓣ (0171) 873 5000.

USA Marketing Ahead Inc., 433 Fifth Avenue, New York, NY 10016,
Ⓣ (212) 686 9213.

RENFE Offices

Cordoba Ronda de los Tejares 10, Ⓣ 95 749 0202.

Granada Reyes Católicos 63, Ⓣ 95 827 1272.

Seville Zaragoza 29, Ⓣ 95 441 4111.

If you are not part of a tour which includes inter-city travel, this is certainly the most convenient way of getting between the cities, and often the most pleasurable. However, there are no petrol concessions or coupons for tourists. Another problem is that only a few hotels—the more expensive ones—have garages or any sort of parking. And in cities parking is always difficult, although a useful tip to remember is that space which appears to be private—e.g. underground car parks of apartment blocks and offices—is often public, and rates are usually modest. Spain's highway network is adequate, usually in good repair, and sometimes impressive. The system of *autovías* (motorways) is constantly expanding. Spanish road building is remarkable for its speed if not always its durability.

To drive in Spain you'll need a pink EU driving licence or an **International Driver's Permit** (IDP), available through the AA or RAC or any auto club in the USA, and a **Green Card** proving limited liability insurance. In some parts of Spain, particularly away from the centres, local police may not recognize the EU driving licence so you are advised to take an IDP in any case. Though it's not compulsory, you are also advised to extend your motor insurance to include a bail bond. Should you be unfortunate enough to have an accident, without a bail bond your car will be impounded and you are just as likely to find yourself in jail for the night. Americans should not be intimidated by driving in Europe. Learn the international road-sign system (charts available to members from most auto clubs), brush up on your gear-changing technique, and get used to the idea of few signals, and traffic constantly converging from all directions. Seat belts are mandatory. The speed limit is 100km (62 miles) per hour on national highways, unless otherwise marked, and 120km (75 miles) per hour on motorways. Drive with the utmost care at all times—having an accident will bring you untold headaches, and to make matters worse, many Spaniards drive without insurance.

Hitchhiking is likely to involve a long, hot wait. Drivers in Andalucía are rarely inclined to give lifts and temperatures in midsummer can soar; few Spaniards ever hitchhike.

car hire

This is moderately cheaper than elsewhere in Europe. The big international companies are the most expensive, and seldom the most service-orientated. Smaller companies will, for example, deliver a car to your hotel when you want it, and collect it again when you no longer require it. Prices for the smallest cars begin at about £100 ($155) per week, which includes unlimited mileage and full insurance (CDW), according to season. An all-in weekly rate for a two-door Opel Corsa in mid-season picked up from and returned to Malaga Airport should run to about 21,000 pts.

If your car rental begins at Malaga Airport, try booking it locally in advance. You will do no better than with **Mustang Rent-a-Car**, Aeropuérto de Malaga, ✆ 95 223 5159, 🖷 05 223 9776. Apart from offering good rates and friendly service, Mustang is also a car-repair garage—worth remembering if your own car breaks down or needs attention; you can hire another while it's being repaired. Two other firms with a good reputation are **Marinsa**, ✆ 95 223 2304, and **Helle Hollis**, ✆ 95 224 5544. Local firms also rent

mopeds and **bicycles**, especially in tourist areas. To pre-book in the UK, try **Transhire**, ℰ (0171) 978 1222, **Holiday Autos** ℰ (0990) 300400 or **Suncars**, ℰ (01444) 456446. However, pre-booked car rentals offer no refunds should your plans change.

taxis

Taxis are still cheap enough for the Spaniards to use them regularly on their shopping trips. The average fare for a ride within a city will be 500–750 pts. Taxis are not always metered, but the drivers are usually quite honest; they are entitled to certain surcharges (for luggage, night or holiday trips, to the train or airport, etc.), and if you cross the city limits they can usually charge double the fare shown. It's rarely hard to hail a cab from the street, and there will always be a few around the stations. If you get stuck where there is none, call information for the number of a radio taxi.

By Bus

With literally dozens of companies providing services over southern Spain, expect choice at the price of confusion. Not all cities have bus stations; in some, including Seville and Cordoba, there may be a dozen little offices spread around town for each firm.

Buses, like the trains, are cheap by northern European standards, but still no bargain; if you're travelling on the cheap, you'll find that transportation is your biggest expense. Usually, whether you go by train or bus will depend on simple convenience; in some places the train station is far from the centre, in others the bus station is. As is the custom at some RENFE stations, tickets on the inter-city bus routes are sometimes sold at the last minute.

If you want to escape the cities and venture out on day trips, small towns and villages can normally only be reached by bus. Buses are usually clean, dependable and comfortable, and there's plenty of room for baggage in the compartment underneath. On the more luxurious buses which link the main cities of Andalucía, as well as the services along the coast, you get air-conditioning and even a movie (*Rambo*, *Kung Fu*, sappy Spanish flicks from the Franco era or locally produced rock videos).

Tourist information offices are the best sources for information.

city buses

Every Spanish city has a perfectly adequate system of public transportation. You won't need to make much use of it, though, for in almost every city all attractions are within walking distance of each other. City buses usually cost 120 pts, and if you intend to use them often there are books of tickets called *abonamientos* or *bono-Bus* or *tarjeta* cards to punch on entry, available at reduced rates from tobacco shops. Bus drivers will give change but don't give them a 1000 pts note. In many cities, the bus's entire route will be displayed on the signs at each stop (*parada*). And don't take it for granted that the bus will stop just because you are waiting—nearly every stop apart from the terminus seems to be a *request* stop. Flamboyant signals and throwing yourself across its path are the only ways of ensuring the bus will stop for you.

Practical A–Z

Children

Spaniards adore children, and they'll welcome yours almost everywhere. Baby foods, etc. are widely available, but don't expect to find babysitters except at the really smart hotels; Spaniards always take their children with them, even if they're up until 4am. Nor are there many special amusements for children, though these are beginning to spring up with Spain's new prosperity, for better or worse; traditionally Spaniards never thought of their children as separate little creatures who ought to be amused.

Ask at a local tourist office for a list of attractions in its area geared towards children.

Climate and When to Go

Andalucía is hot and sunny in the summer, generally mild and sunny by day in the winter—in fact, with an average 320 days of sunshine in the region, you can count on more sun here than anywhere else in Europe. Autumn weather is normally warm and comfortable, but can pack a few surprises, from torrential rains to droughts. The mild winters in coastal regions give way to warm springs with minimal rainfall. Temperatures inland can be considerably lower, especially in the mountainous regions, and the *Levante* wind can make life uncomfortable, even in summer, when it will not only blow your beach umbrella away, but might even make you a bit kooky. For comfort, spring and autumn are the best times to visit; winter is generally pleasant on the Mediterranean coast, though can be damp and chilly inland. You'll probably feel more uncomfortable inside than out; Spanish homes (and hotel rooms) are not made for the winter.

Seasonal temperatures in °C (°F)

	Jan		April		July		Oct	
	max	min	max	min	max	min	max	min
Seville	15 (59)	6 (43)	23 (74)	11 (52)	35 (95)	21 (70)	26 (79)	14 (58)

Average monthly rainfall in mm (inches)

	Jan	April	July	Oct
Seville	99 (4)	80 (3)	0 (0)	37 (1.5)

Disabled Travellers

Facilities for disabled travellers are limited within Spain and public transport is not particularly wheelchair-friendly, though RENFE usually provides wheelchairs at main city stations. You are advised to contact the Spanish Tourist Office, which has compiled a fact sheet and can give general information on accessible accommodation, or any of the organizations that specifically provide services to people with disabilities.

ECOM in Barcelona, ✆ 93 451 5550, is the federation of private Spanish organizations offering services for the disabled. Ask for Emilio Grande, who speaks good English.

ONCE (Organización Nacional de Ciegos de España), Pso. de la Castellana 95, Planta 28, Madrid, ✆ 91 597 4727, is the Spanish association for blind people.

Holiday Care Service, 2 Old Bank Chambers, Station Road, Horley, Surrey RH6 9HW, ✆ (01293) 774535, offers travel information and details of accessible accommodation and care holidays.

RADAR (The Royal Association for Disability and Rehabilitation), 12 City Forum, 250 City Road, London EC1V 8AF, ✆ (0171) 259 3222, has a wide range of travel information.

Royal National Institute for the Blind, 224 Great Portland Street, London W15 5TB, ✆ (0171) 388 1266. Its mobility unit offers a 'Plane Easy' audio-cassette which advises blind people on travelling by plane. It will also advise on accommodation.

Tripscope, The Courtyard, Evelyn Road, London W4 5JL, ✆ (0181) 994 9294, or ✆ (08457) 585641 (calls from within the UK charged at cheap rate), both also minicom, offers practical advice for elderly and disabled travellers.

American Foundation for the Blind, 15 West 16th Street, New York, NY 10011, ✆ (212) 620 2000; toll free ✆ 800 232 5463, is the best source of information in the USA for visually impaired travellers.

Federation of the Handicapped, 211 West 14th Street, New York, NY 10011, ✆ (212) 747 4262, organizes summer tours for members; there is a nominal annual fee.

Mobility International USA, PO Box 3551, Eugene, OR 97403, ✆ (503) 343 1248, offers a service similar to that of its sister organization in the UK.

SATD (Society for the Advancement of Travel for the Disabled), Suite 610, 347 5th Avenue, New York, NY 10016, ✆ (212) 447 7284, offers advice on travel for the disabled for a $5 charge, or free to members ($45, concessions $30).

Electricity

Current is 225 AC or 220 V, the same as most of Europe. Americans will need converters, and the British will need two-pin adapters for the different plugs. If you plan to stay in the less expensive *hostales*, it may be better to leave your gadgets at home. Some corners of Spain, even some big cities, have pockets of exotic voltage—150V for example—guaranteeing a brief display of fireworks. Big hotels always have the standard current.

Embassies and Consulates

Australia	Pso. de la Castellana, 143 Edificio Cuzco, Madrid, ✆ 91 279 8504.
Canada	C/ Núñez de Balboa 35, Madrid ✆ 91 431 4300.
France	C/ Salustiano Olózaga 9, Madrid, ✆ 91 435 5560.
Germany	C/ Fortuny 8, Madrid, ✆ 91 557 9056.
Ireland	C/ Claudio Coello 73, Madrid, ✆ 91 576 3500.
Italy	C/ Joaquín Costa 29, Madrid, ✆ 91 262 5546.
Netherlands	Pso. de la Castellana 178, Madrid, ✆ 91 359 0914.
New Zealand	Plaza de la Lealtad 2, Madrid, ✆ 91 523 0226.
UK	C/ de Fernando el Santo 16, Madrid, ✆ 91 319 0208. Pza. Nueva 8, Sevilla, ✆ 95 422 8875.
	Edificio Duquesa, C/ Duquesa de Parcent 8, Málaga, ✆ 95 221 7571.
	Avda de las Fuerzas Armadas 11, Algeciras, ✆ 95 666 1600.
	Gibraltar: (Vice Consulate) 65 Irish Town, ✆ 78 305.
USA	C/ Serrano 75, Madrid, ✆ 91 587 2200; consular office for passports, around the corner at Pso de la Castellana, 52 Pso de las Delicias 7, Seville, ✆ 95 423 1885.
	C/ Martínez Catena, Portal 6, Apartado 5B, Complejo Sol Playa, Fuengirola (Malaga), ✆ 95 247 9891.

consulate telephone numbers

Austria	✆ 95 235 4313	**Greece**	✆ 95 231 1847
Belgium	✆ 95 239 9007	**Holland**	✆ 95 260 0260
Canada	✆ 95 222 3346	**Ireland**	✆ 95 247 5108
Denmark	✆ 95 222 6373	**Italy**	✆ 95 230 6150
Finland	✆ 95 222 5340	**Norway**	✆ 95 221 0331
France	✆ 95 221 4888	**Sweden**	✆ 95 221 5662
Germany	✆ 95 221 2442	**Switzerland**	✆ 95 221 7266

Festivals

One of the most spiritually deadening aspects of Francoism was the banning of many local and regional fiestas. These are now celebrated with gusto, and if you can arrange your itinerary to include one or two you'll be guaranteeing an unforgettable holiday. Besides those listed below, there are literally thousands of others, and new ones spring up all the time. Many village patronal fiestas feature *romerías* (pilgrimages) up to a venerated shrine.

Getting there is half the fun, with everyone in local costume, riding on horseback or driving covered wagons full of picnic supplies. Music, dancing, food, wine and fireworks are all necessary ingredients of a proper fiesta, while the bigger ones often include bullfights, funfairs, circuses and competitions. *Semana Santa* (Holy Week) is a major tourist event, especially in Seville. The processions of *pasos* (ornate floats depicting scenes from the Passion) carried in a slow march to lugubrious tuba music, and accompanied by children and men decked out in costumes later copied by the Ku Klux Klan, are worth fighting the crowds to see. And while a certain amount of merry-making goes on after dark, the real revelry takes place after Easter, in the unmissable April *feria*. Fiestas or *ferias* are incredibly important to Andalucíans, no matter what the cost in money and lost sleep; they are a celebration of being alive in a society constantly aware of the inevitability of death. Dates for most festivals tend to be fluid, flowing towards the nearest weekend; if the actual date falls on a Thursday or a Tuesday, Spaniards 'bridge' the fiesta with the weekend to create a four-day whoopee. Check dates at the tourist office in advance.

Calendar of Events

January

first week   **Granada**: commemoration of the city's capture by the Catholic Kings.

March

Easter week   **Seville**: sees the most important *Semana Santa*: celebrations, with over 100 processions, broken by the singing of *saetas* (weird laments). **Cordoba**: the city's 26 processions are perhaps the most emotionally charged of all, making their way around the streets of the great Mosque. **Malaga, Granada, Úbeda**: also put on major 'dos'.

April

last week   **Seville**: the capital's *Feria*, originally a horse-fair, has now grown into the greatest festival of Andalucía. Costumed parades of the gentry in fine carriages, lots of flamenco, bullfights, and drinking.

May

first week   **Granada:** everyone dresses up and decorates the streets with carpets and flowers for the *Fiesta de la Santa Cruz.*

second week   **Cordoba:** every third year the *Concurso Nacional de Arte Flamenco* takes place, with 100 singers, guitar players and dancers.

June

mid-month   **Granada:** start of the month-long *Festival Internacional de Música y Danza,* which attracts big names from around the world; classical music, jazz and ballet; also flamenco competitions in odd-numbered years.

July

first Sunday   **Cordoba:** International Guitar Festival—classical, flamenco and Latino.

16   **Malaga:** *Virgen del Carmen*—decorated boats with firework displays.

last two weeks   **Lebrija** (near Seville): flamenco festival.

August

5   **Trevélez** (near Granada) has a midnight pilgrimage up Mulhacén, Spain's highest mountain, so that pilgrims arrive exhausted but in time for prayers at midday.

For a comprehensive guide to Andalucía's *ferias,* festivals, pageants, carnivals and cultural events, get a copy of the excellent free booklet *52 and a half weeks,* available from El Legado Andalusi, C/ Molinos 65, 18009 Granada, toll free © 900 101 409, ✆ 95 822 8644.

Food and Drink

Read an old guidebook to Spain and, when the author gets around to the local cooking, expressions like 'eggs in a sea of rancid oil' and 'mysterious pork parts' or 'suffered palpitations through garlic excess' pop up with alarming frequency. One traveller in the 18th century fell ill from a local concoction and was given a purge 'known on the comic stage as angelic water. On top of that followed four hundred catholic pills, and a few days later...they gave me *escordero* water, whose efficacy or devilry is of such double effect that the doctors call it ambidexter. From this I suffered agony'.

You'll fare better; in fact, the chances are you'll eat some of the tastiest food you've ever had at half the price you would have paid for it at home. The massive influx of tourists has had its effect on Spanish kitchens, but so has the Spaniards' own increased prosperity and, perhaps most significantly, the new federalism. Each region, each town even, has come to feel a new interest and pride in the things that set it apart, and food is definitely one of those; the best restaurants are almost always those that specialize in regional cooking.

The greatest a
cuisine is th
ingredients. Se
and mai...
speciality. (The traditiona... ...
or *adobo*, is a mixture of water,
vinegar, salt, garlic, paprika, cumin
and marjoram.) Other specialities
include the wholesome broth made
with fish, tomato, pepper and paprika,
and the famous cured hams of **Jabugo**
and **Trevélez**. Almost everybody has
heard of *gazpacho*; there are literally
dozens of varieties, ranging from the
pimentón of **Antequera** made with red
peppers, to the thick, tasty Cordovan
version, *salmorejo*. Olives, preserved in cumin, wild marjoram, rosemary, thyme, bay
leaves, garlic, savoury fennel and vinegar are a particular treat, especially the plump green
manzanilla olives from **Seville**. *Boquerones* (often mistaken for the peculiarly English
whitebait but in fact a variety of anchovy) feature widely in restaurants and tapas bars,
along with *pijotas*, small hake that suffer the indignity of being sizzled with tail in mouth.

In **Granada**, an unappetizing mixture of brains, bulls' testicles, potatoes, peas and red
peppers results in a very palatable *tortilla Sacromonte*, and many restaurants in the city
work wonders with slices of beef *filete* or loin larded with pork fat and roasted with the
juice from the meat and sherry. However, watch out for odd little dishes like *revoltillos*,
whose name gives you a fair warning of what flavours to expect in this subtle dish of tripe,
rolled and secured with the animal's intestines, mercifully lined with ham and mint.

The province of **Cordoba** has a fine culinary tradition, including dishes with a strong
Arab and Jewish influence, like *calderetas*, lamb stew with almonds. But Cordoba is also
the home of one of the most famous *andaluz* dishes, *rabo de toro*, a spicy concoction of
oxtail, onions and tomatoes. Also try the *buchón* (rolled fish filled with ham, dipped in
breadcrumbs, then fried). As one might expect, the **Sierras** offer dishes based on the
game and wild herbs found in the mountains. Here freshwater lakes teem with trout, and
wild asparagus grows on the slopes. Delectable salads are a feature of most menus (try
the *pipirrana*).

All over the region you will find *pinchitos*, a spicier version of its Greek cousin the
souvlaki, a mini-kebab of lamb or pork marinated in spices. To finish off your meal there
are any number of desserts (*postres*) based on almonds and custards, and the Arab influence once again shows through in, for example, the excellent sweetmeats from Granada
and the *alfajores* (puff pastry) from Huércal, Almería.

rs for absurd bureaucracy, the Spanish government rates restaurants by forks (this become a bit of a joke—a car repair shop in Granada has rated itself two wrenches). he forks have nothing to do with the quality of the food, though they hint somewhat at the prices. Unless it's explicitly written on the bill (*la cuenta*), service is not included in the total, so tip accordingly. Be careful, though: eating out in southern Spain—especially away from the Costa and big towns—is still a hit-and-miss affair. You will need luck as well as judgement. Spain has plenty of bad restaurants; the worst offenders are often those with the little flags and 10-language menus in the most touristy areas. But common sense will warn you off these.

If you dine where the locals do, you'll be assured of a good deal, if not necessarily a good meal. Almost every restaurant offers a *menú del día*, or a *menú turístico*, featuring an appetizer, a main course, dessert, bread and drink at a set price, always cheaper than if you had ordered the items *à la carte*. These are always posted outside the restaurant, in the window or on the plywood chef at the door; decide what you want before going in if it's a set-price menu, because these bargains are hardly ever listed on the menu the waiter gives you at the table.

One step down from a restaurant are **comedores** (literally, dining-rooms), often tacked on to the backs of bars, where the food and décor are usually drab but cheap, and **cafeterías**, usually those places that feature photographs of their offerings of *platos combinados* (combination plates) to eliminate any language problem. **Asadores** specialize in roast meat or fish; **marisqueras** serve only fish and shellfish—you'll usually see the sign for '*pescados y mariscos*' on the awning. Keep an eye out for **ventas**, usually modest family-run establishments offering excellent *menús del día* for working people. They specialize in typical *andaluz* dishes of roast kid or lamb, rabbit, *paella*, game (partridge crops up often) and many pork dishes, *chorizo* sausage and varieties of ham. Try and visit one on a Sunday lunchtime when all the Spanish families go out—with a bit of luck things may get out of hand, and guitars and castanets could appear from nowhere, in which case abandon all plans for the rest of the day.

If you're travelling on a budget, you may want to eat one of your meals a day at a **tapas bar** or *tasca*. Tapas means 'lids', since they started out as little saucers of goodies served on top of a drink. They have evolved over the years to become the basis of the world's greatest snack culture. Bars that specialize in them have platter after platter of delectable titbits—shellfish, mushrooms baked in garlic, chicken croquettes, *albóndigas*, the ubiquitous Spanish meatball, quails' eggs and stews. (Tortilla is seldom as good as it looks, unless you like eating reheated shoe-leather). All you have to do is pick out what looks best and point to it. At about 150 pts a go, it doesn't really matter if you pick a couple of duds. Order a *tapa* (hors d'œuvre), or a *ración* (big helping) if it looks really good. It's hard to generalize about prices, but on average 750 pts of tapas and wine or beer really fill you up. Sitting down at a table rather than eating at the bar may attract a token surcharge. Another advantage of tapas is that they're available at what most Americans or Britons would consider normal dining hours. Spaniards are notoriously late diners; 2pm is the earliest they would consider sitting down to their huge 'midday' meal. Then after work at 8pm a few tapas at the bar hold them over until supper at 10 or 11pm. After living in Spain for a few months this makes perfect sense, but it's exasperating to the average visitor. On the coasts, restaurants tend to open earlier to accommodate foreigners (some as early as 5pm) but you may as well do as the Spaniards do.

Prices in the guide are an average for two courses, without wine (although many people find that a main course is more than enough). For menu and restaurant **vocabulary** *see* **Language** (pp.165–8).

Drink

No matter how much other costs have risen in Spain, **wine** (*vino*) has remained awesomely inexpensive by northern European or American standards; what's more, it's mostly very good and there's enough variety from the regions for you to try something different every day. If you take an empty bottle into a *bodega*, you can usually bring it out filled with the wine that suits your palate that day. A *bodega* can be a bar, wine cellar or warehouse, and is worth a visit whatever its guise.

While dining out, a restaurant's *vino del lugar* or *vino de la casa* is always your least expensive option; it usually comes out of a barrel or glass jug and may be a surprise either way. Some 20 Spanish wine regions bottle their products under strict controls imposed by the *Instituto Nacional de Denominaciones de Origen* (these almost always have the little maps of their various regions pasted on the back of the bottle). In many parts of Andalucía you may have difficulty ordering a simple bottle of white wine, as, on requesting *una botella de vino blanco de la casa*, you will often be served something resembling diluted sherry. To make things clear, specify a wine by name or by region—for example *una botella de Rioja blanco*—or ask for *un vino seco*, and the problem should be solved. Spain also produces its own champagne, known as *cava*, which seldom has the depth of the French, nor the lightness of an Italian *prosecco*, but is refined enough to drink alone. The principal house, *Cordoniú*, is always a safe bet. Some *andaluz* wines have achieved an international reputation for high quality. Best known is the *jerez*, or what we in English call **sherry**. When a Spaniard invites you to have a *copita* (glass) it will nearly always be filled with this Andalucían sunshine. It comes in a wide range of varieties: *manzanillas* are very dry; *fino* is dry, light and young (the famous *Tío Pepe*); *amontillados* are a bit sweeter and rich and originate from the slopes around Montilla in Cordoba province; *olorosos* are very sweet dessert sherries, and can be either brown, cream, or *amoroso*.

The white wines of **Cordoba** grown in the Villaviciosa region are again making a name for themselves, after being all but wiped out by phylloxera in the last century.

In **Seville**, wine is produced in three regions: Lebrija; Los Palacios (white table wines); and Aljarafe, where full-bodied wines are particular favourites. Jaén also has three wine-producing regions. Torreperogíl, east of Úbeda, produces wine little known outside the area, but extremely classy. Take your bottle along to the local *bodega* when you are here, as many wines are on tap only. In Bailén, the white, rosé and red table wines resemble those of the more famous La Mancha vineyards. In the west of the province, Lopera white wines are also sold from the barrel.

Many Spaniards prefer **beer** (*cerveza*), which is also good, though not quite the bargain wine is. The most popular brands are *Cruzcampo* and *San Miguel*—most bars sell it cold in bottles or on tap; try *Mahón* Five Star if you see it. Imported whisky and other spirits are pretty inexpensive, though even cheaper are the versions Spain bottles itself, which may come close to your home favourites. Gin, believe it or not, is often drunk with Coca-Cola. Bacardi and Coke is a popular thirst-quencher but beware, a *Cuba Libre* is not necessarily a rum and Coke, but Coke with anything, such as gin or vodka—you have to specify; then, with a flourish worthy of a *matador*, the barman will zap an ice-filled tumbler in front of you, and heave in a quadruple measure.

Coffee, tea, all the international soft-drink brands and *Kas*, the locally made orange drink, round out the average café fare. If you want tea with milk, say so when you order, otherwise it may arrive with a piece of lemon. Coffee comes with milk (*café con leche*) or without (*café solo*). Spanish coffee is good and strong, and if you want a lot of it order a *doble* or a *solo grande*; one of those will keep you awake through the guided tour of any museum.

Health and Insurance

There is now a standard agreement for citizens of EU countries, entitling them to a certain amount of free medical care, but it's not straightforward. You must complete all the necessary paperwork before you go to Spain, and allow a couple of months to make sure it comes through in time. Ask for a leaflet entitled *Before You Go* from the Department of Health and fill out form E111, which on arrival in Spain you must take to the local office of the *Instituto Nacional de Seguridad Social* (INSS), where you'll be issued with a Spanish medical card and some vouchers enabling you to claim free treatment from an INSS doctor. At time of writing, the government is trying to implement a much easier system. If you have a particular diet or need special treatment then obtain a letter from your doctor and get it translated into Spanish before you go. In an emergency, ask to be taken to the nearest *hospital de la seguridad social.*

Before resorting to a *médico* (doctor) and his £20 ($30) fee (ask at the tourist office for a list of English-speaking doctors), go to a pharmacy and tell them your woes. Spanish *farmacéuticos* are highly skilled, and if there's a prescription medicine that you know will cure you, they'll often supply it without a doctor's note. (The newspaper *Sur* lists *farmacías* in large cities that stay open all night and every pharmacy displays a duty roster outside so you can locate one nearby which is open.)

No inoculations are required to enter Spain, though it never hurts to check that your tetanus jab is up to date, as well as some of the more exotic inoculations (typhoid, cholera and gamma globulin) if you want to venture on into Morocco.

The tap water is safe to drink in Spain, but of horrendously poor quality after periods of drought. At the slightest twinge of queasiness, switch to the bottled stuff.

insurance

You may want to consider travel insurance, available through most travel agents. For a small monthly charge, not only is your health insured, but your bags and money as well. Some will even refund a missed charter flight if you're too ill to catch it.

Many English and English-speaking doctors now have arrangements with European insurance companies and send their account directly to the company without you, the patient, having to fork out. But whether you pay on the spot or not, be sure to save all doctors' bills, pharmacy receipts and police documents (if you're reporting a theft).

Left Luggage

Since terrorists stopped leaving bombs in rail stations, RENFE has started to reintroduce *consignas*, or left-luggage facilities; you'll have about an even chance of finding one in a bus station or small bus company office, and sometimes bars near train or bus stations are willing to let you leave your bags. But don't rely on it.

Media

The Socialist *El País* is Spain's biggest and best national **newspaper**, though circulation is painfully low at under 400,000; Spaniards just don't read newspapers (the little magazine *Teleprograma*, with television listings, is far and away the best-selling periodical).

El País has the best regional **film** listings, indicating where you can see some great films subtitled instead of dubbed (look out for *versión original* or its abbreviation 'vo'). Films are cheap and Spaniards are great cinema-goers; there are lots of inexpensive outdoor movie theatres in the summer. Hollywood hearthrob Antonio Banderas is a native *malagueño*; his occasional visits to the Costa del Sol are greeted with a media frenzy.

The other big papers are *Diario 16* (centrist), *ABC* (conservative, in a bizarre 1960s magazine format), and the *Alcázar* (neo-fascist). Major British papers are available in all tourist areas and big cities by around 4pm the same day; the American *New York Herald Tribune*, the *Wall Street Journal*, and *USA Today* are readily available wherever Americans go. Most hit the newsstands a day late; issues of *Time* and *Newsweek* often hang about until they find a home.

Money

Spanish **currency** comes in notes of 1000, 2000, 5000, 10,000 **pesetas** (pts), all in different colours, and coins of 1, 5, 10, 25, 100, 200 and 500 pts. At street markets, and in out-of-the-way places, you may hear prices given in *duros* or *notas*. A *duro* is a 5 pta piece, and a *nota* is a 100 pta note.

Exchange rates vary, but until any drastic changes occur £1 is roughly 200 pts, and $1 equivalent to about 150 pts. Think of 100 pts as about 50p or 75 cents—so those green 1000 pta notes, the most common, are worth about £5 or $7.50.

Spain's city centres seem to have a bank on every street corner, and most of them will exchange money; look for the *cambio* or *exchange* signs and the little flags. There is a slight difference in the rates, though usually not enough to make shopping around worthwhile. Beware exchange offices, as they can charge a hefty commission on all transactions. You can often change money at travel agencies, hotels, restaurants or the big department stores. Even big supermarkets tend to have *telebancos* or automatic tellers. There are 24-hour *cambios* at the big train stations in Barcelona and Madrid. A Eurocheque card will be needed to support your British Eurocheques, and even then they may not be welcome.

Traveller's cheques, if they are from one of the major companies, will pass at most bank exchanges. Wiring money from overseas entails no special difficulties; just give yourself two weeks to be on the safe side, and work through one of the larger institutions (Banco Central, Banco de Bilbao, Banco Español de Crédito, Banco Hispano Americano, Banco de Santander, Banco de Vizcaya). All transactions have to go through Madrid.

Credit cards will always be helpful in towns. Direct debit cards are also useful ways of obtaining money, though you should check with your bank before leaving to ensure your card can be used in Spain. But do not rely on a hole-in-the-wall machine as your only source of cash; if, for whatever reason, the machine swallows your card, it usually takes 10 days to retrieve it.

Opening Hours

banks

Most banks are open Mon–Thurs 8.30–2.30, Fri 8.30–2 and Sat in winter 8.30–1.

churches

The less important churches are often closed. Some cities probably have more churches than faithful communicants, and many are unused. If you're determined to see one, it will never be hard to find the *sacristán* or caretaker. Usually they live close by, and would be glad to show you around for a tip. Don't be surprised when cathedrals and famous churches charge for admission—just consider the costs of upkeep.

shops and museums

Shops usually open from 9.30am. Spaniards take their main meal at 2pm and, except in the larger cities most shops shut down for 2–3 hours in the afternoon, usually from 1pm or 2pm. In the south, where it's hotter, the siesta can last from 1pm to 5pm. In the evening most establishments stay open until 7pm or 8pm, or later still in tourist resorts.

Although their opening times have become more chaotic lately, major **mu**, historical sites tend to follow shop hours, but abbreviated in the winter months; ... close on Mondays. We have tried to list the hours for the important sights. Seldom-v ones have a raffish disregard for their official hours, or open only when the mood strik them. Don't be discouraged; bang on doors and ask around.

We haven't bothered to list admission prices for all museums and sites. Usually the sum is trivial and often fluctuating—hardly anything will cost more than 250 pts, usually less; EU nationals are admitted free to many monuments. The **Alhambra** in Granada, **La Mezquita** in Cordoba and **La Giralda** in Seville, all at around 750 pts, are notable exceptions.

Photography

Film is quite expensive everywhere; so is developing it, but in any city there will be plenty of places—many in opticians' shops (*ópticas*) or big department stores—where you can get processing done in a hurry.

Serious photographers must give some consideration to the strong sunlight and high reflectivity of surfaces (pavements and buildings) in towns. If you're there during the summer use ASA100 film.

Police Business

Crime is not really a big problem in Spain and Spaniards talk about it perhaps more than is warranted. Pickpocketing and robbing parked cars are the specialities; in Seville they like to take the whole car. The big cities are the places where you should be careful, especially Seville. You're probably safer in Spain than you would be at home, though; the crime rate is roughly a quarter of that in Britain. Note that in Spain less than 8 grams of cannabis is legal; buying and selling it, however, is not. And anything else may easily earn you the traditional 'six years and a day'.

There are several species of **police**, and their authority varies with the area. Franco's old goon squads, the Policía Armada, have been reformed and relatively demilitarized into the *Policía Nacional*, whom the Spaniards call 'chocolate drops' for their brown uniforms; their duties largely consist of driving around in cars and drinking coffee. They are, however, more highly thought of than the Policía Armada, and their popularity increased when their commander, Lt General José Antonio Sáenz de Santa María, ordered his men to surround the Cortes to foil Tejero's attempted coup in 1981, thereby proving that he and his *Policía Nacional* were strongly on the side of the newly born democracy. The *Policía Municipal* in some towns do crime-control, while in others they are limited to directing traffic.

Mostly in rural areas, there's the *Guardia Civil*, with green uniforms, but no longer do they don the black patent-leather tricorn hats. The 'poison dwarfs of Spain', as Laurie Lee called them, may well be one of the most efficient police forces in the world, but after a century and a half of upholding a sick social order in the volatile countryside they have few friends. They too are being reformed; now they're most conspicuous as a highway patrol, assisting ng out tickets (ignoring 'no passing' zones is the best way to get one). ...s are payable on the spot; the traffic cops have a reputation for upright

...city, regardless of size, seems to have one post office (*correos*) and no more. It will always be crowded, but unless you have packages to mail, you may not ever need to visit one. Most tobacconists sell stamps (*sellos*) and they'll usually know the correct postage for whatever you're sending. The standard charge for sending a letter is 60 pts (European Union) and 87 pts (North America). Send everything air mail (*por avión*) and don't send postcards unless you don't care when they arrive. Mailboxes are bright yellow and scarce. The post offices also handle telegrams, which normally take four hours to arrive within Europe but are very expensive—a one-word message plus address costs around 2000 pts. There is also, of course, the poste restante (general delivery). In Spain this is called *lista de correos*, and it is as chancy as anywhere else. Don't confuse post offices with the Caja Postal, the postal savings banks, which look just like them.

Public Holidays

The Spaniards, like the Italians, try to have as many public holidays as possible. And everything closes. The big holidays, celebrated throughout Spain, are *Corpus Christi* in late May, *Semana Santa* during the week before Easter, *Asunción* on 15 August and *Día de Santiago* on 25 July, celebrating Spain's patron, Saint James. No matter where you are, there are bound to be fireworks or processions on these dates, especially for *Semana Santa* and *Corpus Christi*. But be aware that every region, town, and village has at least one of its own holidays as well (*see* 'Festivals' above).

National Holidays in Spain

1 Jan	Año Nuevo (New Year's Day)
6 Jan	Epifanía (Epiphany)
March/April	Viernes Santo (Good Friday)
1 May	Día del Trabajo (Labour Day)
May/June	Corpus Christi
25 July	Día de Santiago (St James' Day)
15 Aug	Asunción (Assumption)
12 Oct	Día de la Hispanidad (Columbus' Day)
1 Nov	Todos los Santos (All Saints' Day)
6 Dec	Día de la Constitución (Constitution Day)
8 Dec	Inmaculada Concepción (Immaculate Conception)
25 Dec	Navidad (Christmas Day)

There are some delightful tacky to['] 'daggers', plastic bulls and flamenco dol[ ] are also some good buys to be had, [ ] quality **leather goods** from Cord[ ] Ubrique, which has been producing leather-work since Roman times. Moorish craftsmen later had a major influence on the method of treating the cured skin for export. But, though the quality is good, the design seldom compares with its Italian counterpart. While Cordoba is better known for its ornate embossed leather for furniture decoration and **filigree jewellery**, Ubrique specializes in handmade items such as diaries, suitcases, bags and wallets. **Ceramic** plates, pottery and colourful *azulejo* tiles are made all over Andalucía; the quality varies enormously, from the shoddy factory-made products adorning tourist shop shelves, to the sophisticated **ceramic ware** you will find in the Triana district of Seville. Granada is well known for its **inlaid wood** *taracea* work (chests, chessboards and music boxes), although these can be rather crudely produced. Spanish **woven goods** are reasonably priced; Seville produces exquisite *mantillas* and embroidered shawls, and is the centre for the extraordinary designs that adorn the bullfighter's costume. In the Alpujarras a concentrated effort is being made to revive old skills, using the wooden loom particularly, to produce the typical **woollen blankets** and **rugs** for which this area had long been known—a fascinating mixture of ancient Christian and Arab designs. Brightly coloured handwoven blankets are the claim to fame of Grazalema, a village less than 20km to the west of Ronda. In the province of Almería, the village of Níjar produces colourful *jarapas*—woven blankets and mats. To encourage the nation's craftsmen, the government has organized a kind of co-operative, *Artespaña*, with various outlets selling their work, which can be found at Rodríguez Jurado 4, Sevilla; Corral del Carbón, Granada.

The major **department store** chains in Spain, El Corte Inglés and Galerías Preciados, often have good selections of crafts from around the region. All of the above will ship items home for you. You can also get excellent bargains at the roving **weekly markets**, where Spaniards do a good deal of their shopping. Local tourist offices will have details. Good-quality **antiques** can occasionally be picked up at a ***rastro*** (flea market), but they aren't the great finds they once were—Spaniards have learned what they're worth and charge accordingly. Guitars, mandolins and bagpipes, fine wooden furniture and Goya tapestries are some of the bulky, more expensive items you may want to ship home.

EU citizens are not entitled to tax refunds.

nd cafés collect much of the Spaniards' leisure time. They are wonderful institu-
s, where you can eat breakfast or linger over a glass of beer until 4 in the morning; in
any of them you could see an old sailor delicately sipping his camomile tea next to a young
mother, baby under her arm, stopping by for a beer break during her shopping. Some have
music—jazz, rock or flamenco; some have great snacks, or tapas, some have games or
pinball machines. Every Spaniard is a gambler; there seem to be an infinite number of
lotteries run by the State (the *Lotería Deportiva*), for the blind (ONCE), the Red Cross or
the Church; there's at least one bingo-hall in every town and there are **casinos** in all
major resorts. Every bar has a slot machine, doling out electronic versions of *La Cucaracha*
whenever it gets lonely.

Discos, nightclubs, etc. are easily found all three cities and tourist spots; most tend to be
expensive. Ask around for the current favourites. Watch out for posters for **concerts,
ballets**, and especially for **circuses**. The little travelling Spanish troupes with their family
acts, tents, tinsel and names like 'The National Circus of Japan' will charm you; they often
gravitate to the major fiestas throughout the summer.

Football has pride of place in the Spanish heart, and **bullfighting** (*see* **Snapshots**,
pp.67–8) and cycling vie for second place; all are shown regularly on television, which,
despite a heavy fare of dubbed American shows, everyone is inordinately fond of
watching. Both channels are state-run, but with satellite dishes outnumbering *bodegas*,
who watches them anyway?

cycling

Cycling is taken extremely seriously in Spain and you don't often see people using a bike
as a form of transport. Instead, Lycra-clad enthusiasts pedal furiously up the steepest of
hills, no doubt trying to reach the standards set by Miguel Indurain, who was the Spanish
winner of the *Tour de France* for three years running. If you do want to bring your own
bicycle to Spain, you can make arrangements by ferry or train; by air, you'll almost always
have to dismantle it to some extent and pack it in some kind of crate. Each airline seems to
have its own policy. The south of Spain would be suicide to bike through in summer,
though all right in winter. **Information**: call the Cycling Federation of Andalucía, Ferraz
16, 28028 Madrid, © 91 542 0421, © 91 542 0341.

football

Soccer is the most popular sport throughout Spain, and the Spaniards play it well:
FC Barcelona and Real Madrid are the best teams to watch; fans of Sevilla FC and Real
Betis will each argue that their team is the best in Andalucía. The season lasts from
September to June, and matches are usually trouble-free. **Information**: Spanish Football
Federation, Alberto Bosch 13, 28014 Madrid, © 91 420 3321, © 91 420 2094.

hiking and mountaineering

Thousands of hikers and mountaineers are attracted to the paths in the Sierra Nevada
above Granada. The tourist office or the Spanish Mountaineering Federation provide a list

of *refugios*, which offer mountain shelter in many places. Some are well equipped and can supply food. Most, however, do not, so take your own sleeping bags, cooking equipment and food with you. Hiking boots are essential, as is a detailed map of the area, issued by the Instituto Geográfico Nacional, or the Servicio Geográfico Ejército (*see* 'Maps', p.38). **Information**: Spanish Mountaineering Federation, Alberto Aguilera 3, 28015 Madrid, ✆ 91 445 1382.

horse racing

Horse racing is centred in Madrid, but there is a winter season at the Pineda racecourse in Seville. **Information**: Spanish Horse Racing Federation, Calle Montesquinza 8, 28006 Madrid, ✆ 912 577 7892, ✉ 912 575 0770.

pelota

Pelota, although a Basque game by origin, has a following in Andalucía. This is a fast, thrilling game, where contestants wearing long basket-like gloves propel a hard ball with great force at high walls; rather like squash. The fast action on the *jai-alai* court is matched by the wagering frenzy of the spectators. **Information**: Spanish Pelota Foundation, Los Madrazo 11, 28014 Madrid, ✆ 91 521 4299, ✉ 91 532 3879.

skiing

Many of the mountains popular with hikers at other times of the year attract ski crowds in the winter. An hour from Granada you can be among the Iberian Peninsula's highest peaks and Europe's southernmost ski resorts, whose après-ski life is steadily improving. In Spain, it's easy to arrange all-inclusive ski packages through a travel agent.

A typical deal would include six nights' accommodation in a three- or four-star hotel with half board and unlimited use of ski lift for the week, at a cost of around 100,000 pts. With instruction fees, count on 10–15,000 pts extra per week. **Information**: write to the tourist office or the Spanish Winter Sports Federation, Infanta Maria Teresa 14, 28016 Madrid, ✆ 91 344 0944.

tennis

There is just as much fervour for tennis as for golf, inspired by international champion Arantxa Sánchez Vicario, and more recently by Conchita Martínez, both of whom are revered in their native Spain. Again, the best clubs are to be found on the coast, and every resort hotel has its own courts; municipal ones are rare or hard to get to.

Information: Royal Spanish Tennis Federation, Avda. Diagonal 618, 08021 Barcelona, ✆ 93 201 0844.

Emergency Numbers

Spain: *proteccíon civil* ✆ 006   police ✆ 091

Save for a few annoying quirks, Spain has one of the best and cheapest telephone systems in Europe (25 pts for a short local call), although it can be rather confusing to use. All local telephone numbers in Spain contain seven digits plus a code, which now must be dialled even from within a province. In Andalucía, this code is 95. Spain is one of the few countries where you can make an international call conveniently from a phone booth. In newer phone booths there are complete instructions (in English) and the phone itself has a little slide on top that holds coins; keep it full of 100 pts, and you can gab all day as the Spaniards do. This can be done to the USA too, but take at least 3000 pts in change with you in 100s.

Overseas calls from Spain are among the most expensive in Europe; calls to the UK cost about 250 pts a minute, to the USA substantially more. There are central telephone offices (*telefónicas*) in every big city, where you call from metered booths (and pay a fair percentage more for the comfort); they are indispensable, however, for reversed charge or collect calls (*cobro revertido*). *Telefónicas* are generally open 9–1pm and 5–10pm and closed on Sundays. Expect to pay a big surcharge if you do any telephoning from your hotel or any public place that does not have a coin slot. Cheap rate is from 10pm–8am Monday–Saturday and all day Sunday and public holidays.

For calls to Spain from the UK, dial 00 followed by the country code, the area code (remember that if you are calling from outside Spain you drop the '9' in the area code) and the number. For international calls from Spain, dial 07, wait for the higher tone and then dial the country code, etc.

Australia	61	Netherlands	31
Canada	1	New Zealand	64
France	33	Spain	34
Germany	49	UK	44
Italy	39	USA	1

Toilets

Outside bus and train stations, public facilities are rare in Spain. On the other hand, every bar on every corner has a toilet; don't feel uncomfortable using it without purchasing something—the Spaniards do it all the time. Just ask for *los servicios* (on signs they are sometimes referred to as *aseos*). It has to be said that public lavatories and ones in private commercial establishments have improved tremendously over the last decade. Going to the loo in a marble cubicle at an airport or petrol station can be a positively delightful experience!

After receiving millions of tourists each year for the last two decades, no country has more information offices, or more helpful ones, or more intelligent brochures and detailed maps. Every city will have an office, and about two-thirds of the time you'll find someone who speaks English. Sometimes they'll be less helpful in the big cities in the summer. More often, though, you'll be surprised at how well they know the details of accommodation and transportation. Many large cities also maintain **municipal tourist offices**, though they're not as well equipped as those run by the Ministry of Tourism, better known as **Turismo**.

Hours for most offices are Monday to Friday, 9.30 to 1.30 and 4 to 7, open on Saturday mornings, closed on Sundays.

Spanish National Tourist Offices

UK
57–58 St James's Street, London SW1A 1LD,
✆ (0171) 499 1169/0901, ✉ (0171) 629 4257.

USA
Water Tower Place, Suite 915,
East 845 North Michigan Avenue, Chicago, Illinois,
IL 60611, ✆ (312) 642 1992, ✉ (312) 642 9817.

8383 Wilshire Boulevard, Suite 960, Beverly Hills,
CA 90211, ✆ (213) 658 7188, ✉ (213) 658 1061.

665 Fifth Avenue, New York, NY 10022, ✆ (212) 759 8822, ✉ (212) 980 1053.

Australia
203 Castlereagh Street, Suite 21a, PO Box A-685, Sydney,
✆ (2) 264 7966, ✉ (2) 267 5111.

Brazil
Escritorio Espanhol de Turismo, Rua Zequinha de Abreu
78, CEP 01250 São Paulo, ✆ (11) 65 59 99.

Belgium
Avenue des Arts 21–22, 1040 Brussels,
✆ (2) 280 19 26, ✉ (2) 230 21 47.

Canada
102 Bloor Street West, Toronto, Ontario, M5S 1M8,
✆ (416) 961 3131, ✉ (416) 961 1992.

France
43 Avenue Pierre 1 de Serbie, Paris,
✆ 01 47 20 90 54, ✉ 01 47 23 56 38.

Germany
Kurfürstendamm 180, 10707 Berlin,
✆ (30) 882 6036, ✉ (30) 882 6661.

Myliusstraße 14, 60323 Frankfurt,
✆ (69) 72 50 33, ✉ (69) 72 53 13.

Post Fach No. 151940, Schuberterstraße 10, München,
✆ (89) 538 90 75.

Italy	Via del Mortaro 19, interno 5, Roma 00187,-
	© 06 678 3106, *✉* 679 82 72.
	Piazza del Carmine 4, Milano 20221,
	© 02 72 00 46 17, *✉* 02 72 00 43 18.
Netherlands	Laan Van Meerdervoort 8, 2517 's-Gravenhage,
	© (70) 346 5900, *✉* (70) 364 9859.

maps

Cartography has been an art in Spain since the 12th-century Catalans charted their Mediterranean empire in Europe's first great school of map-making. The tourist offices in each city hand out beautifully detailed maps of their town.

If you can't wait until you get to Spain, specialist shops in London include Stanford's at 12 Long Acre, WC2, *©* (0171) 836 1321; and in the USA, The Complete Traveler, 199 Madison Avenue, New York, NY 10022, *©* (212) 685 9007.

Where to Stay

Many people visiting Granada, Seville and Cordoba will have taken advantage of the various city break packages available from tour operators, which will include accommodation and travel between the cities as part of the package. This will often be the cheapest and most efficient way of seeing the cities of southern Spain; however, if you prefer to make independent travel arrangements, hotels in Spain are still bargains—though, as with prices for other facilities, Spain is gradually catching up with the rest of western Europe.

One thing you can still count on is a consistent level of quality and service; the Spanish government regulates hotels intelligently and closely. Room prices must be posted in the hotel lobbies and in the rooms, and if there's any problem you can ask for the complaints book, or *Libro de Reclamaciones*. No one ever writes anything in these; any written complaint must be passed on to the authorities immediately. Hotel keepers would usually rather correct the problem for you.

The prices given in this guide are for double rooms with bath (unless stated otherwise) but do not include VAT (IVA) charged at 7% on all hotel rooms. Prices for single rooms will average about 60 per cent of a double, while triples or an extra bed are around 35 per cent more.

Within the price ranges shown, the most expensive are likely to be in the big cities, while the cheapest places are always in provincial towns.

On the whole, prices throughout Andalucía are surprisingly consistent. No government, however, could resist the chance to insert a little bureaucratic confusion, and the wide range of accommodation in Spain is classified in a complex system. Look out for the little **blue plaques** next to the doors of all *hoteles, hostales,* etc., which identify the classification and number of stars. Local tourist information offices will have a complete accommodation list for their province, and some can be very helpful with finding a room when things are tight.

paradores

The government, in its plan to develop tourism in the 1950s, started this nationwide chain of classy hotels to draw some attention to little-visited areas. They restored old palaces, castles and monasteries for the purpose, furnished them with antiques and installed fine restaurants featuring local specialities.

Paradores for many people are one of the best reasons for visiting Spain. Not all *paradores* are historical landmarks; in resort areas, they are as likely to be cleanly designed modern buildings, usually in a great location with a pool and some sports facilities. As their popularity has increased, so have their prices; in most cases both the rooms and the restaurant will be the most expensive in town. *Paradores* are classed as three- or four-star hotels, and their prices range from 8000 pts in remote provincial towns to 23,000 pts and upwards for the most luxurious. Many offer out-of-season or weekend promotional rates. If you can afford a *parador*, there is no better place to stay. We've mentioned most of them throughout this book.

Advance Booking

Spain	Head office, Requena 3, 28013, Madrid © 91 516 6666.
UK	Keytel International, 402 Edgware Road, London W2 1ED, © (0171) 402 8182.
USA	Marketing Ahead, 433 Fifth Avenue, New York, NY 10016, © (212) 686 9213.

hoteles

Price Ranges

rating	high	average	low
★★★★★	42,000+	26,000	18,000
★★★★	32,000	22,000	13,000
★★★	20,000	14,000	9000
★★	10,000	7000	5000
★	7000	5000	4500

Hoteles (H) are rated with from one to five stars, according to the services they offer. These are the most expensive places, and even a one-star hotel will be a comfortable, middle-range establishment. *Hotel Residencias* (HR) are the same, only without a restaurant. Many of the more expensive hotels have some rooms available at prices lower than those listed. They won't tell you, though; you'll have to ask. You can often get discounts in the off season but will be charged higher rates during important festivals. These are supposedly regulated, but in practice hotel-keepers charge whatever they can get. If you want to attend any of these big events, book your hotel as far in advance as possible.

hostales and pensiones

Price Ranges

rating	high	average	low
★★★	10,000	6000	4000
★★	8000	5000	3500
★	5000	4000	3000

Hostales (Hs) and *Pensiones* (P) are rated with from one to three stars. These are more modest places, often a floor in an apartment block; a three-star *hostal* is roughly equivalent to a one-star hotel.

Pensiones may require full- or half-board; there aren't many of these establishments, only a few in resort areas.

Hostal Residencias (HsR), like *hotel residencias*, do not offer meals except breakfast, and not always that. Of course, *hostales* and *pensiones* with one or two stars will often have rooms without private baths at considerable savings.

fondas, casas de huéspedes and camas

Price Ranges (without bath)

high	average	low
3500	3000	2000

The bottom of the scale is occupied by the *fonda* (F) and *casa de huéspedes* (CH), little different from a one-star *hostal*, though generally cheaper. Off the scale completely are hundreds of unclassified cheap places, usually rooms in an apartment or over a bar and identified only by a little sign reading *camas* (beds) or *habitaciones* (rooms).

You can also ask in bars or at the tourist office for unidentified *casas particulares*, private houses with a room or two; in many villages these will be the best you can do, but they're usually clean—Spanish women are manic housekeepers. The best will be in small towns and villages, and around universities. Occasionally you'll find a room over a bar, run by somebody's grandmother, that is nicer than a four-star hotel—complete with frilly pillows, lovely old furnishings, and a shrine to the Virgin Mary. The worst are inevitably found in industrial cities or dull modern ones. It always helps to see the room first. In cities, the best places to look are right in the centre, not around the bus and train stations. Most inexpensive establishments will ask you to pay a day in advance.

alternative accommodation

Youth hostels exist in Spain, but they're usually not worth the trouble. Most are open only in the summer; there are the usual inconveniences and silly rules, and often hostels are in out-of-the-way locations. You'll be better off with the inexpensive *hostales* and *fondas*—sometimes these are even cheaper than youth hostels—or ask at the local tourist office for rooms that might be available in **university dormitories.**

If you fancy some peace and tranquillity, the national tourist office has a list of 64 **monasteries** and **convents** that welcome guests. Accommodation starts at about £10 a night, meals are simple and guests may usually take part in the religious ceremonies.

camping

Campsites are rated with from one to three stars, depending on their facilities, and in addition to the ones listed in the official government handbook there are always others, rather primitive, that are unlisted. On the whole camping is a good deal, and facilities in most first-class sites include shops, restaurants, bars, laundries, hot showers, first aid, swimming pools, telephones and, occasionally, a tennis court.

Caravans (campers) and trailers converge on the more developed sites, but if you just want to pitch your little tent or sleep out in some quiet field, ask around in the bars or at likely farms. Camping is forbidden in many forest areas because of fears of fire, as well as on the beaches (though you can often get close to some quieter shores if you're discreet). If you're doing some hiking, bring a sleeping bag and stay in the free *refugios* along the major trails.

Price Ranges (per day)

Adult	275–500 pts
Caravan	300–650 pts
Child	200–350 pts
Tent	250–650 pts
Car	300–400 pts

Information: the government handbook *Guía de Campings* can be found in most bookstores and at the Spanish tourist office; further details can be obtained from the Federación Española de Campings, San Bernardo 97–99, Edificio Colomina, 28015 Madrid, ✆ 91 448 1234; or Camping and Caravan Club, Greenfields House, Westwood Way, Coventry CV4 8JH, ✆ (01203) 422 024 (membership necessary, £30).

Reservations for sites can be made through Federación Española de Empresarios de Camping, General Oraa 52, 2° d, 28006 Madrid. ✆ 91 562 9994; or Angel Ganivet 5, 4° a, 18009 Granada, ✆ 95 822 1456.

Women

On the whole, the horror stories of sexual harassment in Spain are a thing of the past—unless you dress provocatively and hang out by the bus station after dark. All Spaniards seem to melt when they see blondes, so if you're fair you're in for a tougher go. Even Spanish women sunbathe topless these days at the international *costa* resorts, but do be discreet elsewhere, especially near small villages. Apart from the coast, it often tends to be the older men who comment on your appearance as a matter of course. Whether you can understand what is being said or not, best to ignore them.

History

EL CID

Prehistory

Southern Spain has been inhabited since the remotest antiquity. Neanderthal man lived in Gibraltar some 50,000 years ago, and later peoples contributed cave paintings around Ronda. A site near the centre of—of all places—Marbella is currently being excavated for its Middle-Palaeolithic remains. Neolithic cultures, with their dolmens and burial mounds, begin to appear around the Iberian coasts *c.* 4000 BC. About 800 BC, the native Iberians were joined by other peoples, notably the Celts from over the Pyrenees, who occupied much of the north and centre of Spain. The great mystery of this era is the fabled kingdom of Phoenician **Tartessos**, roughly modern Andalucía and Murcia, the only place where the anarchistic Iberians ever founded a state. Phoenician records mention it, and in the *Book of Kings* it appears as 'Tarshish', its great navy bringing wares of Spain and Africa to trade with King Solomon. With great wealth from the mines of the Río Tinto and the Sierra Morena, Tartessos reached its height about 800–700 BC, just in time to be digested by more high-powered civilizations from the east.

Phoenicians, Carthaginians, Romans: 1100 BC–AD 50

The **Phoenicians** 'discovered' Spain perhaps as early as 1100 BC, founding *Gades* (Cádiz), claimed to be the oldest city in western Europe. They were after Spain's mineral resources—copper, tin, gold, silver and mercury, all in short supply in the Middle East at this time—and their successful exploitation of Spain made the Phoenicians the economic masters of the Mediterranean. Their rivals, the **Greeks**, arrived about 636 BC, founding a trading post at Mainake near Málaga.

By this time, the Phoenicians of the Levant were in decline and **Carthage**, their western branch office, was building an empire out of their occupied coasts in Spain and North Africa. About 500 BC, the Carthaginians gobbled up the last remains of Tartessos and stopped the Greek infiltration. The Carthaginians contributed little to Spain, but they maintained the status quo until 264–241 BC, when **Rome** drubbed them in the First Punic War. In the rematch, the Second Punic War (218–201 BC), the Romans under Scipio Africanus conquered Spain while Hannibal was chasing rainbows in Italy (with a largely Spanish army).

Unlike their predecessors, the Romans were never content to hold just a part of Spain. Relentlessly, they slogged over the peninsula, subjugating one Celtic or Iberian tribe after another, a job that was not completed until AD 220. Rome had to send its best—Cato, Pompey, Julius Caesar and Octavian (Augustus) were all commanders in the Spanish conquest. Caesar, in fact, was governor in Andalucía, the most prosperous part of the peninsula, and the one that adapted most easily to Roman rule and culture.

Roman Bætica: AD 50–409

At first the Romans called the region simply 'Further Spain', but eventually it settled in as *Bætica*, from the Bætis, the ancient name for the Guadalquivir river. For the next four centuries, it would be a prosperous, contented place; by grace of its mineral and agricultural wealth it was the richest Roman province west of Tunisia. Besides wine, oil and metals, another export was dancing girls—Bætica's girls were reputed to be the hottest in the empire. And for the choicer Roman banquets, there was *garum*, a highly prized condiment made of fish guts. Modern gourmets have been trying to guess the recipe for centuries.

New cities grew up to join Cádiz, Itálica and Málaga. Of these the most important were *Hispalis* (Seville) and *Corduba* (Cordoba). Among the cosmopolitan population were Iberians, Celts, Phoenicians, Italians, and a sizeable minority of Jews. During the Diaspora, Rome settled them here in great numbers, as far from home as they could possibly put them; they played an important and constructive role in Spanish life for the next 1500 years. The province also had a talent for keeping in the mainstream of imperial politics and culture. Vespasian had been governor here, and Bætica gave birth to three of Rome's best emperors: Trajan, Hadrian and Theodosius. It also contributed almost all the great figures of the 'silver age' of Latin literature—Lucan, both Senecas, Martial and Quintilian.

Roman Twilight and the Visigoths: 409–711

By the 4th century, the crushing burden of maintaining the defence budget and the government bureaucracy sent Spain's economy into a permanent recession. Cities declined, and in the countryside the great landowners gradually squeezed the majority of the population into serfdom or outright slavery. Thus when the bloody, anarchic **Vandals** arrived in 409, they found bands of rural guerrillas, or *bagaudae*, to help them in smashing up the remnants of the Roman system. The Vandals moved on to Africa in 428, leaving nothing behind but, maybe, the name Andalucía—perhaps originally *Vandalusia*.

The next uninvited guests were the **Visigoths**, a ne'er-do-well Teutonic folk who had been pushed westwards by the Huns. After sacking Rome in 410, they found their way into Spain four years later. By 478 they had conquered most of it, including Andalucía, and they established an independent kingdom stretching from the Atlantic to the Rhône. The Visigoths were illiterate, selfish and bloody-minded, but persistent enough to endure, despite endless dynastic and religious quarrels; like most Germans, they were Arian heretics. There weren't many of them, only a warrior élite that never formed more than a small fraction of the population. For support they depended on the landowners, who were making the slow but logical transition from Roman *senatores* to feudal lords.

Despite all the troubles, Andalucía at least seems to have been doing well—probably better than anywhere else in western Europe—and there was even a modest revival of learning in the 7th century, the age of St Isidore (*c.* 560–636), famous scholar of Seville. King Leovigild (573–86) was an able leader; his son Reccared converted to Catholicism in 589; both brought their state to the height of its power as much by internal reform as military victories. Allowing the grasping Church a share of power, however, proved fatal to the Visigoths. The Church's depredations against the populace and its persecutions of Jews and heretics made the Visigothic state as many enemies within as it ever had beyond its borders.

The Muslim Conquest: 711–756

The great wave of Muslim Arab expansion that began in Mohammed's lifetime was bound to wash up on Spain's shores sooner or later. A small Arab force arrived in Spain in 710, led by **Tarif**, who gave his name to today's Tarifa on the straits. The following year brought a larger army—still only about 7000 men—under **Tariq ibn-Ziyad** who quickly defeated the Visigoths near Barbate, a battle in which King Roderick was killed. Within five years, the Arabs had conquered most of the peninsula.

The ease of the conquest is not difficult to explain. The majority of the population was delighted to welcome the Arabs and their Berber allies. The overtaxed peasants and persecuted Jews supported them from the first. Religious tolerance was guaranteed under the new rule; since the largest share of taxes fell on non-believers, the Arabs were happy to refrain from seeking converts. The conquest, however, was never completed. A small Christian enclave in the northwest, the kingdom of Asturias, survived following an obscure but symbolic victory over the Moors at Covadonga, and by the beginning of the 10th century the Christians had recaptured León and most of Galicia. At the time, the Arabs could barely have noticed; Muslim control of most of Spain was solid, but hampered almost from the start by dissension between the Arabs and the neglected Berbers, and among the various tribes of the Arabs themselves.

The Emirate of al-Andalus: 756–1031

Far away in Damascus, the political struggles of the caliphate were being resolved by a general massacre of the princes of the Umayyad dynasty, successors of Mohammed; the Abbasids replaced them. One Umayyad escaped—**Abd ar-Rahman**; he fled to Cordoba, and gained the support of Umayyad loyalists there. After a battle in May 756, he proclaimed himself emir, the first leader of an independent emirate of al-Andalus.

Under this new government, Muslim Spain grew strong and prosperous. Political unity was maintained only with great difficulty, but trade, urban life and culture flourished. Though their domains stretched as far as the Pyrenees, the Umayyad emirs referred to it all as *al-Andalus.* Andalucía was its heartland and Cordoba, Seville and Malaga its greatest cities, unmatched by any others in western Europe. Abd ar-Rahman began the Great Mosque in Cordoba, a brilliant and unexpected start to the culture of the new state.

After Abd ar-Rahman, the succession passed without difficulty through Hisham I (788–96), Al-Hakim I (796–822), and Abd ar-Rahman II (822–52). Abd ar-Rahman's innovations, the creation of a professional army and palace secretariat, helped considerably in maintaining stability. The latter, called the *Saqaliba,* a civil service of imported slaves, was made up largely of Slavs and black Africans. The new dynasty seems also to have worked sincerely to establish justice and balance among the various contentious ethnic groups. One weakness, shared with most early Islamic states, was the personal, non-institutional nature of rule. Individuals and groups could address their grievances only to the emir, while governors in distant towns had so much authority that they often began to think of themselves as independent potentates—a cause of frequent rebellions in the reign of Mohammed I (852–86).

In the tenth century, al-Andalus enjoyed its golden age. **Abd ar-Rahman III** (912–61) and **al-Hakim II** (961–76) collected tribute from the Christian kingdoms of the north, and from North African states as far as Algiers. In 929, Abd ar-Rahman III assumed the title of caliph, declaring al-Andalus entirely independent of any higher political or religious authority. When the boy Caliph, Hisham II, came to the throne in 976, effective power was seized by his chamberlain Ibn Abi-Amir, better known as **al-Mansur** (the Victorious), who recaptured León, Pamplona and Barcelona from the Christians, and even raided the great Christian shrine at Santiago de Compostela, in Galicia, stealing its bells to hang up as trophies in the Great Mosque of Cordoba. A more resounding al-Andalus accomplishment was keeping in balance a diverse, sophisticated population—Latinized Bæticans and residual Celt-Iberians, Yemenites, Jews, Arabs, Syrians, Slavs, Berbers, black Africans—all the while accommodating three religions and ensuring mutual tolerance. At the same time, they made it pay. Al-Andalus cities thrived, far more than any of their neighbours, Muslim or Christian, and the countryside was more prosperous than it has been before or since. The Arabs introduced cotton, rice, dates, sugar, oranges and much else. Irrigation, begun under the Romans, was perfected, and even parched Almería became a garden.

At the height of its fortunes, al-Andalus was one of the world's great civilizations. Its wealth and stability sustained an impressive artistic flowering—obvious today, even from the relatively few monuments that survived the Reconquista. Cordoba, with al-Hakim's great library, became a centre of learning; Malaga was renowned for its singers, and Seville for the making of musical instruments. Art and life were also growing closer. About 822, the famous **Ziryab** had arrived in Cordoba from Baghdad. A great musician and poet, Ziryab also revolutionized the manners of the Arabs, introducing eastern fashions, poetic courtesies, and the proper way to arrange the courses of a meal. It wasn't long before the élite of al-Andalus became more interested in the latest graft of Shiraz roses than in riding across La Mancha to cross swords with the malodorous Asturians.

When Christian Europe was just beginning to blossom, al-Andalus and Byzantium were its exemplars and schoolmasters. Religious partisanship and western pride have always obscured the relationship; how much we really owe al-Andalus in scholarship—especially the transmission of Greek and Arab science—in art and architecture, in technology, and in poetry and the other delights of civilization, has never been completely explored. Contacts were more common than is generally assumed. Christian students were not unknown in Toledo or Cordoba—like the French monk who became Pope Sylvester II in 997.

Throughout the 10th century, the military superiority of al-Andalus was great enough to have finally erased the Christian kingdoms, had the caliphs cared to do so; it may have been a simple lack of aggressiveness and determination that held them back. The Muslim–Christian wars of this period cannot be understood as a prelude to the Crusades, or to the bigotry of Ferdinand and Isabella. Religious fanaticism, in fact, was lacking on both sides. Frontier chiefs could switch sides more than once without switching religions. The famous **El Cid** spent more time working for Muslim rulers than Christians; all the kings of León had some Moorish blood, and the mother of Abd ar-Rahman III was a Basque.

After the death of al-Mansur in 1002, the political situation began to change dramatically. His son, Abd al-Malik, inherited his position as vizier and *de facto* ruler and held the state together until his death in 1008, despite increasing tensions. All the while, Hisham II remained a pampered prisoner in the sumptuous palace-city of Medinat az-Zahra, outside Cordoba. The lack of political legitimacy in this ministerial rule, and the increasing distance between government and people symbolized by Medinat az-Zahra, contributed to the troubles that began in 1008. Historians also suggest that the great wealth of al-Andalus had made the nation a bit jaded and selfish, that the rich and powerful were scarcely inclined to compromise or sacrifice for the good of the whole.

Whatever the reason, the caliphate disintegrated with startling suddenness after 1008. Nine caliphs ruled between that year and 1031, most of them puppets of the Berbers, the *Saqaliba* or other factions. Civil wars and city riots became endemic. Medinat az-Zahra itself was destroyed, and Cordoba sacked, by Berber troops in 1013. By 1031, when the caliphate was formally abolished, an exhausted al-Andalus had split into some 30 squabbling states called the *taifas*.

The Reconquista: 1031–1492

The years after 1031 are known as the age of the **taifas**, or 'Party Kings', so-called because most of them owed their position to one of the political factions. Few of these self-made rulers slept easily, in an era of constant intrigues and revolts, shifting alliances and pointless wars. The only relatively strong state was that of Seville, founded by former governor Mohammed ibn-Abbad and continued by his sons, who managed to annexe Cordoba and several other towns.

The total inability of these rulers to work together made the 11th century a party for the Christians. **Alfonso VI**, King of Castile and León, collected tribute from most of the *taifas*, including even Seville. In 1085, with the help of the legendary warrior El Cid, he captured Toledo. The loss of this key fortress-city alarmed the *taifas* enough for them to request assistance from the **Almoravids** of North Africa, fanatical Berbers who had recently established an empire stretching from Morocco to Senegal. The Almoravid leader, Yusuf, crossed the straits and defeated Alfonso in 1086. Yusuf liked al-Andalus so much that he decided to keep it, and by 1110 the Almoravids had gobbled up the last of the surviving *taifas*. Under their rule, al-Andalus became more of a consciously Islamic state than it had ever been before, uncomfortable for the Christian Mozarabs and even for the cultured Arab aristocrats, with their gardens and their poetry.

Popular rebellions put an end to Almoravid rule in 1145, and two years later their power in Africa was defeated and replaced by that of the **Almohads**, a nearly identical military-religious state. By 1172, the Almohads had control of most of southern Spain. Somewhat more tolerant and civilized than the Almoravids, their rule coincided with a cultural reawakening in al-Andalus, a period that saw the building of La Giralda in Seville. Literature and art flourished, and in Cordoba lived two of the greatest philosophers of the Middle Ages: the Arab Ibn Rushd (Averroës), and the Jew Moses Maimonides. The Almohads nevertheless shared many of the Almoravids' limitations. Essentially a military regime, with no deep support from any part of the population, they could win victories over the Christians (as at Alarcos in 1195) but were never able to take advantage of them.

At the same time, the Christian Spaniards were growing stronger and gaining a new sense of unity and national consciousness. The end for the Almohads, and for al-Andalus, came with the **Battle of Las Navas de Tolosa** in 1212, when an army from all Christian Spain under Alfonso VII (1126–57) destroyed Almohad power forever. Alfonso's son, **Fernando III** (1217–52), captured Cordoba (1236) and Seville (1248), and was made a saint for his trouble. **Alfonso X** (the Wise, 1252–84), noted for his poetry and the brilliance of his court, completed the conquest of western Andalucía in the 1270s and 1280s.

In the conquest of Seville, important assistance had been rendered by one of Fernando's new vassals, **Mohammed ibn-Yusuf ibn-Nasr**, an Arab adventurer who had conquered Granada in 1235. The **Nasrid Kingdom of Qarnatah** (Granada) survived partly from its cooperation with Castile, and partly from its mountainous, easily defensible terrain. For the next 250 years it was the only remaining Muslim territory on the peninsula. As a refuge for Muslims from the rest of Spain, Granada became al-Andalus in miniature, a sophisticated and generally peaceful state, stretching from Gibraltar to Almería. It produced the last brilliant age of Moorish culture in the 14th century, expressed in its poetry and in the art of the Alhambra.

In the rest of Andalucía, the Reconquista meant a profound cultural dislocation, as the majority of the Muslim population chose to flee the rough northerners and their priests. The Muslims who stayed behind (the *Mudéjars*, meaning those 'permitted to remain') did not fare badly at first. Their economy remained intact, and many Spaniards remained fascinated by the extravagant culture they had inherited. In the 1360s, King Pedro of Castile (1350–69) was signing his correspondence 'Pedro ben Xancho' in a flowing Arabic script, and spending most of his time in Seville's Alcázar, built by artists from Granada. Throughout the period, though, this culture and the society that created it were becoming increasingly diluted, as Muslims either left or converted, while the Castilians imported large numbers of Christian settlers from the north. Religious intolerance, fostered by the Church, was, to say the least, a growing problem.

Los Reyes Católicos: 1479–1516

The final disaster, for Andalucía and for Spain, came with the marriage in 1469 of **King Fernando II of Aragón** and **Queen Isabel I of Castile** (Ferdinand and Isabella), opening the way, 10 years later, for the union of the two most powerful states in Spain. The glory of the occasion has tended to obscure the historical realities. If Fernando and Isabel did not invent genocide, they did their hypocritical best to sanctify it, forcing a maximalist solution to a cultural diversity they found intolerable. In 1481, they began the final war with Granada. In 1492, the capital fell, completing the Reconquista; Fernando and Isabel expelled the Jews from Spain; their Inquisition was in full swing, terrorizing 'heretical' Christians and converted Jews and Muslims and effectively putting an end to all differences of opinion, religious or political. The same year Columbus sailed from Andalucía to the New World, initiating the Age of Discovery.

Under the conditions of Granada's surrender in 1492, the *Mudéjars* were to be allowed to continue their religion and customs unmolested. Under the influence of the Church, however, Spain soon reneged on its promises and attempted forced conversion, a policy cleverly designed to justify itself by causing a revolt. The First Revolt of the Alpujarras, the string of villages near Granada in the Sierra Nevada, in 1500, resulted in the expulsion of all Muslims who failed to convert—the majority of the population had already fled—as well as decrees prohibiting Moorish dress and institutions such as public bathhouses.

Beyond that, the Spanish purposely impoverished the Granada territories, ruining their agriculture and bankrupting the important silk industry with punitive taxes and a ban on exports. The Inquisition enriched the Church's coffers, confiscating the entire property of any converted Muslims who could be found guilty of backsliding in the faith. A second revolt in the Alpujarras occurred in 1568, after which Felipe II ordered the prohibition of the Arabic language and the dispersal of the remaining Muslim population throughout the towns and cities of Castile. In the same year, the Inquisition began incinerating suspected Protestants in Seville. Intolerance had become the way of life.

The Age of Rapacity: 1516–1700

In the 16th century, the new nation's boundless wealth, energy and talent were squandered by two rulers even more vile than *Los Reyes Católicos*. Carlos I, a Habsburg who gained the throne by marriage when Fernando and Isabel's first two heirs died, emptied the treasury to purchase his election as Holy Roman Emperor. Outside Spain he is better known by his imperial title, **Charles V**, a ghoulish, sanctimonious tyrant who had half of Europe in his pocket and dearly wanted the other half. His megalomaniac ambitions bled Spain dry, a policy continued by his son **Felipe II**, under whom Spain went bankrupt twice.

Throughout the century, Andalucía's ports were the base for the exploration and exploitation of the New World. Trade and settlement were planned from Seville, and gold and silver poured into the city each year from the Indies' treasure fleet. What did not immediately go to finance the wars of Charles and Felipe was gobbled up by the nobility, the Genoese bankers, or by inflation—the 16th-century 'price revolution' caused by the riches from America. The historical ironies are profound: amidst all this opulence, Andalucía was rapidly declining from one of the richest and most cultured provinces of Europe to one of the poorest and most backward. Ferdinand and Isabella had begun the process, distributing the vast confiscated lands of the Moors to their friends, or to the Church and military orders; from its birth the new Andalucía was a land of huge estates, exploited by absentee landlords and worked by sharecroppers—the remnants of the original population as well as the hopeful colonists from the north, reduced in a generation or two to virtual serfdom.

By the 17th century, the destruction of Andalucía was complete. The Church's terror had done its work, eliminating any possibility of intellectual freedom and reducing the population to the lowest depths of superstition and subservience. Their traders and manufacturers ruined, the cities stagnated; agriculture suffered as well, as the complex irrigation systems of the Moors fell into disrepair and were gradually abandoned. The only opportunity for the average man lay with emigration, and Andalucía contributed more than its share to the American colonies. The shipments of American bullion peaked about 1610–20, and after that the decline was precipitous.

Bourbons, on the Rocks: 1700–1931

For almost the next two centuries, Andalucía has no history at all. The perversions of Spain's rulers had exhausted the nation. Scorned for its backwardness, Spain was no longer even taken seriously as a military power. The War of the Spanish Succession, during which the English seized (and were later ceded) Gibraltar (1704), replaced the Habsburgs with the **Bourbons**, though their rule brought little improvement. The one bright spot in the 18th century was the reign of **Carlos III** (1759–88), a reformer who expelled the Jesuits, attempted to revive trade and resettled the most desolate parts of Andalucía. New towns were founded—the *Nuevas Poblaciones*—such as La Carolina and Olavide.

Despite three centuries of decay, Andalucíans responded with surprising energy to the French occupation during the Napoleonic Wars. The French gave them good reason to, stealing as much gold and art as they could carry, and blowing up castles and historical buildings just for sport. As elsewhere in Spain, irregulars and loyal army detachments assisted the British under Wellington. In 1808, a force made up mostly of Andalucíans defeated the French at the Battle of Bailén. In 1812, a group of Spanish liberals met in Cádiz to declare a constitution, and under this the Spanish fitfully conducted what they call their **War of Independence**.

With victory, however, came not reforms and a constitution, but reaction and the return of the Bourbons. The confusing century that followed would see the loss of the American colonies, coups, counter-coups, civil wars on behalf of pretenders to the throne (the two Carlist Wars of the 1830s and 1870s), a short-lived First Republic in 1874 and several *de facto* dictatorships. Andalucía, disappointed and impoverished as ever, contributed many liberal leaders. The desperate peasantry, meanwhile, had become one of the most radicalized rural populations in Europe.

At first, this manifested itself as simple outlawry, especially in the Sierra Morena. In 1870, an Italian agitator and associate of Bakunin (the Russian writer and anarchist) named Fanelli brought **Anarchism** to Andalucía. In a land where government had never been anything more than institutionalized oppression, the idea was a hit. Anarchist-inspired guerrilla warfare and terrorism increased steadily, reaching its climax in the years 1882–6, directed by a secret society called the *Mano Negra*. Violence continued for decades, met with fierce repression by the hated but effective national police, the *Guardia Civil*.

The Second Republic and the Civil War: 1931–9

The coming of the democratic Second Republic in 1931 brought little improvement. Peasant rebellions intensified, especially under the radical right-wing government of 1934–6, when attempted land seizures led to incidents such as the massacre at Casas Viejas in 1934. Spain's alarmed Left formed a Popular Front to regain power in 1936, but street fighting and assassinations were becoming daily occurrences, and the new government seemed powerless to halt the country's slide into anarchy. In July 1936 the army uprising, orchestrated by Generals Francisco Franco and Emilio Mola, led to the **civil war**. The Army of Africa, under Franco's command, quickly captured eastern Andalucía, and most of the key cities in the province soon fell under Nationalist control. In Seville, a flamboyant officer named Gonzalo Queipo de Llano (later famous as the Nationalists' radio propaganda voice) singlehandedly bluffed and bullied the city into submission, and in archreactionary Granada, the authorities and local fascists massacred thousands of workers and republican loyalists. Thereafter Andalucía saw little fighting, though its people shared fully in Nationalist reprisals and oppression.

1939 to the Present

After the war, in the dark days of the 1940s, Andalucía knew widespread destitution and, at times, conditions close to famine. Emigration, which had been significant ever since the discovery of America, now became a mass exodus, creating the huge Andalucían colonies in Madrid and Barcelona, and smaller ones in nearly every city of northern Europe.

Economic conditions improved marginally in the 1950s, with American loans to help get the economy back on its feet, and the birth of the Costa del Sol, on the empty coast west of Malaga. A third factor, often overlooked, was the quietly brilliant planning of Franco's economists, setting the stage for Spain's industrial take-off of the 1960s and '70s. In Andalucía, their major contributions were industrial programmes around Seville and Cadiz and a score of dams, providing cheap electricity and ending the endemic, terrible floods.

When King Juan Carlos ushered in the return of democracy, Andalucíans were more than ready. Felipe González, the Socialist charmer from Seville, ran Spain from 1982 to 1996 (when the many political scandals of 1995 and his disastrous domestic economic policies finally discouraged the electorate from returning him to office) and other Andalucíans are well represented in every sector of government and society. They took advantage of the revolutionary regional autonomy laws of the late 1970s, building one of the most active regional governments, and giving Andalucía some control over its destiny for the first time since the Reconquista. And in other ways history seems to be repeating itself over the last 20 years: the Arabs have returned in force, building a mosque in the Albaicín in Granada, making a home from home along the Western Costa del Sol, and bringing economic if not exactly cultural wealth to the area; and Jews once more are free to worship, and do so, in small communities in Malaga, Marbella and Seville. In 1978 the first synagogue to be built since the Inquisition was consecrated at El Real in Malaga province.

Five centuries of misery and misrule, however, cannot be redeemed in a day. The average income is less than half of that in Catalunya or the Basque country; the unemployment rate, despite the relief which tourism brings along the coast, is brutal. None of this will be readily apparent, unless you visit the more dismal suburbs of Seville or Malaga, or the mountain villages of Almería province, where the new prosperity is still a rumour. In the flashy, vibrant cities and the tidy whitewashed villages, Andalucíans hold fast to their ebullient, extrovert culture, living as if they were at the top of the world.

Art and Architecture

Until the coming of the Moors, southern Spain produced little of note, or at least little that has survived. To begin at the beginning, there are the 25,000-year-old cave drawings at the Cueva de la Pileta, near Ronda, and Neolithic dolmens near Antequera and Almería. No significant buildings have been found from the Tartessians or the Phoenicians, though remains of a 7th-century BC temple have been dug up at Cadiz. Not surprisingly, with their great treasury of metals, the people of the region were skilled at making jewellery and figurines in silver and bronze (also ivory, traded up from North Africa where elephants were still common).

Real art begins with the arrival of the Greeks in the 7th century BC. The famous Lady of Elche in the Madrid museum, though found in the region of Murcia, may have been typical of the Greek-influenced art of all the southern Iberians; their pottery, originally decorated in geometrical patterns, began to imitate the figurative Greek work in the 5th century BC. The best collections of early work are in the Archaeological Museum at Seville and the museum at Malaga.

During the long period of Roman rule, Spanish art continued to follow trends from the more civilized east (ruins and amphitheatres at Itálica, Carmona, Ronda; a reconstructed temple at Cordoba; museums in Seville, Cordoba and Cadiz). Justinian's invasion in the middle of the 6th century BC brought new influences from the Greek world, though the exhausted region by that time had little money or leisure for art. Neither was Visigothic rule ever conducive to new advances. The Visigoths were mostly interested in gaudy jewellery and trinkets (best seen not in Andalucía, but in the museums of Madrid and Toledo). Almost no building work survives; the Moors purchased and demolished all of the important churches, but made good use of one Visigothic architectural innovation, the more-than-semicircular 'horseshoe' arch.

Moorish Art

The greatest age for art in Andalucía began not immediately with the Arab conquest, but a century and a half later, with the arrival of Abd ar-Rahman and the establishment of the Umayyad emirate. The new emir and his followers had come from Damascus, the old capital of Islam, and they brought with them the best traditions of emerging Islamic art from Syria. 'Moorish' art, like 'Gothic', is a term of convenience that can be misleading. Along with the enlightened patronage of the Umayyads, this new art catalysed the dormant culture of Roman Spain, creating a brilliant synthesis; of this, the first and finest example is **La Mezquita**, the Great Mosque of Cordoba.

La Mezquita was recognized in its own time as one of the wonders of the world. We are fortunate it survived, and it is chilling to think of the literally thousands of mosques, palaces, public buildings, gates, cemeteries and towers destroyed by the Christians: the methodical effacement of a great culture. We can discuss this art from its finest production, and from little else. As architecture, La Mezquita is full of subtleties and surprises (*see* pp.136–9). Some Westerners have tended to dismiss the Moorish approach as 'decorative art', without considering the philosophical background, or the expression of ideas inherent in the decoration. Figurative art being prohibited in Islam, artists used other forms: Arabic calligraphy, which soon became an Andalucían speciality; repetitive geometric patterns, mirroring a Pythagorean strain that had always been present in Islam; and a meticulously clever arrangement of forms, shapes and spaces, meant to elicit surprise and delight. The infinite elements of this decorative universe (*see* **Snapshots**, pp.62–4) come together in the most unexpected of conclusions—a reminder that unity is a basic principle of Islam.

The 'decorative' sources are wonderfully eclectic, and easy enough to discern. From Umayyad Syria came the general plan of the rectangular, many-columned mosques, along with the striped arches; from Visigothic Spain the distinctive horseshoe arch. The floral arabesques and intricate, flowing detail, whether on a mosque window, a majolica dish or a delicately carved ivory, are the heritage of late-Roman art, as can be clearly seen on the recycled Roman capitals of La Mezquita itself. The Umayyads in Syria had been greatly impressed by Byzantine mosaics, and had copied them in their early mosques. This continued in Spain, often with artists borrowed from Constantinople. Besides architectural decoration, the same patterns and motifs appear in the minor arts of al-Andalus, in painted ceramics, textiles and in metalwork, a Spanish speciality since prehistoric times—an English baron of the time might have traded a village for a fine Andalucían dagger or brooch.

Such an art does not seek progress and development, in our sense; it shifts slowly, like a kaleidoscope, carefully and occasionally finding new and subtler patterns to captivate the eye and declare the unity of creation. It carried on, without decadence or revolutions, until the end of al-Andalus and beyond. Under the Almohads, who made their capital at Seville, it created the **Torre del Oro** and **La Giralda**, model for the great minarets of Morocco.

The Christian conquest of Cordoba, Seville, and most of the rest of al-Andalus (1212–80), did not put an end to Moorish art. The tradition continued intact, with its Islamic foundations, for another two centuries in the kingdom of Granada. In the rest of Spain, Muslim artists and artisans found ready employment for nearly as long; their *mudéjar* art briefly contended with imported styles from northern Europe to become the national art of Spain. Most of its finest productions are not in Andalucía at all—the churches of Toledo, the towers of Teruel and many other towns of Aragón. The trademarks of *mudéjar* building are geometrical decoration in *azulejo* tiles and brickwork, and elaborately carved wooden *artesonado* ceilings.

Granada, isolated from the rest of the Muslim world and constantly on the defensive, produced no great advances, but this golden autumn of Moorish culture brought the decorative arts to a state of serene perfection. In the **Alhambra** (continued throughout the 14th century), where the architecture incorporates gardens and flowing water, the emphasis is on panels of ornate plaster work (*see* back cover photograph), combining floral and geometric patterns with calligraphy—not only Koranic inscriptions, but the deeds of Granada's kings and contemporary lyrical poetry. Another feature is the stucco *muqarnas* ceilings, translating the Moorish passion for geometry into three dimensions.

Granada's art and that of the *mudéjares* cross paths at Seville's **Alcázar**, expanded by Pedro the Cruel in the 1360s; artists from Granada did much of the work. Post-1492 *mudéjar* work can also be seen in some Seville palaces, such as the **Palacio de las Dueñas** or the **Casa de Pilatos**. The smaller delights of late Moorish decorative arts include painted majolica ware, inlaid wooden chests and tables (the *taracea* work, still a speciality of Granada), and exquisite silver and bronze work in everything from armour to astronomical instruments; the best collection is in the Alhambra's Museo Nacional de Arte Hispano-Musulmán.

Gothic and Renaissance

For art, the Reconquista and the emergence of a united Spain was a mixed blessing. The importation of foreign styles gave a new impetus to painting and architecture, but it also gradually swept away the nation's Moorish and *mudéjar* tradition, especially in the south, where it put an end to 800 years of artistic continuity. In the 13th century, churches in the reconquered areas were usually built in straightforward, unambitious Gothic, as with **Santa Ana** in Seville, built under Pedro the Cruel, and the simple and elegant parish churches of Cordoba. In the next century, Gothic lingered on without noticeable inspiration; Seville's squat and ponderous **cathedral**, the largest Gothic building anywhere, was probably the work of a German or Frenchman.

The Renaissance was a latecomer to Andalucía. In 1506, when the High Renaissance had already hit Rome, the Spaniards were building a Gothic chapel in Granada for the tombs of Ferdinand and Isabella. This time, though, they had an architect of distinction; **Enrique de Egas**, who had already created important works in Toledo and Santiago de Compostela, made the **Capilla Real** Spain's finest late-Gothic building, in the lively style called 'Isabelline Gothic' or 'plateresque', roughly corresponding to the contemporary French Flamboyant or English Perpendicular. The Plateresque in the decorative arts had already been established in Seville (the huge cathedral *retablo*, begun in 1482), and would continue into the next century (the cathedral's **Capilla Real** and **sacristy**). Other noteworthy figures of this period are the Siloés: **Gil de Siloé**, a talented sculptor, and his son **Diego**, who began the cathedrals at Granada (1526) and at Úbeda.

Genuine Renaissance architecture arrived with **Pedro Machuca**, who had studied in Italy. Strongly influenced by the monumental classicism of Bramante, his imposing **Palacio de Carlos V** (1527–8), in the Alhambra at Granada, actually antedates the celebrated Roman palaces it so closely resembles. Andalucía's Renaissance city is Úbeda, with an ensemble of exceptional churches and palaces; its **Sacra Capilla del Salvador** contains some of the finest Renaissance reliefs and sculpture in Spain.

In the stern climate of the Counter-Reformation, architecture turned towards a disciplined austerity, the *estilo desornamentado* introduced by **Juan de Herrera** at Felipe

II's palace-monastery of El Escorial, near Madrid. Herrera gave Seville a textbook example in his **Lonja**, a business exchange for the city's merchants. His most accomplished follower, **Andrés de Vandelvira**, brought the 'unornamented style' to a striking conclusion with his **Hospital de Santiago** in Úbeda, and other works in Úbeda and Baeza; he also began the ambitious **cathedral** at Jaén.

Baroque and Beyond

This style, like the Renaissance, was slow in reaching southern Spain. One of the most important projects of the 17th century, the **façade** for the unfinished Granada cathedral, wound up entrusted to a painter, **Alonso Cano** (1664). The idiosyncratic result, with its three gigantic arches, shows a little appreciation for the new Roman style, though it is firmly planted in the Renaissance. Real baroque arrived three years later, with Eufrasio López de Rojas's **façade** for Jaén cathedral. The most accomplished southern architect in the decades that followed was **Leonardo de Figueroa**, who combined Italian styles with a native Spanish delight in colour and patterns in brickwork; he worked mostly in Seville (**El Salvador**, begun 1699, **Colegio San Telmo**, 1724, and the **Convento de la Merced**, now the Museo de Bellas Artes). Baroque sculpture was largely a matter of gory realism done in wood, as in the work of **Juan Martínez Montañés** (Seville cathedral) and his disciple **Juan de Mena**.

The 17th century has often been described as a 'golden age' of painting in Andalucía. Giving ample room for exaggeration, there is still **Velázquez** (1599–1660), a native *sevilleno* who left the region forever in 1623 when he became painter to the king. Almost none of his work remains in the south. Of those who stayed behind, there is **Alonso Cano**, whose work often has a careful architectonic composition that betrays his side career as an architect, but seldom ranges above the pedestrian and devotional. **Francisco Herrera** of Seville (1576–1656) shows more backbone, in keeping with the dark and stormy trends of contemporary Italian painting.

Best of all is an emigrant from Extremadura, **Francisco de Zurbarán**, who arrived in Seville in 1628. He is often called the 'Spanish Caravaggio', and though his contrasts of light and shadow are equally distinctive, this is as much a disservice as a compliment. Set in stark, bright colours, Zurbarán's world is an unearthly vision of monks and saints, with portraits of heavenly celebrities that seem painted from life, and uncanny, almost abstract scenes of monastic life like the *Miracle of Saint Hugo* in the Seville Museo de Bellas Artes. Seeing the rest of his best work would require a long trip across two continents; the French under Maréchal Soult stole hundreds of his paintings, and there are more than 80 in the Louvre alone.

In the next generation of southern painters, the worst qualities of a decaying Spain are often painfully evident. **Bartolomé Esteban Murillo** (1617–82), another *sevilleno*, is the best of them; two centuries ago he was widely considered among the greatest painters of all time. Modern eyes are often distracted by the maudlin, missal-illustration religiosity of his saints and Madonnas, neglecting to notice the exceptional talent and total sincerity that created them.

Even harder to digest is **Juan de Valdés Leal** (1622–90), obsessed with the Hallowe'en blood-and-bones side of Counter-Reformation Catholicism to an extent that will often evoke either laughter or disgust (these two artists can be compared in Seville's museum and at the Hospital de la Caridad).

If any style could find a natural home in Spain, it would be the **rococo**. Eventually it did, though a lack of energy and funds often delayed it. **Vicente Acero** introduced the tendency early on, with a striking **façade** for the cathedral at Guadix. He had a chance to repeat it on a really important building project, the new Cadiz cathedral, but the money ran out, and the result was a stripped-down baroque shell—ambition without the decoration. The great **Fábrica de Tabacos** in Seville (1725–65), the largest project of the century in Andalucía, met a similar end, leaving an austere work, an unintentional precursor of the neoclassical. Whenever the resources were there, Andalucían architects responded with a tidal wave of eccentric embellishment worthy of the Moors—or the Aztecs. Pre-Columbian architecture may have been a bigger influence on Spain than is generally credited; judge for yourself at the chapel and sacristy of the **Cartuja** in Granada (1747–62), the most blatant interior in Spain.

Elsewhere, the decorative freedom of the rococo led to some unique and delightful build- ings, essentially Spanish and often incorporating eclectic references to the styles of centuries past. José de Bada's church of **San Juan de Dios** (1737–59) in Granada is a fine example. In Cordoba, there is the elegant **Convento de la Merced** (1745), and the **Coro** of the Cathedral, inside La Mezquita, a 16th-century Gothic work redecorated (1748–57) with elaborate stucco decoration by **Juan de Oliva** and stalls and overall design by **Pedro Duque Cornejo**. Seville, in its decline, was still building palaces, blending the new style with the traditional requirements of a patio and grand staircase; the best of the century's palaces, however, is in Écija, the **Palacio de Peñaflor** (1728). Many smaller towns, responding to the improved economic conditions under Felipe V and Carlos III, built impressive churches, notably in Priego de Cordoba, Lucena, Utrera, Estepa and Écija.

In view of all Andalucía's troubles, it should not be surprising that little has been produced in the last two centuries. **Pablo Picasso**, of Malaga, was the outstanding example of the artist who had to find his inspiration and his livelihood elsewhere.

Despite the lack of significant recent architecture, Andalucíans hold on to the glories of their past with tenacity; splashes of *azulejo* tiles and Moorish decoration turn up in everything from bus stations and market houses to simple suburban cottages.

THE PARTAL
ALHAMBRA.

Snapshots

You're on the road to Cordoba, passing the hours through some of the loneliest landscapes in Europe. For a long time, there's been nothing to see but olive trees—gnarled veterans, some of them planted in the time of Ferdinand and Isabella. You may see a donkey pulling a cart. At twilight, you arrive in the city and find yourself in the Avenida del Gran Capitán, an utterly Parisian boulevard of chic boutiques and pompous banks, booming with traffic. The loudspeakers from Galerías Preciados department store broadcast he latest chart singles. In a different way, southern Spanish cities have probably had much the same bustling ambience for over 2000 years; the atmosphere may be hard to recapture, but we can learn a lot by looking at decoration and design.

We know little about city life in Roman times—only that for relatively small populations, towns such as Itálica had amphitheatres and other amenities comparable to any in the empire. The cities of Moorish Spain were a revelation—libraries, public gardens and street lighting, at a time when feudal Europe was scratching its carrot rows with a short stick. Their design, similar to that of North African and Middle Eastern cities, can be discerned (with some difficulty) in parts of Granada, Cordoba and Seville today. It is difficult to say what aspects of the design of Andalucía's Moorish cities are legacies from Roman Bætica, and what was introduced by the Moors themselves. Enclosure was the key word in Moorish architecture: a great mosque and its walled courtyard occupied the centre, near the fortified palace (*alcázar* or *alcazaba*) and its walled gardens. Along with the markets and baths, these were located in the *medina*, and locked up behind its walls each night. The residential quarters that surrounded the *medina* were islands in themselves, a maze of narrow streets where the houses, rich or poor, looked inwards to open patios while turning blank walls to the street. Some of these survive, with their original decoration, as private homes in Granada's Albaicín.

In Roman times, the patio was called a *peristyle*. The gracious habit of building a house around a colonnaded central court was perfected by the Greeks, and became common across the Roman Mediterranean. Today, while most of us enjoy the charms of our cramped flats and dull, squarish houses, the Andalucíans have never given up their love of the old-fashioned way. In Cordoba especially, the patios of the old quarters spill over with roses, wisteria and jasmine; each year there is a competition for the prettiest. Besides the houses, some of the cellular quality of Moorish cities survived the Reconquista. In 16th-century Seville, thick with artful bandits, the silversmiths had their own walled quarter (and their own cops to guard it). The Moorish urban aesthetic evolved gracefully into the modern Andalucían: the simple, unforgettable panorama of almost any town—an oasis of brilliant white rectangularity, punctuated sharply by upright cypresses and by the warm sandstone of churches, palaces and towers.

One Spanish invention, combining Italian Renaissance planning with native tradition, was the arcaded, rectangular square usually called *Plaza Mayor*. The best are in Madrid and Salamanca, but many Andalucían towns have one, and there is a huge dilapidated specimen in Cordoba. Architecturally unified—the four walls often seem like a building

turned inside-out—the *Plaza Mayor* translated the essence of the patio into public space. Such a square made a perfect stage for the colourful life of a Spanish city. Spanish theatres in the great age of Lope de Vega and Calderón took the same form, with three sides of balconies, the fourth for the stage, on the narrow end, and a Shakespearean 'pit' at ground level. In the last two centuries, while the rest of Spain continued to create innovations in urban design and everyday pageantry, impoverished Andalucía contributed little—some elegant bullrings, certain exquisite redesigns of the old Moorish gardens, a few grand boulevards like the *paseos* of Granada, and some eccentric decorations, such as the gigantic, sinister stone birds of prey that loom over most city centres—symbols of an insurance company.

Modern Spain, even in the worst of times, never lost its talent for city building. The world's planners honour the memory of Arturo Soria, who in the 19th century proposed the *Ciudad Lineal* as a new form for the industrial age, a dense ribbon of city, three blocks wide but stretching for miles, where everyone would be a block or two from open countryside, and transportation to any point made easy and quick by a parallel railway line. A Ciudad Lineal was actually begun northeast of Madrid, though it has long since been swallowed up by the expanding suburbs.

During the last 30 years, the time of Spain's 'take-off' into a fully fledged industrial economy, *urbanización* has continued at a furious pace—in all senses of the word. As migrants streamed into the cities during the 1960s, endless blocks of high-rise suburban developments grew up, ugly but unavoidable. To the people who moved into them from poor villages or ancient tenements, they must have represented an exciting new way of life. The name for these is *urbanizaciones,* and the Spanish also use the word for their big seaside vacation developments, where they package northerners into urbanized holidays on the beach.

Since the 1970s and the end of Francoism, one can sense a slickness gathering momentum: a touch of anonymous good design in a shop sign, new pavements and lighting, ambitious new architecture with a splash of colour and surprise. The *El Corte Inglés* department store in Malaga has been known to be entirely covered in computer-controlled electric lights at Christmas, nearly a vertical acre of permanent fireworks, flashing peacock tails and other patterns in constantly changing, brilliant colours—as spectacular and futuristic a decoration as any city has ever had. Watch out for these sharp

Andalucíans—and for Spaniards in general. While we fog-bound northerners are nodding off with Auntie at twelve o'clock, they may well be plotting the delights of the future.

Castrum

In laying out their military camps, as in anything else, the Romans liked to go by the book. From Britain to Babylonia, they established hundreds of permanent forts (*castrum* in Latin) all seemingly stamped out of the same press, with a neatly rectangular circuit of walls and two straight streets, the *cardo* and *decumanus*, crossing in the middle. Many of these grew into towns—any place in Britain, for example, that ends in -chester or -caster.

In Spain, where the Roman wars of conquest went on for 200 years, there are perhaps more of these than anywhere else, and it's interesting to try and trace out the outlines of the Roman *castrum* while you're exploring a Spanish city. In Barcelona's Barri Gòtic, the plan is obvious, and in Ávila and Cáceres the streets and walls have hardly changed since Roman times. With a little practice and a good map, you can find the *castra* hiding inside Cordoba and a score of other towns.

Roses of the Secret Garden

Western art and Islamic art are two worlds that will never agree. Even today, the sort of folk who believe in the divinity of Michelangelo or the essential greatness of the Baroque can be found in print, sniffing at the art of the Alhambra as merely 'decorative'. On the other side, you will discover a state of mind that can dismiss our familiar painting and sculpture as frivolous, an impious obsession with the appearances of the moment that ignores the transcendent realities beneath the surface. A powerful idea was in the air in the 7–8th centuries, perhaps a reaction against the worldliness and incoherence that drowned classical civilization. It was not limited to Islam alone; the 'iconoclastic' controversy in Byzantium, following the attempt of Emperor Leo III to end the idolatrous veneration of icons, was about the same issue.

However this argument started, Islam grew up with an aversion to figurative art. At the same time, Islam was gaining access to the scientific and mathematical heritage of Greece and Rome, and finding it entirely to its liking. A new approach to art gradually took form, based on the sacred geometry of Byzantine architecture, and on a trend of mathematical mysticism that goes back to Pythagoras. Number, proportion, and symmetry were the tools God used to create the world. The same rule could be found in every aspect of creation, and could be reproduced in art by the simple methods of Euclidean geometry. This geometry now found its place not only in the structure of a building, but also in its decoration.

Once the habit of thinking this way was established, it profoundly affected life and art in all the Islamic world, including Spain. The land itself became a careful mosaic, with neat rows of olive trees draped over the hills and the very beans and carrots in the gardens laid out in intricate patterns (Andalucían farmers still do it). While nature was being made to imitate art, Muslim artists, consciously or not, often imitated the hidden

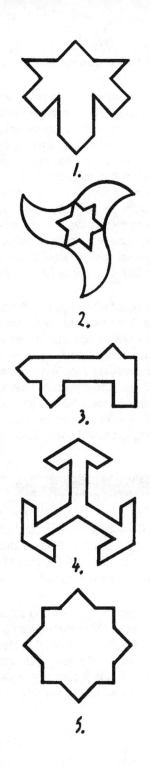

1.

2.

3.

4.

5.

processes of nature—the Cordoba mosque grew like a crystal with the columns and aisles of each new addition. Often, they created novelties by changing scales, reducing and replicating old forms to make new, more complex ones. One example of this is the Visigothic horseshoe arch. You can see it in its simplest form at Cordoba or nearby Madinat az-Zahra; later, as in Seville's Alcázar, the same arch is made of smaller versions of itself. And in the Alhambra, you'll see arches made of arches made of arches, seeming to grow organically down from the patterns on the walls. A tree or a snowflake finds its form in much the same way. Fans of chaos theory, take note—the Moors had anticipated fractals and Koch curves 600 years ago.

Three dimensions is the domain of the mundane shell, the worldly illusion. The archetypes, the underlying reality, can be more fittingly expressed in two. With their straight-edge and compass, Islamic artists developed a tradition of elaborate geometrical decoration, in painted tiles, stucco, or wooden grilles and ceilings. The highest levels of subtlety reached by this art were in Isfahan, Persia, in Egypt, and in Granada. The foundation, as in all constructive geometry, is the circle—*man's heart is the centre, heaven the circumference*, as a medieval Christian mystic put it. From this, they wove the exquisite patterns that embellish the Alhambra, exotic blooms interlaced in rhythms of 3, 5, 6, 8 or 12. This is not the shabby, second-hand symbolism of our times. A 12-pointed flower does not *symbolize* the firmament and the 12 signs of the zodiac, for example; it *recalls* this, and many other things as well. For philosophers, these patterns could provide a meditation on the numerical harmony of creation; for the rest of us, they stand by themselves, lovely, measured creations, whispering a sweet invitation to look a bit more closely at the wonders around us. The patterns of the Alhambra haunt Andalucía to this day. In Granada especially, these geometric flowers are endlessly reproduced on *azulejo* tiles in bars and restaurants, and in the *taracea* (marquetry) work boxes and tables sold in the Alcaicería.

One of the favourite games of the Islamic artists was filling up space elegantly, in the sense that a mathematician understands that word. In geometry, only three regular polygons, when repeated, can entirely fill a flat plane: the hexagon (as in a honeycomb); the square (as on a chessboard); and the equilateral triangle. Some not-so-regular polygons (any triangle or parallelogram, for example) can do it too. Try and find some more complex forms; it isn't easy. One modern artist fascinated by these problems was M. C. Escher, whose tricks of two-dimensional space are beloved of computer programmers and other Pythagoreans of our own age. The first four figures on the previous page can fill a plane. The first, with a little imagination and geometrical know-how, could be made into one of Escher's space-filling birds or fish. The third doesn't quite do the job, but properly arranged it creates a secondary pattern of eight-pointed stars (fig.5) in between. For a puzzle, try and multiply each of the four on paper to fill a plane. Answers can be found on the walls of the Alhambra.

By now, you may suspect that these shapes were not employed without reason. In fact, according to the leading authority on such matters, Keith Critchlow (in his book *Islamic Patterns*), the patterns formed by figs.1 and 3 mirror the symmetrical arrangement of numbers in a magic square. Triangular figs.2 and 4 are based on the *tetractys*, a favourite study of the Pythagoreans. But a Spanish Muslim did not need to be a mathematician to appreciate the lesson of this kind of geometry. Everyone understood the basic tenet of Islam—that creation is One: harmonious and complete. Imagine some cultured minister of a Granadan king, musing under the arcades of the Court of the Lions, reflecting perhaps on the nature that shaped the roses in the court, and how the same laws are proclaimed by the ceramic blossoms within.

Flamenco

For many people, flamenco is the soul of Spain—like bullfighting—an essential part of the culture that sets it apart from the rest of the world. Good flamenco, with that ineffable quality of *duende*, has a primitive, ecstatic allure that draws in its listeners until they feel as if their very hearts were pounding in time with its relentless rhythms, their guts seared by its ululating Moorish wails and the sheer drama of the dance. Few modern experiences are more cathartic.

As folklore goes, however, flamenco is newborn. It began in the 18th century in Andalucía, where its originators, the gypsies, called one another '*flamencos*'—a derogatory term dating back to the days when Charles V's Flemish (*flamenco*) courtiers bled Spain dry. These gypsies, especially in the Guadalquivir delta cities of Seville, Cádiz, and Jerez, sang songs of oppression, lament and bitter romance, a kind of blues that by the 19th century began to catch on among all the other downtrodden inhabitants of Andalucía.

Yet despite flamenco's recent origins, the Andalucían intelligentsia, especially Lorca and Manuel de Falla, found (or invented) much to root it deeply in the south's soil and soul. Its rhythms and Doric mode are as old as Andalucía's ancient Greek settlers; its spirit of improvisation and spontaneity date from the famous Cordoba school of music and poetry, founded in 820 by Abu al-Hassan Ali ibn Nafi, better known as Ziryab, the 'Blackbird' (see **History**, p.47); the half-tonal notes and lyrics of futility of the *cante jondo*, or deep song, the purest flamenco, seem to go straight back to the Arab troubadours of al-Andalus.

But just how faithfully the music of al-Andalus was preserved among the gypsies and others to be reincarnated as flamenco will never be known; the Arabs knew of musical notation, but disdained it in their preference for improvisation.

By the late 19th century, flamenco had gone semi-public, performed in the back rooms of cafés in Seville and Malaga. Its very popularity in Spain, and the enthusiasm set off by Bizet's *Carmen* abroad, began seriously to undermine its harsh, true quality. At the same time, flamenco's influence spread into the popular and folk repertories to create a happier, less intense genre called the *sevillana* (often songs in praise of you know where). When schoolchildren at a bus stop in Cadiz burst into an impromptu dance and hand-clapping session, or when some old cronies in Malaga's train-station bar start singing and reeling, you can bet they're doing a *sevillana*.

In the 1920s attempts were made to establish some kind of standards for the real thing, especially *cante jondo*, though without lasting results; the 'real, original flamenco' was never meant to be performed as such, and will only be as good as its 'audience'. This should ideally be made up of other musicians and flamenco *aficionados*, whose participation is essential in the spontaneous, invariably late-night combustion of raw emotion, alcohol, drugs and music, to create *duende*.

Flamenco not only remains popular in Spain, but is undergoing something of a renaissance. It all started in the 1970s and 1980s when Paco de Lucia, a native of Algeciras, took his art to the international stage, fusing it with jazz. Paco's music is a must for any lover of flamenco guitar and he continues to produce traditional records as well as recording crossover with other musicians like John McLaughlin and Al Di Meola. Within Spain, Ketama, a popular gypsy band from Granada, have fused flamenco with rock, and singers like Niña Pastori are following in their wake. On a pop level, flamenco has achieved an international audience thanks to the Gypsy Kings (who are French) and the Michael Flatley-style dance spectaculars of Joaquin Cortés.

Andalucía for itself, for Spain and for Humanity

So reads the proud device on the regional escutcheon, hurriedly cooked up by the Andalucíans after the regional autonomy laws of the 1970s made them masters in their own house once again. Above the motto we see a strong fellow, mythologically under-dressed and accompanied by two lions. Though perhaps more familiar to us for his career among the Hellenes, he is also the first Andalucían—HERCULES DOMINATOR FUNDATOR.

The Greeks themselves admit that Hercules found time for two extended journeys to the distant and little-known West. In the eleventh of his Twelve Labours, the Apples of the Hesperides caper, he made it as far as the environs of Tangier, where he dispatched the giant Antaeus. The tenth Labour brought Hercules into Spain, sailing in the golden goblet of Helios and using his lion skin for a sail. In the fabled land of Tartessos, on the 'red island' of Erytheia, he slew the three-headed titan Geryon and stole his cattle. Before heading back to Greece, he founded the city of Gades, or Cadiz, on the island (Cadiz, surrounded by marshes is almost an island). He also erected his well-known Pillars, Gibraltar and Mount Abyle, across the way in Africa. His return was one of the all-time bad trips; whenever you're crazed and dying on some five-hour 'semi-direct' Andalucían bus ride (say, Granada to Cordoba via Rute), think of Hercules, marching Geryon's cows through Spain and over the Pyrenees, then making a wrong turn that took him halfway down the Italian peninsula before he noticed the mistake. After mortal combats with several other giants and monsters, he finally made it to Greece—but then his nemesis, Hera, sent a stinging blue-tail fly to stampede the cattle. They didn't stop until they reached the Scythian Desert.

To most people, Hercules is little more than mythology's most redoubtable Dog Warden, rounding up not only Cerberus, the Hound of Hell, but most of the other stray monsters that dug up the roses and soiled the footpaths of the Heroic Age. But there is infinitely more than this to the character of the most-travelled, hardest-working hero of them all. In antiquity, wherever Hercules had set foot the people credited him with founding nations and cities, building roads and canals, excavating lakes and draining swamps. And there is the intellectual Hercules, the master of astronomy and lord of the zodiac, the god of prophecy and eloquence who taught both the Latins and the Spaniards their letters. One version has it that the original Pillars of Hercules were not mountains at all, but columns, like those of the Temple of Jerusalem, and connected with some alphabetical mysticism.

Ancient mythographers had their hands full, sorting out the endless number of deities and heroes known to the peoples of Europe, Africa and the Middle East, trying to decide whether the same figure was hiding behind different names and rites. Varro recorded no fewer than 44 Hercules, and modern scholars have found the essential Herculean form in myths from Celtic Ireland to Mesopotamia. Melkarth, the Phoenician Hercules, would have had his temples in southern Spain long before the first Greek ever saw Gibraltar. Not a bad fellow to have for a founding father—and a reminder that in Andalucía the roots of culture are as strong and as deep as in any corner of Europe.

Bullfights

In Spanish newspapers, you will not find accounts of the bullfights (*corridas*) on the sports pages; look in the 'arts and culture' section, for that is how Spain has always thought of this singular spectacle. Bullfighting combines elements of ballet with the primal finality of Greek tragedy. To Spaniards it is a ritual sacrifice without a religion, and it divides the nation irreconcilably between those who find it brutal and demeaning, an echo of the old Spain best forgotten, and those who couldn't live without it. Its origins are obscure. Some claim it derives from Roman circus games, others that it started with the Moors, or in the Middle Ages, when the bull faced a mounted knight with a lance.

There are bullrings all over Spain, and as far afield as Arles in France and Guadalajara, Mexico, but modern bullfighting is quintessentially Andalucían. The present form had its beginnings around the year 1800 in Ronda, when Francisco Romero developed the basic pattern of the modern *corrida*; some of his moves and passes, and those of his celebrated successor, Pedro Romero, are still in use today.

The first royal *aficionado* was Fernando VII, the reactionary post-Napoleonic monarch who also brought back the Inquisition. He founded the Royal School of Bullfighting in Seville, and promoted the spectacle across the land as a circus for the discontented populace. Since the Civil War, bullfighting has gone through a period of troubles similar to those of boxing in the USA. Scandals of weak bulls, doped-up bulls and bulls with the

BULLFIGHTING
SEVILLE

points of their horns shaved have been frequent. Attempts at reform have been made, and all the problems seem to have decreased bullfighting's popularity only slightly.

In keeping with its ritualistic aura, the *corrida* is one of the few things in Andalucía that begins strictly on time. The show commences with the colourful entry of the *cuadrillas* (teams of bullfighters or *toreros*) and the *alguaciles*, officials dressed in 17th-century costume, who salute the 'president' of the fight. Usually three teams fight two bulls each, the whole taking only about two hours. Each of the six fights, however, is a self-contained drama performed in four acts. First, upon the entry of the bull, the members of the *cuadrilla* tease him a bit, and the *matador*, the team leader, plays him with the cape to test his qualities. Next comes the turn of the *picadores*, on padded horses, whose task is to slightly wound the bull in the neck with a short lance or *pica*, and the *banderilleros*, who agilely plant sharp darts in the bull's back while avoiding the sweep of its horns. The effect of these wounds is to weaken the bull physically without diminishing any of its fighting spirit, and to force it to keep its head lower for the third and most artistic stage of the fight, when the lone *matador* conducts his pas de deux with the deadly, if doomed, animal. Ideally, this is the transcendent moment, the *matador* leading the bull in deft passes and finally crushing its spirit with a tiny cape called a *muleta*. Now the defeated bull is ready for 'the moment of truth'. The kill must be clean and quick, a sword thrust to the heart. The corpse is dragged out to the waiting butchers.

More often than not the job is botched. Most bullfights, in fact, are a disappointment, especially if the *matadores* are beginners, or *novios*, but to the *aficionado* the chance to see one or all of the stages performed to perfection makes it all worthwhile. When a *matador* is good, the band plays and the hats and handkerchiefs fly; a truly excellent performance earns as a reward from the president one, or both, of the bull's ears; or rarely, for an exceptionally brilliant performance, both ears and the tail.

You'll be lucky to see a bullfight at all; there are only about 500 each year in Spain, mostly coinciding with holidays or a town's fiesta. During Seville's *feria* there is a bullfight every afternoon at the famous Maestranza ring, while the rings in Malaga and Puerto de Santa María near Cádiz are other major venues. Tickets can be astronomically expensive and hard to come by, especially for a well-known *matador*; sometimes touts buy out the lot. Get them in advance, if you can, and directly from the office in the *plaza de toros* to avoid the hefty commission charges. Prices vary according to the sun—the most expensive seats are entirely in the shade.

Dust in the Wind

The poets of al-Andalus devoted most of their attention to sensuous songs of love, nature, wine, women and boys, but amidst all the lavish beauty there would linger, like a *basso continuo*, a note of refined detachment, of melancholy and futility. Instead of forgetting death in their man-made paradises, the poets made a point of reminding their listeners of how useless it was to become attached to these worldly delights. After all, only God is forever, and why express love to something that would one day turn to dust? Why even attempt to build something perfect and eternal—the main ingredients of the lovely, delicate Alhambra are plaster and wood. The Nasrid kings, were they to return, might be appalled to find it still standing.

The Christians who led the Reconquista had no time for futility. In their architecture and art they built for eternity, plonking a soaring church right in the middle of the Great Mosque and an imperial palace on the Alhambra—literal, lapidarian, emanating the power and total control of the temporal Church and State. Their oppression reduced the sophisticated songs of the Moorish courts to a baser fatalism. The harsh realities of everyday life encouraged people to live for the moment, to grab what happiness they could in an uncertain world. This uncertainty was best expressed by the 17th-century Spanish playwright Pedro Calderón de la Barca, especially in his great *La Vida es Sueño* (Life is a Dream), known as the Catholic answer to *Hamlet.*

There wasn't much poetry in Granada between 1492 and the advent of Federico García Lorca, born in 1898 in the Vega just outside of town. Lorca, a fine musician as well as a poet and playwright, found much of his inspiration in what would be called nowadays Granada's 'alternative' traditions, especially those of the gypsies. In 1922, Lorca was a chief organizer of Granada's first *cante jondo* festival, designed to bring flamenco-singing to international attention and prevent it from sliding into a hackneyed Andalucían joke. In 1927, he published the book of poems that made him the most popular poet in Spain, the *Romancero Gitano* (Gypsy Ballads); his plays, like *Bodas de Sangre* (Blood Wedding) and *Yerma* (The Barren One), have the lyrical, disturbing force of the deepest *cante jondo*. But of post-Reconquista Granada he was sharply critical, accusing Ferdinand and Isabella of destroying a much more sophisticated civilization than their own—and as for the modern inhabitants of Granada, they were an imported reactionary bourgeois contingent from the north, not 'real' Andalucíans. Lorca criticized, but he kept coming back, and had dreams of bringing the city's once great culture back to life.

In Granada, a commemorative park at Víznar marks the spot where, on 18 August 1936, local police or rebel soldiers took Lorca and shot him dead. No one knows who gave the orders, or the reason why; the poet had supported the Republic but was not actively political. When news of his secret execution leaked out, it was an embarrassment to Franco, who managed to hush up the affair until his own death. But most historians agree that the killing was a local vendetta for Lorca's outspoken views of his home town, a blood sacrifice to the stone god of Ferdianad and Isabella and Charles V who fears all change, closing (one can only hope) once and for all the circle of bittersweet futility, frustration, and death.

Hot-blooded Andalucían Women

Andalucía holds roughly a fifth of Spain's people, which means one twelfth of the population consists of the most sultry, sensuous women in Europe. Ah, *señores*, how they arch their supple torsos in an improvised *sevillana*, clicking their magic castanets! *Dios*, how provocative they are behind the iron grilles of their windows with their come-hither burning black eyes over flickering fans, serenaded by their handsome guitar-strumming *caballero*, tossing him a red rose of promise and desire!

Ever since the first boatload of dancing girls from Cádiz docked at the slave-markets of ancient Rome, the women of Andalucía have had to put up with this—an extraordinary reputation for grace, beauty, and amorous dispositions. Travellers' accounts and novels elaborate on their exotic charms, spiced by the languor of the Moorish harem odalisque and the supposed promiscuity of the passionate gypsy. After all, when Leporello counts off his master's conquests in Mozart's *Don Giovanni*, which country comes out on top? Spain, of course, with 1003 victims to the arch-libertine's art of persuasion.

Nothing kept this fond male fancy afloat as much as the fact that nubile Andalucían women were tantalizingly inaccessible, thanks to a rigid Latin code of honour second to none. It took the Industrial Revolution, the Seville tobacco factory, and a French visitor, Prosper Mérimée, to bring this creature of the imagination out into the open, in the form of the beautiful gypsy tomato *Carmen* (1845), rendered immortally saucy in Bizet's opera of 1873. Step aside, Don Juan, or be stepped on! This new stereotype was as quick to light up a cheroot as to kick aside her sweetheart for a strutting matador in tight trousers. Not surprisingly, it wasn't long before the Tobacco Factory and its steamy, scantily-clad examples of feminine pulchritude (labouring for a handful of pesetas a day) attracted as many tourists as the Giralda tower.

Alas, where is the kitsch of yesteryear? Modern young Andalucían women are, like modern Andalucían men, among the most normal, mentally well-balanced people in the world. Ask them about the cloistered *señoritas* of the past and they'll laugh. Ask them about the unbridled Carmen, and they'll laugh. Ask them about the bizarre wind called the *solano* that troubles Cádiz in the springtime, a wind that in the old days drove the entire female population en masse to the beach, where they would fling off their clothes and dive into the sea to seek relief while the local cavalry regiment stood guard. Ask them about it, and they'll just laugh.

Spain and Britain

Where would the English be without Spain? Where would they get their brussels sprouts in January, or canaries, or Seville oranges for marmalade? Long ago the ancient Iberians colonized Cornwall (of course historians can be found who say they arrived in Spain *from* Britain), and ever since, these two lands have been bound by the oldest of crossed destinies, either as the closest of allies, as in the Hundred Years War, or the most implacable of enemies.

Strange little connections would fill a book. Morris dancing, or *Moorish* dancing if you like, is said to have come up with John of Gaunt after his unsuccessful campaign to snatch the throne of Castile. One of Elizabeth II's biggest crown jewels was a gift from Pedro the Cruel to the Black Prince; Pedro had murdered an ambassador from Muslim Granada to get it off his turbann. In politics, we can thank Spain for words like *propaganda*, *Fifth Column* (both from the Civil War), and *liberal* (from the 1820s), and among the Jews expelled by Ferdinand and Isabella in 1492 were the ancestors of Disraeli.

In Spain, the Welsh may feel right at home in the green mining country of Asturias, and the Irish can honour the memory of the 19th-century prime minister O'Donnell, the famous governor of Cádiz, Conde O'Reilly, or the thousands of their countrymen who escaped persecution to settle in Galicia in the 16th century. The true Scotsman will make a pilgrimage to the Vega of Granada to look for the heart of Robert the Bruce, hero of the battle of Bannockburn. In 1329 Sir James Douglas was taking the Bruce's heart to be buried in the Holy Land, when crusading zeal side-tracked him to Spain. In battle against the Moors of Granada, Douglas and his knights became surrounded beyond hope of rescue. Spurring his horse for a last attack, Douglas flung the Bruce's heart into the enemy ranks, crying, 'Go ye first, as always!'

Bats

A fine country for bats, is Spain. Almost everywhere in the country (but especially in Aragón and around Granada) you'll see clouds of them cavorting in the twilight, zooming noiselessly past your ears and doing their best to ensure you get a good night's sleep by gobbling up all the mosquitoes they can. Spaniards don't mind them a bit, and the medieval kings of Aragón even went so far as to make them a dynastic emblem, derived from a Muslim Sufi symbol.

Lots of bats, of course, presumes lots of caves, and Spain has more than its share. The famous grottoes of Nerja, Aracena, and Valporquero (near León) are only a few of the places where you can see colossal displays of tinted, aesthetically draped stalactites. Hundreds were decorated in one way or another by Palaeolithic man; even though the most famous, at Altamira, are closed to the public, you can still see some cave art by asking around for a guide in Albarracín in Aragón, in the villages west of Cuenca, at Puente Viesgo near Santander, or around Vélez Rubio west of Murcia. This last area, from Vélez as far west as Granada, actually has a huge population still living in caves—quite cosily fitted out these days—and in Granada itself you can visit the 'gypsy caves' for a little histrionic flamenco and diluted sherry.

THE
ALHAMBRA,
GRANADA.

Granada

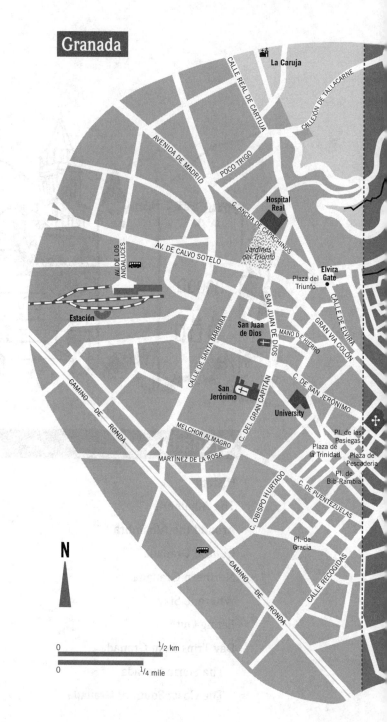

Granada

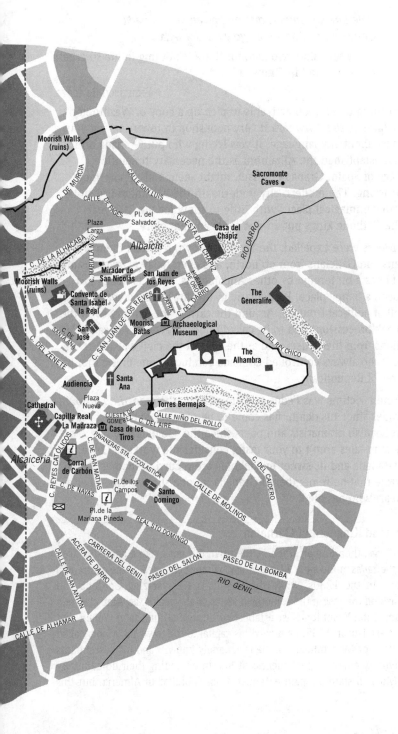

Moorish Walls
(ruins)

C. DE MURCIA

CALLE DE PAGES

CALLE SAN LUIS

Sacromonte
Caves ●

Plaza
Larga

Pl. del
Salvador

CUESTA DEL CHAPIZ

Casa del
Chapiz

C. DE LA ALHACABA

Albaicín

RIO DARRO

C. MARIA LA MIEL

Mirador de
San Nicolás

San Juan de
los Reyes

Moorish Walls
(ruins)

Convento de
Santa Isabel
la Real

C. DE SANTA ANA

San
José

C. SAN JUAN DE LOS REYES

C. DEL ZAFRA

HORNO DE ORO

C. DEL DARRO

The
Generalife

C. DEL ZENETE

Moorish
Baths

Archaeological
Museum

C. DEL REY CHICO

The
Alhambra

Audiencia

Santa
Ana

Plaza
Nueva

CUESTA DE GOMEREZ

Cathedral

Torres Bermejas

Capilla Real
La Madraza

C. DEL AIRE

CALLE NIÑO DEL ROLLO

Casa de los
Tiros

PAVANERAS STA. ESCOLÁSTICA

Alcaicería

C. REYES CATÓLICOS

C. DE SAN MATÍAS

Corral
de Carbón

C. DE NAVAS

Pl.de los
Campos

Santo
Domingo

CALLE DE MOLINOS

C. DEL CAIDERO

Pl.de la
Mariana Pineda

REAL STO DOMINGO

CARRERA DEL GENIL

ACERA DE DARRO

CALLE DE SAN ANTÓN

PASEO DEL SALÓN

PASEO DE LA BOMBA

RIO GENIL

CALLE DE ALHAMAR

Dale limosna mujer, que no hay en la vida nada
Como la pena de ser ciego y en Granada.

(Give him alms, woman, for there is nothing in life so cruel as being blind in Granada.)

Francisco de Icaza

The first thing to do upon arrival is to pick up a copy of Washington Irving's *Tales of the Alhambra*. Every bookshop in town can sell you one in just about any language. It was Irving who put Granada on the map, and established the Alhambra as the necessary romantic pilgrimage of Spain. Granada, in fact, might seem a disappointment without Irving. The modern city underneath the Alhambra is a stolid, remarkably unmagical place, with little to show for the 500 years since the Catholic kings put an end to its ancient glory.

As the Moors were expelled, the Spanish Crown replaced them with Castilians and Galicians from up north, and even today *granadinos* are thought of as a bit foreign by other Andalucíans. Their Granada has never been a happy place. Particularly in the last hundred years it has been full of political troubles. Around the turn of the century even the Holy Week processions had to be called off for a few years because of disruptions from the leftists, and at the start of the civil war the reactionaries who always controlled Granada conducted one of the first big massacres of Republicans.

One of their victims was Federico García Lorca, the *granadino* who, in the decades since his death, has come to be recognized as one of the greatest Spanish dramatists and poets since the 'Golden Age'. If Irving's fairy-tales aren't to your taste, consider the works of Lorca, in which Granada and its sweet melancholy are recurring themes. Lorca once wrote that he remembered Granada 'as one should remember a sweetheart who has died'.

History: the Nasrid Kingdom of Qarnatah

First Iberian *Elibyrge*, then Roman *Illiberis*, the town did not make a name for itself until the era of the *taifas* in the early 11th century, when it emerged as the centre of a very minor state. In the 1230s, while the Castilians were seizing Córdoba and preparing to polish off the rest of the Almoravid states of al-Andalus, an Arab chieftain named Mohammed ibn-Yusuf ibn-Nasr established himself around Jaén. When that town fell to the Castilians in 1235, he moved his capital to the town the Moors called *Qarnatah*. Ibn Nasr (or Mohammed I, as he is generally known) and his descendants in the Nasrid dynasty enjoyed great success at first in extending their domains. By 1300 this last Moorish state of Spain extended from Gibraltar to Almería, but this accomplishment came entirely at the expense of other Moors. Mohammed and his successors were in fact vassals of the kings of Castile, and aided them in campaigns more often than they fought them.

Qarnatah at this time is said to have had a population of some 200,000—almost as many as it has now—and both its arts and industries were strengthened by refugees from the fallen towns of al-Andalus. Thousands came from Córdoba, especially, and the Albaicín quarter was largely settled by the former inhabitants of Baeza. Although a significant Jewish population remained, there were very few Christians. In the comparatively peaceful 14th century, Granada's conservative, introspective civilization reached its height, with the last flowering of Arabic-Andaluz lyric poetry and the architecture and decorative arts of the Alhambra.

This state of affairs lasted until the coming of the Catholic kings. Isabella's religious fanaticism made the completion of the Reconquista the supreme goal of her reign; she sent Ferdinand out in 1484 to do the job, which he accomplished in eight years by a breathtakingly brilliant combination of force and diplomacy. Qarnatah at the time was suffering the usual curse of al-Andalus states—disunity founded on the egotism of princes. In this fatal feud, the main actors were Abu al-Hasan Ali (Mulay Hassan in Irving's tales), king of Qarnatah, his brother El Zagal ('the valiant') and the king's rebellious son, Abu abd-Allah, better known to posterity as Boabdil el Chico. His seizure of the throne in 1482 started a period of civil war at the worst possible time. Ferdinand was clever enough to take advantage of the divisions; he captured Boabdil twice, and turned him into a tool of Castilian designs. Playing one side against the other, Ferdinand snatched away one Nasrid province after another with few losses.

When the unfortunate Boabdil, after renouncing his kingship in favour of the Castilians, finally changed his mind and decided to fight for the remnants of Qarnatah (by then little more than the city itself and the Sierra Nevada), Ferdinand had the excuse he needed to mount his final attack. Qarnatah was besieged and, after two years, Boabdil agreed to surrender under terms that guaranteed his people the use of their religion and customs. When the keys of the city were handed over on 2 January 1492, the Reconquista was complete.

Under a gentlemanly military governor, the Conde de Tendilla, the agreement was kept until the arrival in 1499 of Cardinal Ximénez de Cisneros, the most influential cleric in Spain and a man who made it his personal business to destroy the last vestiges of Islam and Moorish culture. The new Spanish policy—planned, gradual genocide (*see* **History**, p.49)—was as successful in the former lands of Granada as it was among those other troublesome heathens of the same period, the Indians of Central and South America. The famous revolt in Las Alpujarras (1568) was followed by a rising in the city itself, in the Albaicín. Between 1609 and 1614, the last of the Muslims were expelled, including most of those who had converted to Christianity, and their property confiscated. It is said that, even today, there are old families in Morocco who sentimentally keep the keys to their long-lost homes in Granada.

Such a history does not easily wear away, even after so many centuries. The Castilians corrupted Qarnatah to *Granada*; just by coincidence that means 'pomegranate' in Spanish, and the pomegranate has come to be the symbol of the city. With its associations with the myth of Persephone, with the mysteries of death and loss, no symbol could be more suitable for this capital of melancholy.

Getting Around

by air

There are two flights daily to Madrid (Mon–Sat), two daily to Barcelona (Mon–Fri) and flights three times a week to the Balearics and Canaries. The airport is 16km west of Granada, near Santa Fé. **Information:** © 95 822 75 92.

by train

Granada has connections to Guadix and Almería (three daily), to Algeciras, Sevilla, and Córdoba by way of Bobadilla Junction (they are sometimes complicated) and two daily to Madrid and Barcelona; three daily to Alicante, one a day to Valencia. The station is at the northern end of town, about a mile from the centre, on Avenida de los Andaluces; the city ticket office is on Calle Reyes Católicos, off Piaza Nueva. **Information:** © 95 822 34 97.

by bus

Nearly all intercity buses leave from the the new main bus station, on the outskirts of town on the Carretera de Jaén. **Information:** © 95 818 50 10. Bus no.3 runs between the bus station and the city centre. Buses to the ski resorts and the Alpujarras leave from the corner of Paseo de los Basilios and Prof Tierno Golvan.

The '*Alhambra*' bus from the Plaza Nueva will save you the trouble of climbing up to the Alhambra.

by car

Parking is a problem, so if you plan staying overnight make sure that your hotel has parking facilities and check whether there is a charge or not—it can cost as much as the accommodation in some places. Traffic police are extremely vigilant. Fines of up to 20,000 pts are payable on the spot if you are a tourist. Ignore people at the bottom of the Alhambra trying to persuade you to park before you reach the top; there's plenty of parking space by the entrance and it's a steep walk to get there.

Tourist Information

Provincial tourist office, Pza. Mariana Pineda 10, © 95 822 66 88. *Open Mon–Fri 9.30–7 and Sat 10–2.*

There's a smaller office inside the Corral del Carbón, C/ Liberos 2, © 95 822 59 90. *Open Mon–Sat 9–7 and Sun 10–2.*

A Sentimental Orientation

In spite of everything, more of the lost world of al-Andalus can be seen in Granada than even in Cordoba. Granada stands where the foothills of the Sierra Nevada meet the fertile Vega de Granada, the greenest and best stretch of farmland in Andalucía. Two of those hills extend into the city itself. One bears the **Alhambra,** the fortified palace of the Nasrid kings, and the other the **Albaicín,** the most evocative of the 'Moorish' neighbourhoods of Andalucían cities.

Parts of old Qarnatah extended down into the plain, but they have been largely submerged into the new city. How much you enjoy Granada will depend largely on how successful you are in ignoring the new districts, in particular three barbarically ugly streets that form the main automobile route through Granada: the **Gran Vía Colón** chopped through the centre of town in the 19th century, the **Calle Reyes Católicos,** and the **Acera del Darro.** The last two are paved over the course of the Río Darro, the little stream that ran picturesquely through the city until the 1880s.

Before these streets were built, the centre of Granada was the **Plaza Nueva,** a square that is also partly built over the Darro. The handsome building that defines its character is the **Audiencia** (1584), built by Felipe II for the royal officials and judges. **Santa Ana** church, across the plaza, was built in 1537 by Diego de Siloé, one of the architects of Granada's cathedral. From this plaza the ascent to the Alhambra begins, winding up a narrow street called the **Cuesta de Gomérez,** past guitar-makers' shops and gypsies with vast displays of tourist trinkets, and ending abruptly at the **Puerta de las Granadas,** a monumental gateway erected by Charles V.

The Alhambra

Open daily 9–7.45, Sun 9–5.45, also open Tues, Thurs and Sat evenings 10–midnight (summer), 8–10pm (mid season); adm 750pts. Admission times constantly change, so always check beforehand with the ticket office, © 95 822 09 12.

The grounds of the Alhambra begin here with a bit of the unexpected. Instead of the walls and towers, not yet even in view, there is a lovely grove of great elms, the **Alameda**; even more unexpectedly, they are the contribution of the Duke of Wellington, who took time off from chasing the French to plant them during the Peninsular War. Take the path to the left—

The Alhambra

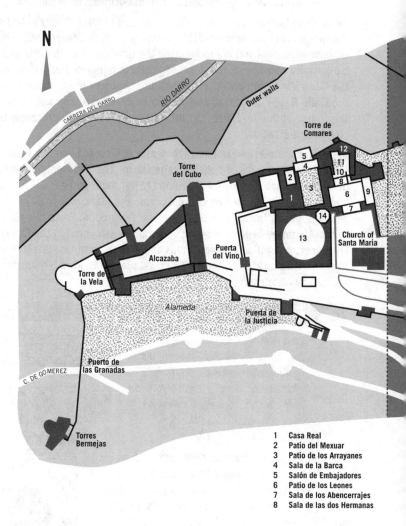

N

CARRERA DEL DARRO

RIO DARRO

Outer walls

Torre de Comares

Torre del Cubo

12
5
4
11
10
2
8
3
1
6
9
7
14
13

Church of Santa Maria

Alcazaba

Puerta del Vino

Torre de la Vela

Alameda

Puerta de la Justicia

Puerto de las Granadas

C. DE GOMEREZ

Torres Bermejas

1 Casa Real
2 Patio del Mexuar
3 Patio de los Arrayanes
4 Sala de la Barca
5 Salón de Embajadores
6 Patio de los Leones
7 Sala de los Abencerrajes
8 Sala de las dos Hermanas

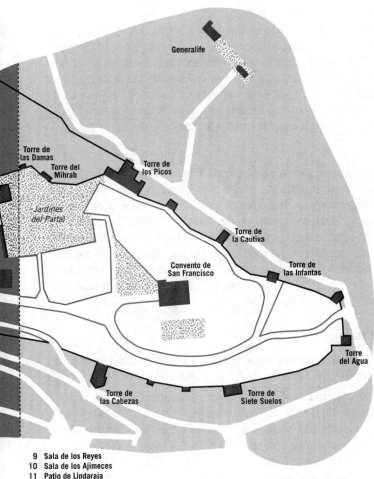

Generalife

Torre de
las Damas

Torre del
Mihrab

Torre de
los Picos

Jardines
del Partal

Torre de
la Cautiva

Convento de
San Francisco

Torre de
las Infantas

Torre
del Agua

Torre de
las Cabezas

Torre de
Siete Suelos

 9 Sala de los Reyes
10 Sala de los Ajimeces
11 Patio de Lindaraja
12 Queen's Chamber
13 Palacio de Carlos V /
    Museo de Bellas Artes/
    Museo Nacional de Arte Hispano-Musulmán
14 Chapel and Crypt

it's a stiff climb—and in a few minutes you'll arrive at the **Puerta de Justicia**, entrance of the Alhambra. The orange tint of the fortress walls explains the name *al-hamra* (the red), and the unusual style of the carving on the gate is the first clue that here is something very different. The two devices, a hand and a key, carved on the inner and outer arches, are famous. According to one of Irving's tales, the hand will one day reach down and grasp the key; then the Alhambra will fall into ruins, the earth will open, and the hidden treasures of the Moors will be revealed.

From the gate, a path leads up to a broad square. Here are the ticket booth, and the **Puerta del Vino**, so called from a long-ago Spanish custom of doling out free wine from this spot to the inhabitants of the Alhambra. To the left you'll see the walls of the **Alcazaba,** the fort at the tip of the Alhambra's narrow promontory, and to the right the huge **Palacio de Carlos V**; signs point your way to the entrance of the **Casa Real** (Royal Palace), with its splendidly decorated rooms that are the Alhambra's main attraction. Visit again after dark; seeing it under the stars is the treat of a lifetime.

The Alcazaba

Not much remains of the oldest part of the Alhambra. This citadel probably dates back to the first of the Nasrid kings. Its walls and towers are still intact, but only the foundations of the buildings that once stood within it have survived. The **Torre de la Vela** at the tip of the promontory has the best views over Granada and the Vega. Its big bell was rung in the old days to signal the daily opening and closing of the water gates of the Vega's irrigation system; the Moors also used the tower as a signal post for sending messages. The Albaicín, visible on the opposite hill, is a revelation; its rows of white, flat-roofed houses on the hillside, punctuated by palm trees and cypresses, provide one of Europe's most exotic urban landscapes.

Casa Real (Royal Palace)

Palace visits are limited to ½hr and the time must be specified at time of ticket purchase, otherwise it will be arranged for approximately 1½hrs later.

Words will not do, nor will exhaustive descriptions help, to communicate the experience of this greatest treasure of al-Andalus. This is what people come to Granada to see, and it is the surest, most accessible window into the refinement and subtlety of the culture of Moorish Spain—a building that can achieve in its handful of rooms what a work like Madrid's Royal Palace cannot even approach with its 2800.

It probably never occurs to most visitors, but one of the most unusual features of this palace is its modesty. What you see is what the Nasrid kings saw; your imagination need add only a few carpets and tapestries, some well-crafted furniture of wood inlaid with ivory, wooden screens, and big round braziers of brass for heat or incense, to make the picture complete. Most of the actual building is wood and plaster, cheap and perishable, like a World Fair pavilion; no good Muslim monarch would offend Allah's sense of propriety by pretending that these worldly splendours were anything more than the pleasures of a moment (much of the plaster, wood, and all of the tiles, are the products of careful restorations over the last 100 years). The Alhambra, in fact, is the only substantially intact medieval Muslim palace—anywhere.

Like so many old royal palaces (those of the Hittites, the Byzantines or the Ottoman Turks, for example), this one is divided into three sections: one for everyday business of the palace and government; the next, more secluded, for the state rooms and official entertainments of the kings; and the third, where few outsiders ever reached, for the private apartments of the king and his household.

The Mexuar

Of the first, the small Mexuar, where the kings would hold their public audiences, survives near the present-day entrance to the palace complex. The adjacent **Patio del Mexuar**, though much restored, is one of the finest rooms of the Alhambra. Nowhere is the meditative serenity of the palace more apparent (unless you arrive when all the tour groups do) and the small fountain in the centre provides an introduction to an important element of the architecture—water. Present everywhere, in pools, fountains and channels, water is as much a part of the design as the wood, tile and stone.

Patio de los Arrayanes

If you have trouble finding your way around, remember the elaborately decorated portals never really lead anywhere; the door you want will always be tucked unobtrusively to the side; here, as in Sevilla's Alcázar, the principle is to heighten the sense of surprise. The entrance to the grand Patio de los Arrayanes (Court of the Myrtles), with its long goldfish pond and lovely arcades, was the centre of the second, state section of the palace; directly off it, you pass through the **Sala de la Barca** (Hall of the Boat), so called from its hull-shaped wooden ceiling, and into the **Salón de Embajadores** (Hall of Ambassadors), where the kings presided over all important state business. The views and the decoration are some of the Alhambra's best, with a cedarwood ceiling and plaster panels (many were originally painted) carved with floral arabesques or Arabic calligraphy. These inscriptions, some Koranic scripture (often the phrase 'Allah alone conquers', the motto of the Nasrids), some eulogies of the kings, and some poetry, recur throughout the palace. The more conspicuous are in a flowing script developed by the Granadan artists; look closely and you will see others, in the angular Kufic script, forming frames for the floral designs.

In some of the chambers off the Patio de los Arrayanes, you can peek out over the domed roofs of the baths below; opposite the Salón de Embajadores is a small entrance (often closed) into the dark, empty **crypt** of the Palace of Charles V, with curious echo effects.

Patio de los Leones

Another half-hidden doorway leads you into the third and most spectacular section, the king's residence, built around the Patio de los Leones (Court of the Lions). Here the plaster and stucco work is at its most ornate, the columns and arches at their most

THE
FOUNTAIN
OF LIONS
ALHAMBRA

delicate, with little pretence of any structural purpose; balanced on their slender shafts, the façades of the court seem to hang in the air. As in much of Moorish architecture, the overripe arabesques of this patio conceal a subtle symbolism. The 'enclosed garden' that can stand for the attainment of truth, or paradise, or for the cosmos, is a recurring theme in Islamic mystical poetry. Here you may take the 12 endearingly preposterous lions who support the fountain in the centre as the months, or signs of the zodiac, and the four channels that flow out from the fountains as the four corners of the cosmos, the cardinal points, or, on a different level, the four rivers of paradise.

The rooms around the patio have exquisite decorations: to the right, from the entrance, the **Sala de los Abencerrajes**, named after the legend of the noble family that Boabdil supposedly had massacred at a banquet here during the civil wars just before the fall of Granada; to the left, the **Sala de las dos Hermanas** (Hall of the Two Sisters). Both of these have extravagant domed *muqarnas* ceilings. The latter chamber is also ornamented with a wooden window grille, another speciality of the Granadan artists; this is the only one surviving in the Alhambra. Adjacent to the Sala de las dos Hermanas is the **Sala de los Ajimeces**, so called for its doubled windows. The **Sala de los Reyes** (Hall of the Kings), opposite the court's entrance, is unique for the paintings on its ceiling, works that would not be out of place in any Christian palace of medieval Europe. The central panel may represent six of Granada's 14th-century kings; those on the side are scenes of a chivalric court. The artist is believed to have been a visiting Spanish Christian painter, possibly from Sevilla. From the Sala de las dos Hermanas, steps lead down to the **Patio de Lindaraja** (or Mirador de Daraxa), with its fountain and flowers, Washington Irving's favourite spot in the Alhambra. Originally the inner garden of the palace, it was remodelled for the royal visits of Charles V and Felipe V. Irving actually lived in the **Queen's Chamber**, decorated with frescoes of Charles V's expedition to Tunis—in 1829, apartments in the Alhambra could be had for the asking! Just off this chamber, at ground-floor level, is the beautifully decorated **hammam**, the palace baths.

Follow the arrows, out of the palace and into the outer gardens, the **Jardines del Partal**, a broad expanse of rose terraces and flowing water.

The northern walls of the Alhambra border the gardens, including a number of well-preserved towers: from the west, the **Torre de las Damas**, entered by a small porch, the **Torre del Mihrab**, near which is a small mosque, now a chapel; the **Torre de los Picos**; the **Torre de la Cautiva** (Tower of the Imprisoned Lady), one of the most elaborately decorated; and the **Torre de las Infantas**, one of the last projects in the Alhambra (*c.* 1400).

Palacio de Carlos V

Anywhere else this elegant Renaissance building would be an attraction in itself. Here it seems only pompous and oversized, and our appreciation of it is lessened by the mind-numbing thought of this emperor, with a good half of Europe to build palaces in, having to plop it down here—ruining much of the Alhambra in the process. Once Charles had smashed up the place, he lost interest, and most of the palace, still unfinished, was not built until 1616. The original architect, Pedro Machuco, had studied in Italy, and he took the opportunity to introduce into Spain the chilly, Olympian High Renaissance style of Rome.

At the entrances are intricately detailed sculptural **reliefs** showing scenes from Charles's campaigns and military 'triumphs' in the antique manner: armoured torsos on sticks amidst heaps of weapons. This is a very particular sort of art, arrogant and weird, and wherever it appears around the Mediterranean it will usually be associated with the grisly reign of the man who dreamt of being Emperor of the World. Inside, Machuco added a pristinely classical circular courtyard, based perhaps on a design by Raphael. For all its Doric gravity, the patio was used almost from its completion for bull-fights and mock tournaments.

The Museums

Museo de Bellas Artes, © 95 822 48 43; Museo Nacional de Arte Hispano-Musulmán, © 95 822 62 79. Opening times are the same as the Alhambra, but the museums are closed at night.

On the top floor of the Palace is the **Museo de Bellas Artes**, a largely forgettable collection of religious paintings from Granada churches. Downstairs, the **Museo Nacional de Arte Hispano-Musulmán** contains perhaps Spain's best collection of Moorish art, including some paintings, similar to those in the Moorish palace's Sala de los Reyes. Also present are original *azulejo* tiles and plaster arabesques from the palace, and some exceedingly fine wooden panels and screens. There is a collection of ceramic ware with fanciful figurative decoration—elephants and lady musicians—and some lovely astronomical instruments. Tucked in a corner of the museum are four big copper balls stacked on a pole, an ornament that once stood atop a Granada minaret. These were a typical feature of Andalucían minarets (as on La Giralda in Seville) and similar examples can be seen in Morocco today.

Behind Charles's palace a street leads into the remnants of the town that once filled much of the space within the Alhambra's walls, now reduced to a small collection of restaurants and souvenir stands. In Moorish times the Alhambra held a large permanent population, and even under the Spaniards it long retained the status of a separate municipality. At one end of the street, the church of **Santa María** (1581), designed by Juan de Herrera, architect of El Escorial, occupies the site of the Alhambra's mosque; at the other, the first Christian building on the Alhambra, the **Convento de San Francisco** (1495) has been converted into a *parador*.

The Generalife

> *Opening hours are the same as for the Alhambra; adm included in Alhambra ticket.*

The Generalife (*Djinat al-Arif*: high garden) was the summer palace of the Nasrid kings, built on the height the Moors called the Mountain of the Sun. Many of the trillions of visitors the Alhambra receives each year have never heard of it, and pass up a chance to see the finest garden in Spain. To get there, it's about a five-minute walk from the Alhambra along a lovely avenue of tall cypresses. The buildings here hold few surprises if you've just come from the Alhambra. They are older than most of the Casa Real, which was probably begun around 1260. The gardens are built on terraces on several levels along the hillside, and the views over the Alhambra and Albaicín are transcendent. The centrepiece is a long pool with many water sprays that passes through beds of roses. A lower level, with a promenade on the hill's edge, is broken up into secluded bowers by cypress bushes cut into angular shapes of walls and gateways. There is no evidence that the original Moorish gardens looked anything like this; everything here has been done in the last 200 years.

If you're walking down from the Alhambra, you might consider a different route, across the Alameda and down through the picturesque streets below the **Torres Bermejas**, an outwork of the Alhambra's fortifications built on foundations that date back to the Romans. The winding lanes and stairways around Calle del Aire and Calle Niño del Rollo, one of the most beautiful quarters of Granada, will eventually lead you back down near the Plaza Nueva.

Albaicín

Even more than the old quarters of Córdoba, this hillside neighbourhood of whitewashed houses and tall cypresses has successfully preserved some of the atmosphere of al-Andalus. Its difficult site and the fact that it was long the district of Granada's poor explain the lack of change, but today the Albaicín looks as if it is becoming fashionable again.

From the Plaza Nueva, a narrow street called the **Carrera del Darro** leads up the valley of the Darro between the Alhambra and Albaicín hills; here the little stream has not been covered over, and you can get an idea of how the centre of Granada looked in the old days. On the Alhambra side, old stone bridges lead up to a few half-forgotten streets hidden among the forested slopes; here you'll see some 17th-century Spanish houses with curious painted *esgrafiado* façades. Nearby, traces of a horseshoe arch can be seen where a Moorish wall once crossed the river; in the corner of Calle Baruelo there are well-preserved **Moorish baths** (*open Tues–Sat 10–2*). Even more curious is the façade of the **Casa Castril** on the Darro, a flamboyant 16th-century mansion with a portal carved with a phoenix, winged scallop shells and other odd devices that have been interpreted as elements in a complex mystical symbolism. Over the big corner window is an inscription 'Waiting for her from the heavens'. The house's owner, Bernardo de Zafra, was once a secretary to Ferdinand and Isabella, and seems to have got into trouble with the Inquisition.

Casa Castril has been restored as Granada's **archaeological museum** (*open Tues 3–8, Wed–Sat 9–8, Sun 9–2.30*) with a small collection of artefacts from the huge number of caves in Granada province, many inhabited since Palaeolithic times, and a few Iberian settlements. There is a Moorish room, with some lovely works of art, and finally, an even greater oddity than Casa Castril itself. One room of the museum holds a collection of beautiful alabaster burial urns, made in Egypt, but found in a Phoenician-style necropolis near Almuñécar. Nothing else like them has ever been discovered in Spain, and the Egyptian hieroglyphic inscriptions on them are provocative in the extreme (translations given in Spanish), telling how the deceased travelled here in search of some mysterious primordial deity.

Farther up the Darro, there's a small park with a view up to the Alhambra; after that you'll have to do some climbing, but the higher you go the prettier the Albaicín is, and the better the views. Among the white houses and white walls are some of the oldest Christian churches in Granada. As in Córdoba, they are tidy and extremely plain, built to avoid alienating a recently converted population unused to religious imagery. **San Juan de los Reyes** (1520) on Calle Zafra and **San José** (1525) are the oldest; both retain the plain minarets of the mosques they replaced. Quite a few Moorish houses survive in the Albaicín, and some can be seen on **Calle Horno de Oro**, just off the Darro; on **Calle Daralhorra,** at the top of the Albaicín, are the remains of a Nasrid palace that was largely destroyed to make way for Isabel's **Convento de Santa Isabel la Real** (1501).

Here, running parallel to Cuesta de la Alhacaba, is a long-surviving stretch of Moorish wall. There are probably a few miles of walls left, visible around the hillsides over Granada; the location of the city made a very complex set of fortifications necessary. In this one, about halfway up, you may pass through **Puerta de las Pesas**, with its horseshoe arches. The heart of the Albaicín is here, around the pretty, animated **Plaza Larga**; only a few blocks away the **mirador de San Nicolás**, in front of the church of that name, offers the most romantic view imaginable of the Alhambra with the snow-capped peaks of the Sierra Nevada behind it. Note the brick, barrel-vaulted fountain on the mirador, a typical Moorish survival; fountains like this can be seen throughout the Albaicín and most are still in use. Granada today has a small but growing Muslim community, and they are beginning to build a mosque just off the mirador. Construction hasn't started yet; apparently they are facing some difficulties with the city government.

On your way back from the Albaicín you might take a different route, down a maze of back streets to the **Puerta de Elvira**; one of the most picturesque corners of the neighbourhood.

Tortilla al Sacromonte

 Regional dishes include cod rissole soup, chick peas and onions, plus, of course, the famous *tortilla al Sacromonte* made from a delightful concoction of brains, lamb's testicles, vegetables and eggs. The name originates from the Sacromonte gypsies. Broad beans Granadine, cooked with fresh artichokes, tomatoes, onions, garlic, breadcrumbs and a smattering of saffron and cumin may seem less adventurous compared to *Sacromonte* but it's just as typical of Granadinas dishes. If you're in Las Alpujarras, try the fresh goats' cheese, and in Trevélez you'll be hard pushed to avoid its famous ham. But if you're west of Granada near Santafé, make a detour to sample its sumptuous *piononos*— babas with cream.

Sacromonte

For something completely different, you might strike out beyond the Albaicín hill to the **gypsy caves of Sacromonte**. Granada has had a substantial gypsy population for several centuries now. Some have become settled and respectable, others live in trailers on vacant land around town. The most visible are those who prey on the tourists around the Alhambra and the Capilla Real, handing out carnations with a smile and then attempting to extort huge sums out of anyone dumb enough to take one (of course, they'll tell your fortune, too). The biggest part of the gypsy community, however, still lives around Sacromonte in streets of some quite well-appointed cave homes, where they wait to lure you in for a little display of flamenco. For a hundred years or so, the consensus of opinion has been that the music and dancing are usually indifferent, and the gypsies' eventually successful attempts to shake out your last peseta can make it an unpleasantly unforgettable affair. Hotels sell tours for around 2000 pts. Nevertheless, if you care to match wits with the experts, proceed up the Cuesta del Chapiz from the Río Darro, turn right at the **Casa del Chapiz**, a big 16th-century palace that now houses a school of Arab studies, and keep going until some gypsy child drags you home with him. The bad reputation has been keeping tourists away lately so it's now much safer and friendlier as the gypsies are worried about the loss of income. Serious flamenco fans will probably not fare better elsewhere in Granada except during the festivals, though there are some touristy flamenco nightspots—the **Reina Mora** by Mirador San Cristóbal is the best of them. On the third Sunday of each month, though, you can hear a **flamenco mass** performed in the San Pedro Church on the Carrera del Darro at 9am.

Central Granada

The old city wall swung in a broad arc from Puerta de Elvira to Puerta Real, now a small plaza full of traffic where Calle Reyes Católicos meets the Acera del Darro. Just a few blocks north of here, in a web of narrow pedestrian streets that make up modern

Granada's shopping district, is the pretty **Plaza de Bib-Rambla**, full of flower stands and toy shops, with an unusual fountain supported by leering giants at its centre. This was an important square in Moorish times, used for public gatherings and tournaments of arms. The narrow streets leading off towards the east are the **Alcaicería**. This was the Moorish silk exchange, but the build-ings you see now, full of tourist souvenir shops, are not original; the Alcaicería burned down in the 1840s and was rebuilt in more or less the same fashion with Moorish arches and columns.

The Cathedral

Pza. de Pasiegas, © 95 822 29 59. Open Mon–Sat 10.30–1.30 and 4–7, Sun 4–7.

The best way to see Granada's **cathedral** is to approach it from Calle Marqués, just north of the Plaza Bib-Rambla. The unique façade, with its three tall, recessed arches, is a striking sight, designed by the painter Alonso Cano (1667). On the central arch, the big plaque bearing the words 'Ave María' commemorates the exploit of the Spanish captain who sneaked into the city one night in 1490 and nailed this message up on the door of the great mosque this cathedral has replaced.

The other conspicuous feature is the name 'José Antonio Primo de Rivera' carved on the façade. Son of the 1920s dictator, Miguel Primo de Rivera, José Antonio was a mystic fascist who founded the Phalangist Party. His thugs provoked many of the disorders that started the civil war, and at the beginning of the conflict he was captured by the loyalists and executed. Afterwards his followers treated him as a sort of holy martyr, and chis-elled his name on every cathedral in Spain. That you can still see it here says a lot about Granada today.

The rest of the cathedral isn't up to the standard of its façade, and there is little reason to go in and explore its cavernous interior or dreary museum. Work was begun in 1521, after the Spaniards broke their promise not to harm the great mosque. As in many Spanish cathedrals, the failure of this one stems from artistic indecision. Two very talented architects were in charge: Enrique de Egas, who wanted it Gothic, like his adjacent Capilla Real, and (five years later) Diego de Siloé, who decided Renaissance would look much nicer. A score of other architects got their fingers in the pie before its completion in 1703. Some features of the interior: the grandiose **Capilla Mayor**, with statues of the apostles, and of Ferdinand and Isabella, by Alonso de Mena, and enor-mous heads of Adam and Eve by Alonso Cano, whose sculptures and paintings can be seen all over the cathedral; the **Retablo de Jesús Nazareno** in the right aisle, with paintings by Cano and Ribera, and a *St Francis* by El Greco; the Gothic **portal** leading into the Capilla Real (now closed) by de Egas. At the foot of the bell tower is a **museum**; its only memorable work is a subject typical of the degenerate art of the 1700s—a painted wooden head of John the Baptist.

Capilla Real

Gran Vía de Colón, © 95 822 92 39; open daily 10.30–1 and 4–7, Sun 11–1; adm 250 pts.

Leaving the cathedral and turning left, you pass the outsized **sacristy**, begun in 1705 and incorporated in the cathedral façade. Turn left again at the first street, Calle de los Oficios, a narrow lane paved in charming patterns of coloured pebbles—a Granada speciality; on the left, you can pay your respects to *Los Reyes Católicos*, in the Capilla Real. The royal couple had already built a mausoleum in Toledo, but after the capture of Granada they decided to plant themselves here. Even in the shadow of the bulky cathedral, Enrique de Egas's chapel (1507) reveals itself as the outstanding work of the Isabelline Gothic style, with its delicate roofline of traceries and pinnacles. Charles V thought it not nearly monumental enough for his grandparents, and only the distraction of his foreign wars kept him from wrecking it in favour of some elephantine replacement.

Inside, the Catholic Kings are buried in a pair of Carrara marble sarcophagi, decorated with their recumbent figures, elegantly carved though not necessarily flattering to either of them. The little staircase behind them leads down to the crypt, where you can peek in at their plain lead coffins and those of their unfortunate daughter, Juana the Mad, and her husband, Felipe the Handsome, whose effigies lie next to the older couple above. Juana was Charles V's mother, and the rightful heir to the Spanish throne. There is considerable doubt as to whether she was mad at all; when Charles arrived from Flanders in 1517, he forced her to sign papers of abdication, and then locked her up in a windowless cell for the last 40 years of her life, never permitting any visitors. The interior of the chapel is sumptuously decorated—it should be, considering the huge proportion of the crown revenues that were expended on it. The iron *reja* by Master Bartolomé de Jaén and the *retablo* are especially fine; the latter is largely the work of a French artist, Philippe de Bourgogne. In the chapel's sacristy you can see some of Isabel's personal art collection—works by Van der Weyden, Memling, Pedro Berruguete, Botticelli (attributed), Perugino and others, mostly in need of some restoration—as well as her crown and sceptre, her illuminated missal, some captured Moorish banners, and Ferdinand's sword.

Across the narrow street from the Capilla Real, an endearingly garish, painted baroque façade hides **La Madraza**, a domed hall of the Moorish *madrasa* (Islamic seminary); though one of the best Moorish works surviving in Granada, it is hardly ever open to visitors (just walk in if the building is open). The Christians converted it into a town hall, whence its other name, the Casa del Cabildo.

Across Calle Reyes Católicos

Even though this part of the city centre is as old as the Albaicín, most of it was rebuilt after 1492, and its age doesn't show. The only Moorish building remaining is also the only example left in Spain of a *khan* or *caravanserai*, the type of merchants' hotel common throughout the Muslim world. The 14th-century **Corral del Carbón**, just off Reyes Católicos, takes its name from the time, a century ago, when it was used as a coal warehouse. Under the Spaniards it also served time as a theatre; its interior courtyard with balconies lends itself admirably to the purpose, being about the same size and shape as a Spanish theatre of the classic age, like the one in Almagro (La Mancha). Today it houses a government handicrafts outlet, and much of the building is under restoration.

The neighbourhood of quiet streets and squares behind it is the best part of Spanish Granada and worth a walk if you have the time. Here you'll see the *mudéjar* **Casa de los Tiros**, a restored mansion built in 1505 on Calle Pavaneras, with strange figures carved on its façade; it houses a **museum** of the city's history. **Santo Domingo** (1512), the finest of Granada's early churches, is just a few blocks to the south. Ferdinand and Isabella endowed it, and their monograms figure prominently on the lovely façade.

This neighbourhood is bounded on the west by the Acera del Darro, the noisy heart of modern Granada, with most of the big hotels. It's a little discouraging but, as compensation, just a block away the city has adorned itself with a beautiful string of wide boulevards very like the Ramblas of Barcelona, a wonderful spot for a stroll. The **Carretera del Genil** usually has some sort of open-air market on it, and further down, the **Paseo del Salón** and **Paseo de la Bomba** are quieter and more park-like, joining the pretty banks of the Río Genil.

Northern Granada

From the little street on the north side of the cathedral, the Calle de la Cárcel, Calle San Jerónimo skirts the edge of Granada's markets and leads you towards the old **university** district. Even though much of the university has relocated to a new campus half a mile to the north, this is still one of the livelier spots of town, and the colleges themselves occupy some fine, well-restored baroque structures. The long yellow College of Law is one of the best, occupying a building put up in 1769 for the Jesuits; a small botanical garden is adjacent. Calle San Jerónimo ends at the Calle del Gran Capitán, where the landmark is the church of **San Juan de Dios**, with a baroque façade and a big green and white tiled dome. **San Jerónimo**, a block south, is another of the oldest and largest Granada churches (1520); it contains the tomb of Gonzalo de Córdoba, the 'Gran Capitán' who won so many victories in Italy for the Catholic Kings; adjacent are two Gothic cloisters.

Here you're not far from the Puerta de Elvira, in an area where old Granada fades into anonymous suburbs to the north. The big park at the end of the Gran Vía is the

Jardines del Triunfo, with coloured, illuminated fountains the city hardly ever turns on. Behind them is the Renaissance **Hospital Real** (1504–22), designed by Enrique de Egas. A few blocks southwest, climbing up towards the Albaicín, your senses will be assaulted by the gaudiest baroque chapel in Spain, in the **Cartuja**, or Carthusian monastery, on Calle Real de Cartuja (*open daily except Mon, 10–1 and 4–8, © 95 816 19 32*). Gonzalo de Córdoba endowed this Charterhouse, though little of the original works remain. The 18th-century chapel and its sacristy, done in the richest marble, gold and silver, and painted plaster, fairly oozes with a froth of twisted spiral columns, rosettes and curlicues. It has often been described as a Christian attempt to upstage the Alhambra, but the inspiration more likely comes from the Aztecs, via the extravagant Mexican baroque.

Lorca

Outside Spain Federico García Lorca is popularly regarded as Spain's greatest modern dramatist and poet. The Spanish literati would acknowledge others from the generation of 1925 and from the previous generation of 1898 to have at least equal stature. The Galician dramatist and poet Ramón del Valle-Inclán springs to mind. But Lorca's murder certainly enhanced his reputation outside Spain. Under Franco, any mention of him was forbidden (understandably so, since it was Franco's men who shot him).

Today the *granadinos* are coming to terms with Lorca, and seem determined to make up for the past. Lorca fans pay their respects at two country houses, now museums, where the poet spent many of his early years: the **Huerta de San Vicente**, on the outskirts of town at Virgen Blanca, and the **Museo Lorca** at Fuente Vaqueros, the village where he was born, 17km away to the west near the Córdoba road (*both open for guided tours every hour, 10–1 and 5–8, daily except Mon*).

Granada ✉ *18000*   ***Where to Stay***

If you are travelling independently and need to find your own hotel, the city centre, around the Acera del Darro, is full of hotels, and there are lots of inexpensive *hostales* around the Gran Vía—but the less you see of these areas, the better. Fortunately, you can choose from a wide range around the Alhambra and in the older parts of town if you take the time to look.

expensive

Right in the Alhambra itself, the ★★★★**Parador Nacional San Francisco**, © 95 822 14 40, @ 95 822 22 64, is perhaps the most famous of all *paradores*, housed in a convent where Queen Isabel was originally interred. It's beautiful, expensive, and small; you'll always need to book well in advance—a year would not be unreasonable (*33,000 pts*).

An alternative choice very near the Alhambra would be the outrageously florid, neo-Moorish ★★★★**Alhambra Palace**, C/ Peña Portida 2, ✆ 95 822 14 68, ✉ 95 822 64 04, where most rooms have terrific views over the city (*20,500 pts*).

The ★★★★**Hotel Triunfo–Granada**, Pza. del Triunfo 19, ✆ 95 820 74 44, ✉ 95 827 90 17, stands by the Moorish Puerta de Elvira at the foot of the Albaicín. It's a quiet place with a restaurant that's popular with locals (*16,800 pts*).

moderate

The old ★★★**Washington Irving**, Pso. del Generalife 2, ✆ 95 822 75 50, ✉ 95 22 88 40, is a little faded but still classy (*10,500 pts*).

On the slopes below the Alhambra you can get a pool and air-conditioning at ★★★**Los Ángeles**, Cuesta Escoriaza 17, ✆ 95 822 14 24, ✉ 95 822 21 25 (*10,500 pts*). Nearby is the **Hotel Kenia**, C/ Molinos 65, ✆ 95 822 75 06, a quiet old mansion.

There's one other hotel in the Alhambra, the ★**Hotel América**, Real de la Alhambra 53, ✆ 95 822 74 71, ✉ 95 822 74 70, with simple, pretty rooms for *11,500 pts* and a delightful garden and patio but, as for the *parador*, book well in advance.

The **Casa del Aljarife**, Placeta de la Cruz Verde 2, ✆ and ✉ 95 822 24 25, most @mx3.redestb.es, a 17th-century Moorish house with tastefully refurbished rooms, is the only hotel in the Albaicín, and one of the most delightful places to stay in the city, with a view of the Alhambra that you won't better elsewhere. There are only three rooms so be sure to book in advance (*8500 pts*). The friendly owners can arrange parking and will even collect you from the train station or airport.

inexpensive

For inexpensive *hostales*, the first place to look is the Cuesta de Gomérez, the street leading up to the Alhambra from Plaza Nueva. Besides the ★★**Britz**, at No.1, ✆ 95 822 36 52 (*4000 pts with bath, 3000 pts without*) and the ★**Gomérez**, at No.10, ✆ 95 822 44 37 (*2300 pts, no bath*), both nice, there are plenty of other spots nearby.

Off Calle San Juan de Dios, in the university area, there are dozens of small *hostales* used to accommodating students. The ★**San Joaquín**, C/ Mano de Hierro, ✆ 95 828 28 79, is one, with a pretty patio (*4000 pts*).

Centrally placed are the immaculate *hostal* ★★**Lisboa**, Pza. del Carmen 29, ✆ 95 822 14 13 (*5200 pts*), and the Casa de Huéspedes González, C/ Buensuesco (*4600 pts*).

Eating Out

Granada isn't known for its cuisine. There are too many touristy places around the Plaza Nueva, with very little to distinguish between them.

expensive

Best known and best loved is the famous **Sevilla**, C/ Oficios 12, ✆ 95 822 12 23, where Lorca often met fellow poets and intellectuals. The character of the restaurant has been preserved and the specialities are still the local dishes of Granada and Andalucía (*3500–4500 pts*). *Closed Sun eve.* Both are near the cathedral.

Some of the finest cooking in Granada can be found at the **Ruta del Veleta** on the Ctra. de la Sierra, Km 50, ✆ 95 848 61 34, 5km away from the city towards the Sierra Nevada. Dishes include partridge with onion ragôut and salad of angler fish with vegetable stuffing (*5000 pts*).

moderate

The *granadinos* trust dining out at **Cunini**, Pza. de Pescadería 14, ✆ 95 825 07 77, where the menu depends on availability (*2500–3500 pts*). *Closed Mon.*

For agreeable dining in an intimate family-run restaurant, there is no better in Granada than **Mesón Antonio**, Ecce Homo 6, ✆ 95 822 95 99, which serves international dishes of meat and fish (*2700 pts*). *Closed Sun, July and Aug.* You should try to get up to the Albaicín for dinner on at least one night.

The **Mirador de Morayma**, Pianista García Carrillo 2, Albaicín, ✆ 95 822 82 90, is in a charming 16th-century house with views over the Alhambra from the top-floor dining room; *la sopa de espárragos verdes de Huétor* (asparagus soup) is particularly good, and be sure to leave room for an *andaluz* pudding (*3200 pts*). *Closed Sun eve.*

A place popular with *granadinos* is **Chikito**, Pza. de Campillo 9, ✆ 95 822 33 64, serving classic Granada dishes in an intimate atmosphere (*3500 pts*). **Gargantua**, Placeta Silleria 7, near C/ Reyes Católicos, is noted for its atmosphere.

Locals go to the **Nueva Bodega**, C/ Cettimeriem 3, and a younger crowd to the **Mesón Yunque**, Plaza San Miguel Bajo. **Patio Andaluz**, Escudo del Carmen 10, is also very cheap.

inexpensive

Everyone's favourite rock-bottom, filling 750 pts menu is served up at the tiny **Cepillo** on Calle Pescadería. It's a few doors away from the Cunini and is one of the few places where you can get paella for one—order fish or squid.

For *bocadillos* (hot and cold sandwiches) try **Bar Aliatar** in a small street between Plaza de Bib-Rambla and Calle Reyes Católicos. If you like ice creams, head for **Los Italianos** at Gran Vía 4. Delicious.

Granada is one of the best places in Andalucia to catch flamenco. Though there are touristy shows in the caves of Sacromonte, there are also some more spontaneous venues, and it's well worth heading up to Sacromonte to wander around—try **Los Faroles**, one of the last and best of the atmospheric cave flamenco bars, **Peña Platería** at Patio de los Aljibes 13, near San Nicholas, or the popular **El Niño de los Almendras**, in Calle Muladar de Dona Sancha, near Plaza San Miguel Bajo in the Albaicín.

There are a number of discos popular with the locals in Sacromonte, the most famous of which is **El Camborio**, which is packed on Friday and Saturday nights.

Good atmospheric central bars such as **Bar Sabanilla**, C/ San Sebastian 14, and **Bodegas Casteñeda**, C/ Elvira, are traditional yet buzzy and stay open till midnight or later.

Day Trips from Granada

The Sierra Nevada and Las Alpujarras

From everywhere in Granada, the mountains peer over the tops of buildings. Fortunately, Spain's loftiest peaks are also its most accessible; from the city centre you can be riding on Europe's highest mountain road in a little more than an hour. If you're without a car, there's a daily bus from town that makes the Sierra Nevada an easy day trip (*see* below).

Dress warmly, though. As the name implies, the Sierra Nevada is snowcapped nearly all year, and even in late July and August, when the road is clear and you can travel right over the mountains to the valley of Las Alpujarras, it's as chilly and windy as you would expect it to be, some 3300m above sea level. These mountains, a geological curiosity of sorts, are just an oversized chunk of the Penibetic System, the chain that stretches from Arcos de la Frontera almost to Murcia. Their highest peak, **Mulhacén** (3481m), is less than 40km from the coast. From Granada you can see nearly all of the Sierra: a jagged snowy wall without really distinctive peaks. The highest expanses are barren and frosty, but on a clear day they offer a view to Morocco. Mulhacén and especially its sister peak **Veleta** (3392m) can be climbed without too much exertion; the road goes right by Veleta, and in August you can even drive to the top.

Getting Around

For the Sierra Nevada, there is a daily **bus** from the Bar El Ventorrillo, in Granada's Paseo del Violón, to the Albergue Universitario some 12km from the peak of Veleta. Departures are at 9am, returning at 5.30. Bus **tours** are run by Autocares Bonal, *©* 95 827 31 00; check at the Granada tourist office for other companies. Most of them cost around 3000 pts and run only at weekends, provided there are enough passengers.

If you're going by **car**, the road is open in August; it's a rough trip but worth it for the views. For **road snow reports** in English and Spanish, call © 95 824 91 19. Some 20km before you reach Veleta, you'll enter the **Solynieve** ski area, beginning at its main resort **Pradollano**, and continuing up to Veleta. From Pradollano there are cable cars up to the peak itself.

For Las Alpujarras: some **buses** on the Granada–Motril route stop in Lanjarón, but to penetrate the more isolated sections of the valley, you'll have to take a bus from Granada to Orjiva, the base for connecting buses to the other villages. With the area growing in popularity, routes are constantly being extended and increased, so it's always worth checking with the bus companies. For destinations further east, the Bacoma line (from Avenida de los Andaluces in front of Granada's train station) runs daily **buses** to Murcia and Alicante which stop in Guadix.

Tourist Information

For skiing information contact the tourist office in Granada or the Federación Andaluza de Montaña, Pso. de Ronda 101, © 95 829 13 40. *Open Mon–Fri 8.30–10.30pm.*

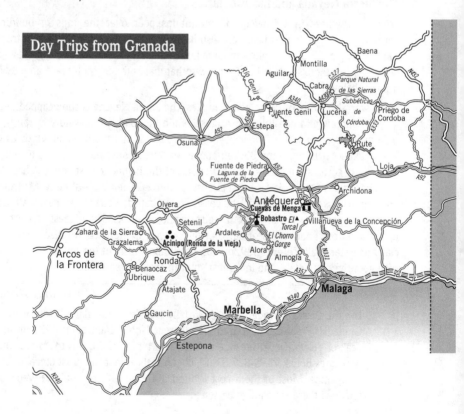

Day Trips from Granada

If you're adventurous and the road is clear, you can continue onwards from Veleta down into **Las Alpujarras**, a string of white villages along the valley of the Río Guadalfeo, between the Sierra Nevada and the little Contraviesa chain along the sea coast. In Moorish times this was a densely populated region, full of vines and orchards. Much of its population was made up of refugees from the Reconquista, coming mainly from Sevilla. Under the conditions for Granada's surrender in 1492, the region was granted as a fief to Boabdil el Chico but, with forced Christianization and the resulting revolts, the entire population was expelled and replaced by settlers from the north.

Though often described as one of the most inaccessible corners of Spain, this region has attracted growing numbers of visitors since Gerald Brenan wrote *South from Granada*. The roads wind past stepped fields, cascades of water, high pastures and sudden drops, and when the almond trees are in blossom it is at its most appealing. Unlike the rest of Andalucían villages with their red-tiled roofs, the *pueblos* of Las Alpujarras are flat-roofed. Although it is a long way off the beaten track, you won't be alone if you visit Las Alpujarras. Nevertheless, they're hardly spoiled; and with the villages relatively close to each other, and plenty of wild country on either side, it's a great spot for hiking or just finding some well-decorated peace and quiet.

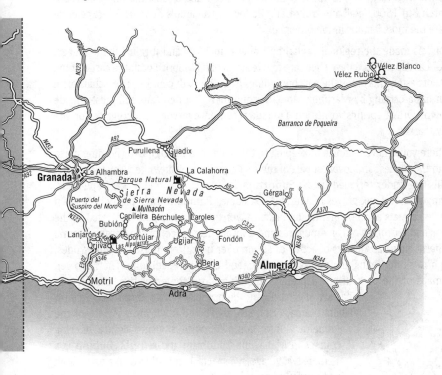

Most visitors don't chance the Sierra Nevada route to Capileira, but use the front door to Las Alpujarras, off the main road from Granada to Motril. On the way, just outside the city, you'll pass the spot called **Suspiro de Moro**, where poor Boabdil sighed as he took his last look back over Granada. His mother was less than sympathetic—'Weep like a woman for what you were incapable of defending like a man,' she told him. It gave Salman Rushdie the title for his novel *The Moor's Last Sigh* (1995).

The last 33km (20½ miles) of this route, where the road joins the Guadalfeo valley down to Motril, is one of the most scenic in Spain, but if you want to see Las Alpujarras, you'll have to take the turn-off for **Lanjarón**, the principal tourist centre in the region. Lanjarón has been attracting visitors to its spas since Roman times and now markets its bottled water all across Spain. There are eight springs in all, each offering a different blend of natural chemicals, while shops along the elegant main street offer complementary remedies for whatever ails you. The ruined Moorish castle on the hill saw the Moors' last stand against the Imperial troops on March 8th 1500. Well and truly Catholic today, Lanjaran's *Semana Santa* celebrations are the most famous in the province.

ROCK FLOWERS
SIERRA NEVADA.

Orjiva was made the regional capital by Isabel II in 1839 and it remains the biggest town of Las Alpujarras today. There are few remains of its Moorish past; the castle of the Counts of Sástago may look the part but it dates from the 17th century. The Renaissance church has a carving by Martínez Montañés and there is a Benizalte mill, just outside the town. Orjiva springs to life on Thursdays, when everyone congregates for the weekly market.

From here you'll have a choice of keeping to the main road for **Ugíjar** or heading north through the highest and loveliest part of the region, with typical white villages climbing the hillsides under terraced fields. **Soportújar**, the first, has one of Las Alpujarras' surviving primeval oak groves behind it. Next comes **Pampaneira**, a pretty little town of cobbled streets and flowers. In the Plaza Mayor there's a museum dedicated to the customs and costumes of Las Alpujarras and a locally run office for the Parque Natural de la Sierra Nevada. All sorts of activities are on offer here, from horse or donkey rides, through to skiing, hang-gliding, nature walks and caving expeditions. They also sell good maps of the park. If you'd prefer something more contemplative, the Tibetan Monastery of Clear Light, the birthplace of a reincarnated Spanish Tibetan lama, Osel, sits above the town on the sides of the Poqueira Gorge, complete with a visitor centre offering courses in Mahayana Buddhism and retreats. **Bubión** is a Berber-style village in a spectacular setting with a textile mill and tourist shops.

RANUNCULUS
ACETOSELLIFOLIUS
RARE BUTTERCUP
OF SIERRA NEVADA

All these villages are within sight of each other on a short detour along the edge of the beautiful (and walkable) ravine called **Barranco de Poqueira. Capileira**, the last village on the mountain-pass route over Mulhacén and Veleta, sees more tourists than most. Its treasure, in the church of Nuestra Señora de la Cabeza, is a statue of the Virgin donated to the village by Ferdinand and Isabella. North from here a tremendously scenic road takes you up across the Sierra Nevada and eventually to Granada. In winter this pass is snowbound, and even in summer you need to take extra care—it's steep and dangerous with precipitous drops down the ravines. However, the beautiful scenery makes the risks worthwhile. Alternatively, continue on the GR421 to **Pitres**, centre of a Hispano-Japanese joint venture that produces and exports handcrafted ballet shoes, of all things. There is a ruined hill-top mosque, and the remains of a few other Moorish buildings litter the village.

The road carries on through the villages of **Pórtugos**, a pilgrimage centre for Our Lady of Sorrows, and **Busquistar**, before arriving in **Trevélez**, on the slopes of Mulhacén. Trevélez likes to claim it's the highest village in Europe. It's also famous in Andalucía for its snow-cured hams—Henry Ford and Rossini were fans—and a ham feast is held in their honour every August. This is the main starting point for climbers heading for the summit of Mulhacén and the other peaks in the Sierra Nevada, but, despite the tacky tourist shops, there's little to detain other visitors. From there the road slopes back downwards to **Juviles** and **Bérchules**, one of the villages where the tradition of carpet-weaving has been maintained since Moorish times. **Yegen**, some 10km further, became famous as the long-time home of British writer Gerald Brenan. His house is still in the village—ask for 'El Casa del Inglés'. After that come more intensively farmed areas on the lower slopes, with oranges, vineyards and almonds; you can either hit Ugíjar and the main roads to the coast and Almería, or detour to the seldom-visited villages of **Laroles** and **Mairena** on the slopes of **La Ragua**, one of the last high peaks of the Sierra Nevada.

Further east, through countryside that rapidly changes from healthy green to dry brown, the village of **Fondón** is of particular interest; an Australian architect, Donald Grey, and his Spanish partner, José Antonio Garvayo, have set up a school to teach the traditional crafts of ironwork, carpentry, tile- and brick-making, so most of the buildings have been restored, and Fondón is now a model village. The church tower was once a mosque's minaret.

Around the Sierra Nevada: Guadix

It's a better road entering Granada from the west than that leaving it to the east. Between the city and Murcia are some of the emptiest, bleakest landscapes in Spain. The first village you pass through is **Purullena**, long famous for its pretty ceramic ware; the entire stretch of highway through it is lined with enormous stands and displays.

The poverty of this region has long forced many of its inhabitants to live in caves, and nowhere more so than in **Guadix**. Several thousand of this city's population, most of

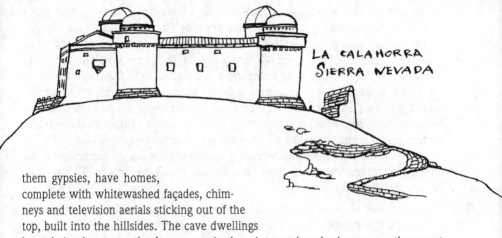

LA CALAHORRA
SIERRA NEVADA

them gypsies, have homes, complete with whitewashed façades, chimneys and television aerials sticking out of the top, built into the hillsides. The cave dwellings have their advantages: they're warmer in the winter and cooler in summer than most Andalucían homes, relatively spacious and well ventilated—and when the time comes to build a new room, all you need is a pick and shovel.

The centre of Guadix is dominated by a Moorish **Alcazaba**, largely rebuilt in the 16th century; near the arcaded central **Plaza Mayor** stands the huge **cathedral**, begun by Diego de Siloé, builder of Granada's cathedral, and given its magnificent façade in the 1700s by Andalucía's great rococo eccentric, Vicente Acero. The ornate traceries of the church, and the imposing castle, appearing together out of the empty, queerly eroded hills make a striking sight.

There's not much else to distract you in this corner of Spain. If you're headed for Almería and the coast (N324), you'll pass near **La Calahorra**, with an unusual Renaissance castle with domed turrets, and **Gérgal**, whose equally singular, perfectly preserved castle was built by the Moors. They claim you can see the stars more clearly here than anywhere in Europe, and Spain has built its national observatory outside the town. The N342 from Guadix west to Murcia is even lonelier; here the surprisingly elegant little whitewashed villages of **Vélez Blanco** and **Vélez Rubio** will provide a pleasant break in your travels. There are several caves in the neighbourhood where a wealth of 4000-year-old rock paintings of abstract patterns and symbols have been found.

Eating Out

Sierra Nevada

Most restaurants are open only in the skiing season, and most are a little pretentious—but that's ski resorts for you. **Rincón de Pepe Reyes** in Pradollano has good Andaluz cooking (*2000–3000 pts*). You can take the cable car up to the frenetic and none-too-clean **Borreguiles** café/restaurant, ℘ 95 848 00 79, halfway up Veleta, and sit out on the terrace to take in the view.

In Edificio Bulgaria, try the **Ruta de Veleta**, ✆ 95 848 12 28 (*4000 pts*).

Las Alpujarras

In Trevélez, **Mesón Haraiçel**, ✆ 95 885 85 30, serves delicious Arab-influenced food with plenty of almond sauces and meat dishes. Try a *soplillo* for dessert (honey and almond meringue, *80 pts*). A three-course meal will cost around *1500 pts*.

La Fragua, Barro del Medio, ✆ 95 885 85 73, concentrates on Alpujarras specialities, with several dishes featuring mountain-cured ham (*2000–3000 pts*). The **Alpujarras Grill** in Orgiva, Ctra. de Trevélez, ✆ 95 878 55 49, does a wonderful roast kid, while the **Finca Los Llanos**, Ctra. de Sierra Nevada, ✆ 95 876 30 71, in Capileira, is known for its speciality: aubergines in honey.

In Ugíjar, the **Hostal Vidaña**, Ctra. de Almería, ✆ 95 876 70 10 serves up humungous portions of delicious mountain fare, such as partridge, goat and rabbit.

The Coast South of Granada

If you feel the need for a breath of sea air, a couple of coastal resorts are within easy reach of Granada by road.

Nerja

Approaching this town, the scenery becomes impressive as the mountains grow closer to the sea. Sitting at the base of the Sierra de Tejeda, Nerja itself is pleasant and quiet for a Costa resort. In Moorish times the town was a major producer of silk and sugar, an industry that fell into rapid decline after their departure. An earthquake in 1884 partially destroyed Nerja, and from then to the early 1960s it had to eke a living out of fishing and farming.

Its attractions are the **Balcón de Europa**, a promenade with a fountain overlooking the sea, and a series of secluded beaches under the cliffs—the best are a good walk away on either side of the town. A few kilometres east, the **Cueva de Nerja** is one of Spain's fabled grottoes, full of Gaudiesque formations and needle-thin stalactites—one, they claim, is the longest in the world. The caves were discovered in 1959, just in time for the tourist boom, and they have been fitted out with lights and music, with photographers lurking in the shadows who'll try to sell you a picture of yourself when you leave. The caves were popular with Cro-Magnon man (first found in a cave of that name in France), and there are some Palaeolithic artworks. Occasionally, this perfect setting is used for ballets and concerts.

Almuñécar and Salobreña

The coastal road east of Nerja, bobbing in and out of the hills and cliffs, is the best part of the Costa, where avocado pears and sugar cane keep the farming community busy; the next resort, however, **Almuñécar**, is better left alone; a nest of dreary high-rises around a beleaguered village. Its only interesting feature is the **Moorish castle**, which houses the local cemetery. Outside the town are the remains of a Roman aqueduct. **Salobreña** is much better, though it may not stay that way. The village's dramatic setting, slung down a steep, lone peak overlooking the sea, is the most stunning on the coast, and helps to insulate it just a little from the tourist industry. The beaches, just starting to become built up, are about 2km (1¼ miles) away.

Eating Out

Nerja ✉ 29780

A popular restaurant in Nerja is the **Rey Alfonso**: there is nothing special about the cuisine but the view is superb, on cliffs directly under the Balcón de Europa (*3500 pts*). You can dine in genuine old Spanish surroundings in the restaurant at the hotel **Cala Bella**, C/ Puerta del Mar 10, ✆ 95 252 07 00, complete with wrought iron, ceramics and cool tiled floors, and views of Calahonda Bay and the Balcón; *salmón con salsa de anchoa* (salmon in anchovy sauce), *perdiz a la almijara* (partridge with local herbs), plus a selection of meats (*3500 pts*). Reservations are essential at **De Miguel**, C/ Pintada 2, ✆ 95 252 29 96, celebrated for its international meat and fish dishes, not least for the flambéd strawberries (*closed Mon and Feb*). **Jiménez** on the Plaza de la Marina serves a wide range of fish and seafood tapas for *under 1000 pts.*

Almuñécar ✉ 18690

Los Geranios, Pza. Rosa 4a, ✆ 95 263 07 24, is a cheerful restaurant in Almuñécar, full of geraniums and owned by a Hispano-Belgian couple; the menu is international with a Spanish bias (*about 3000 pts*). *Closed Sun and Nov.* The **Bodega Francisco**, C/ Real 15, ✆ 95 263 01 68, is a wonderful watering-hole serving inexpensive tapas and the usual *andaluz* staples (*1000–1500 pts*).

Salobreña ✉ 18680

Salobreña has one good restaurant: the **Mesón Durán**, N340, Km 323, specializing in meat and some *andaluz* dishes (*2500 pts*). *Closed Mon.* If you're in the Motril area and hungry, head for Gualchos, 17km (10½ miles) to the east. There you'll find **La Posada**, Pza. de la Constitución 9, ✆ 95 264 60 34, a delightful old coaching inn where you can stay as well as eat. They serve spinach with fish mousse, red mullet with *andaluz* mayonnaise, swordfish with garlic, cream and wine, and duck in Jerez vinegar and raisins (*2000–3000 pts*). *Closed Mon.*

Seville

Qui non ha vista Sevilla, non ha vista maravilla
(Who hasn't seen Seville, has seen no wondrous thing)

Hijo de Sevilla, uno bueno por maravilla
(You'll be lucky if you find a good *sevillano*)

Andalucían sayings

Apart from the Alhambra in Granada, the place where the lushness and sensuality of al-Andalus survives best is Andalucía's capital. Seville may be Spain's fourth-largest city, but it is a place where you can pick oranges from the trees, and see open countryside from the centre of town. Come in spring if you can, when the gardens are drowned in birdsong and the air becomes intoxicating with the scent of jasmine and a hundred other blooms. If you come in summer, you may melt; the lower valley of the Guadalquivir is one of the hottest places in Europe.

The pageant of Seville unfolds in the shadow of La Giralda, the Moorish tower that means so much to Seville ('the mother of artists, the mould for bullfighters' according to a *sevillano* poet). It is still the loftiest tower in Spain, and its size and the ostentatious play of its arches and arabesques make it the perfect symbol for this city, full of the romance of the south and the perfume of excess.

At times Seville has been a capital, and it remains Spain's eternal city; neither past reverses nor modern industry have been able to shake it from its dreams. That its past glories should return and place it alongside Venice and Florence as one of the jewels in the crown of Europe, a true metropolis with full international recognition, is the first dream of every *sevillano*. Crimped and prinked for Expo '92, Seville opened her doors to the world. The new 'Golden Gate' bridge, soaring higher than La Giralda itself, beckoned would-be suitors to the pavilions on the Isla de la Cartuja and the Age of Discoveries. Fresh romance and excess mingled with the old. New roads, a new opera house, the *Alamillo* (the harp), another wonderfully stringed bridge, combined with Moorish palaces and monuments in a vainglorious display that attracted 16 million visitors. And just when the whole shebang was over and the city had got back to normal (inasmuch as the Andalucían capital could ever be described as *normal*), and Cartuja island had started to look a little faded, the King and Queen of Spain announced the engagement of their elder daughter, the Infanta Elena, and that the marriage would take place not in Madrid, as might have been expected, but in the Royal Palace in Seville. The route between the Alcázar and the cathedral was re-paved for the occasion.

Seville is still a city very much in love with itself. When a *sevillano* sings in the street or in a café, which charmingly enough he often does, the subject of the song is invariably the city itself, and posters advertise concerts with the theme *'Seville, ¿por qué te quiero?'* ('Seville, why do I love you?'). Even the big celebration during Holy Week—although enjoyable to the foreigner (anyone from outside the city) with revelry in every café and on every street corner, is essentially a private one; the *sevillanos* celebrate in their own *casitas* with friends, all the time aware that they are being observed by the general public, who can peek but may not enter, at least not without an *enchufe* ('the right connection').

Seville is much like a beautiful, flirtatious woman; she'll tempt you to her doorstep and allow you a peck on the cheek—whether you get over the threshold depends entirely on your charm.

History: from Hispalis to Isbiliya to Sevilla

One of Seville's distinctions is its long historical continuity. Few cities in western Europe can claim never to have suffered a dark age, but Seville flourished after the fall of Rome—and even after the coming of the Castilians. Roman *Hispalis* was founded on an Iberian settlement, and soon became one of the leading cities of the province of Bætica. So was Itálica, the now ruined city just to the northwest (*see* p.128); it is difficult to say which was the more important. During the Roman twilight, Seville seems to have been a thriving town. Its first famous citizen, St Isidore, was one of the Doctors of the Church and the most learned man of the age, famous for his great *Encyclopedia* and his *Seven Books Against the Pagans*, an attempt to prove that the coming of Christianity was not the cause of Rome's fall. Seville was an important town under the Visigoths, and after the Moorish conquest it was second only to Cordoba as a political power and a centre of learning. For a while after the demise of the western caliphate in 1023, it became an independent kingdom, paying tribute to the kings of Castile. Seville suffered under the Almoravids after 1091, but enjoyed a revival under their successors, the Almohads.

The disaster came for Muslim Isbiliya in 1248, 18 years after the union of Castile and León. Fernando III's conquest of the city is not a well-documented event, but it seems that more than half the population found exile in Granada or Africa preferable to Castilian rule; their property was divided among settlers from the north. Despite the dislocation, the city survived, and found a new prosperity as Castile's window on the Mediterranean and South Atlantic trade routes (the Río Guadalquivir is navigable as far as Seville). Everywhere in the city you will see its emblem, the word NODO (knot) with a double knot between the O and D. It recalls the civil wars of the 1270s, when Seville was one of the few cities in Spain to remain loyal to Alfonso the Wise. *'No m'a dejado'* ('She has not forsaken me'), Alfonso is recorded as saying; *madeja* is another word for knot, and placed between the syllables NO and DO it makes a clever rebus besides a tribute to Seville's loyalty to medieval Castile's greatest king.

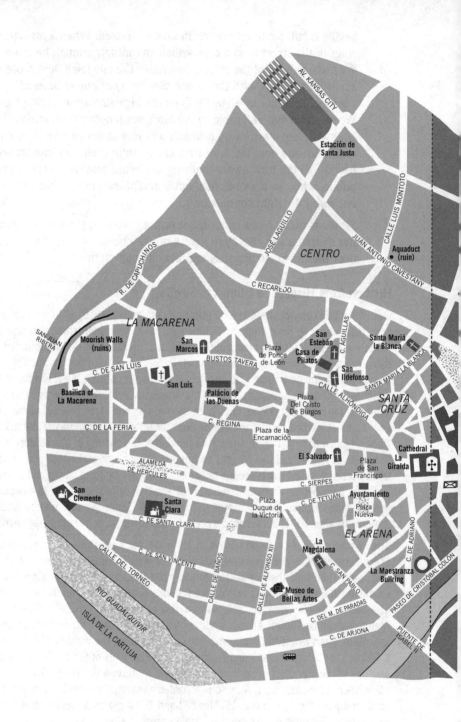

AV. KANSAS CITY

Estación de
Santa Justa

CALLE LUIS MONTOTO

JOSÉ LAGUILLO

CENTRO

JUAN ANTONIO CAVESTANY

Aquaduct
• (ruin)

C RECAREDO

R. DE CAPUCHINOS

LA MACARENA

SAN JUAN
RIBERA

Moorish Walls
(ruins)

San
Marcos

BUSTOS TAVERA

Plaza
de Ponce
de León

San
Esteban

Casa de
Pilatos

C. AGUILLAS

Santa Mariá
la Blanca

San
Ildefonso

SANTA MARÍA LA BLANCA

C. DE SAN LUIS

San Luis

Palácio de
las Duenas

CALLE ALHÓNDIGA

SANTA
CRUZ

Basilica of
La Macarena

C. DE LA FERIA

C. REGINA

Plaza
Del Cristo
De Burgos

Plaza de la
Encarnación

ALAMEDA
DE HERCULES

El Salvador

Plaza
de San
Francisco

Cathedral

La
Giralda

San
Clemente

Santa
Clara

C. DE SANTA CLARA

Plaza
Duque de
la Victoria

C. SIERPES

C. DE TETUÁN

Ayuntamiento

Plaza
Nueva

EL ARENA

C. DE ADRIANO

CALLE DEL TORNEO

C. DE SAN VINCENTE

CALLE DE BAÑOS

CALLE DE ALFONSO XII

La
Magdalena

C. SAN PABLO

La Maestranza
Bullring

PASEO DE CRISTOBAL COLÓN

RIO GUADALQUIVIR

ISLA DE LA CARTUJA

Museo de
Bellas Artes

C. DEL M. DE PARADAS

C. DE ARJONA

PUENTE DE
ISABEL II

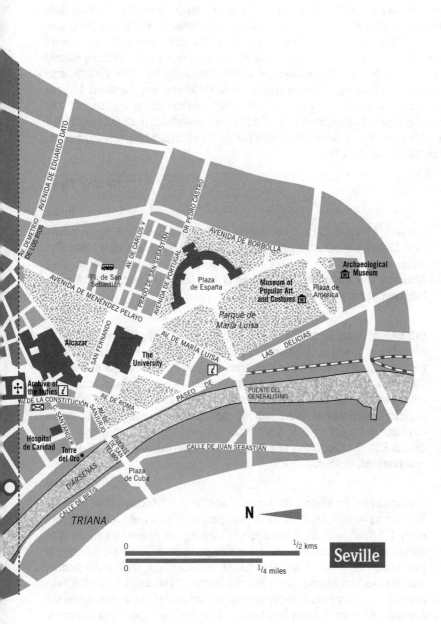

AVENIDA DE EDUARDO DATO

AV. DEMETRIO DE LOS RIOS

AV. DE CARLOS V

PRADO DE SAN SEBASTIÁN

AVENIDA DE PORTUGAL

DR PEDRO CASTRO

AVENIDA DE BORBOLLA

AVENIDA DE MENÉNDEZ PELAYO

Pl. de San Sebastián

Plaza de España

Museum of Popular Art and Customs Ⓜ

Plaza de América

Archaeological Museum Ⓜ

Parque de María Luisa

C. SAN FERNANDO

Alcázar

The University

AV. DE MARÍA LUISA

LAS DELICIAS

AV. DE ROMA

ℹ

AV. DE LA CONSTITUCIÓN

Archive of the Indies ℹ

✠

✉

C. SANTANDER

PASEO DE

PUENTE DEL GENERALISIMO

AV. DE SANJURJO

Hospital de Caridad

Torre del Oro

PUENTE DE SAN TELMO

CALLE DE JUAN SEBASTIÁN

DÁRSENAS

Plaza de Cuba

CALLE DE BETIS

TRIANA

N ◀━━

0 ————————————— ¹/₂ kms

0 ————————————— ¹/₄ miles

Seville

From 1503 to 1680, Seville enjoyed a legal monopoly of trade with the Americas. The giddy prosperity this brought, in the years when the silver fleet ran full, contributed much to the festive, incautious atmosphere that is often revealed in Seville's character. Seville never found a way to hold on to much of the American wealth, and what little it managed to grab was soon dissipated in showy excess. It was in this period, of course, that Seville was perfecting its charm. Poets and composers have always favoured it as a setting. Bizet's Carmen rolled her cigars in the Royal Tobacco Factory (*see* p.118), and for her male counterpart Seville contributed Don Juan Tenorio, who evolved through Spanish theatre in plays by Tirso de Molina and Zorrilla to become Mozart's Don Giovanni; the same composer also used the city as a setting for *The Marriage of Figaro*. Though modern Seville has been loath to leave all this behind, the World Fair allowed it to show off not only the Seville of orange blossoms and guitars, but also the Seville of the future.

Getting There

by air

Seville has regular flights from Madrid, Malaga and Barcelona, less regularly from Lisbon, the Canary Islands and Valencia. San Pablo airport is 12km (7½ miles) east of the city, and the airport bus leaves from Bar Iberia on Calle Almirante Lobos, near the southern end of Avenida de la Constitución. **Airport information:** ✆ 95 467 2981.

by train

Estación de Santa Justa, in the surreally named Avenida Kansas City in the northeast of town, is the modern Expo showpiece. There are train connections—to Madrid by AVE in a staggeringly quick 2 hours 15 minutes, a daily *Talgo* to Valencia and Barcelona, and to Cordoba, Jerez and Cadiz, among the other frequent regular services to these cities; for trains to Malaga, Ronda and Algeciras, you should watch out for possible train changes at Bobadilla Junction, the black hole of Andalucían railways where all lines cross. The central RENFE office is at Calle Zaragoza 29. **Information,** ✆ 95 454 0202; **reservations,** ✆ 95 422 2693.

by bus

Almost all lines for Madrid, the Levante, Andalucía and Portugal leave from the Estación de Autobuses, Plaza de Armas. Buses for Jerez and Cádiz run about every 1½ hours, and there are frequent connections to most other points in Andalucía (five daily to Granada, four to Málaga, three to Cordoba and Úbeda, at least two to the Costa del Sol, Aracena, Almería, La Línea, Tarifa and Algeciras, also three each to Madrid, Valencia and Barcelona). For destinations within the province (e.g. Carmona, Écija), buses depart from outside this station, across the Avenida de Carlos V. Buses for Matalascañas, Huelva, Badajoz and Ayamonte leave from Calle Segura 18, while those for Santiponce and the ruins leave from

Marqués de Parada every hour or so during the day. **Information** on routes and timetables is available from the tourist office.

Tourist Information

The permanent tourist office is very helpful; it's near the cathedral at Avenida de la Constitución 21, ✆ 95 422 1404 (*open weekdays 9–7*). The municipal information centre is near the Parque de María Luisa, next to the US consulate off Avenida de María Luisa, ✆ 95 423 4465. There's an information centre at the airport, ✆ 95 444 9128.

Around the Cathedral

La Giralda

Open Mon–Sat 10.30–5; Sun and hols 2–6; adm 200 pts, or 700 pts including entrance to the cathedral.

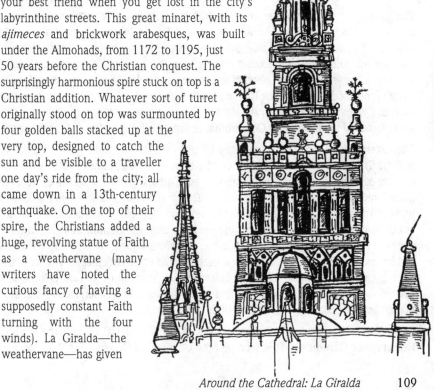

A good place to start your tour of Seville is at one of Andalucía's most famous monuments. You can catch the 319ft tower of **La Giralda** peeking over the rooftops from almost anywhere in Seville; it will be your best friend when you get lost in the city's labyrinthine streets. This great minaret, with its *ajimeces* and brickwork arabesques, was built under the Almohads, from 1172 to 1195, just 50 years before the Christian conquest. The surprisingly harmonious spire stuck on top is a Christian addition. Whatever sort of turret originally stood on top was surmounted by four golden balls stacked up at the very top, designed to catch the sun and be visible to a traveller one day's ride from the city; all came down in a 13th-century earthquake. On the top of their spire, the Christians added a huge, revolving statue of Faith as a weathervane (many writers have noted the curious fancy of having a supposedly constant Faith turning with the four winds). La Giralda—the weathervane—has given its name to the tower as a whole. The climb to the top is easy; instead of stairs there are shallow ramps—wide enough for Fernando III to have ridden his horse up for the view after the conquest in 1248.

The Cathedral: the Biggest Gothic Cathedral in the Whole World

The same opening hours as Le Giralda—you visit both on one ticket.

For a while after the Reconquista, the Castilians who repopulated Seville were content to use the great Almohad mosque, built at the same time as La Giralda. At the turn of the 1400s, in a fit of pious excess, it was decided to build a new cathedral so grand that 'future ages shall call us mad for attempting it'. If they were mad, at least they were good organizers—they got it up in slightly over a century. The architects are unknown, though there has been speculation that the original master was either French or German.

The exterior, with its great rose window and double buttresses, is as fine as any of the Gothic cathedrals of northern Spain—if we could only see it. Especially on the west front, facing the Avenida de la Constitución, the buildings close in; walking around its vast bulk, past the fence of Roman columns joined by thick chains, is like passing under a steep and ragged cliff. Before it was cleaned to look pretty for the World Fair, the grime contributed to the effect. Some of the best original sculptural work is on the two portals flanking the main door: the **Puerta del Bautismo** (left), and the **Puerta del Nacimiento** (right).

The groundplan of this monster, roughly 400ft by 600ft, probably covers the same area as did the mosque. On the northern side, the **Patio de los Naranjos** (Patio of the Orange Trees, and planted accordingly) preserves the outline of the mosque courtyard. The Muslim fountain (built around a basin from the previous Visigothic cathedral) survives, along with some of the walls and arches. In the left-hand corner, the Moorish 'Gate of the Lizard' has hanging from it a stuffed crocodile, said to have been a present from an Egyptian emir asking for the hand of a Spanish infanta. Along the eastern wall is the entrance of the **Biblioteca Colombina**, an archive of the explorer's life and letters.

The cavernous interior overpowers the faithful with its size more than its grace or beauty. The main altarpiece is the world's biggest *retablo*, almost 120ft high and entirely covered with carved figures and golden Gothic ornaments; it took 82 years to make, and takes about a minute to look at. The cathedral is dark and cold inside, and without the usual nave and transept; the enormous space is ill-defined and disorientating. Just behind the Capilla Mayor and the main altar, the **Capilla Real** contains the tombs of San Fernando, conqueror of Seville, and of Alfonso the Wise; Pedro the Cruel and his mistress, María de Padilla, are relegated to the crypt underneath. The art of the various chapels around the cathedral is lost in the gloom, but there are paintings by Murillo in the Capilla de San Antonio (in the north aisle), and an altarpiece by Zurbarán in the Capilla de San Pedro (to the left of the Capilla Real).

In the southern aisle, four stern pallbearers on a high pedestal support the tomb of **Christopher Columbus**. They represent the kingdoms of Castile, León, Navarre, and

Aragón. Columbus has been something of a refugee since his death. In the 16th century his remains were moved for unknown reasons from Valladolid to the island of Santo Domingo, and after Dominican independence from there to Havana Cathedral. In 1899, after Cuba became independent, he was brought to Seville, and this idiosyncratic monument put up to honour him. In the Dominican Republic, they'll tell you Columbus is still buried in Santo Domingo. Of course, most Spaniards are convinced Columbus was born in Spain, so it is appropriate that the life of this most elusive character should have mysteries at both ends.

The Sacristy

Most of the cathedral's collections are housed in a few chambers near the turnstiles at the main entrance. In the **Sala Capitular**, which has an *Immaculate Conception* by Murillo, Seville's bishop can sit on his throne and pontificate under the unusual acoustics of an elliptical baroque ceiling. The adjacent **sacristy** contains paintings by Zurbarán, Murillo, Van Dyck and others, most in dire need of restoration. Spare a moment for the reliquaries. Juan de Arfe, maker of the world's biggest silver monstrances, is represented here with one that seems almost a small palace, complete with marble columns. Spain's most famous and possibly most bizarre reliquary is the **Alfonsine Tables**, filled with over 200 tiny bits of tooth and bone. They were said to have belonged to Alfonso the Wise and were made to provide extra-powerful juju for him to carry into battle.

The Archive of the Indies

Open weekdays, 10–1; research, by appointment, 8–3; © 95 421 1234.

In common with most of its contemporaries, parts of Seville's cathedral were public ground, and the porches, the Patio de los Naranjos and often even the naves and chapels were used to transact all sorts of business. A 16th-century bishop put an end to this practice, but prevailed upon Felipe II to construct next to the cathedral an exchange, or **Lonja**, for the merchants. Felipe sent his favourite architect, Juan de Herrera, then still busy with El Escorial, to design it. The severe, elegant façades are typically Herreran, and the stone balls and pyramids on top are practically the architect's signature. By the 1780s, little commerce was still going on in Seville, and what was left of the American trade passed through Cadiz, so Carlos III converted the lonely old building to hold the **Archive of the Indies**, the repository of all the reports, maps, drawings and documents the crown collected during the age of exploration. The collection, the richest in the world, has not even yet been entirely sifted through by scholars, but they are always worth a look.

The Alcázar

Open Tues–Sat 9.30–7, Sun and hols 9.30–5; adm 600 pts.

It's easy to be fooled into thinking this is simply a Moorish palace; some of its rooms and courtyards seem to come straight from the Alhambra. Most of them, however, were built by Moorish workmen for King Pedro the Cruel of Castile in the 1360s. The Alcázar and its king represent a fascinating cul-de-sac in Spanish history and culture, and allow the possibility that al-Andalus might have assimilated its conquerors rather than have been destroyed by them.

Pedro was an interesting character. In Froissart's *Chronicle*, we have him described as 'full of marveylous opinyons...rude and rebell agaynst the commandements of holy churche'. Certainly he didn't mind having his Moorish artists, lent by the kings of Granada, adorn his palace with sayings from the Koran in Kufic calligraphy. Pedro preferred Seville, still half-Moorish and more than half-decadent, to Old Castile, and he filled his court here with Moorish poets, dancers and bodyguards—the only ones he trusted. But he was not the man for the job of cultural synthesis. The evidence, in so far as it is reliable, suggests he richly deserved his honorific 'the Cruel'; although to *sevillanos* he was Pedro the Just. His brother Don Fadrique is only one of many he is said to have assassinated in this palace. One of the biggest rubies among the British crown jewels was a gift from Pedro to the Black Prince—he murdered an ambassador from Granada to get it off his turban.

Long before Pedro, the Alcázar was the palace of the Moorish governors. Work on the Moorish features began in 712 after the capture of Seville. In the 9th century it was transformed into a palace for Abd ar-Rahman II. Important additions were made under the Almohads; the Alcázar was their capital in al-Andalus. Almost all the decorative work you see now was done under Pedro, some by the Granadans and the rest by Muslim artists from Toledo; altogether it is the outstanding production of *mudéjar* art in Spain.

The Alcázar is entered through a little gate on the Plaza del Triunfo, on the south side of the cathedral. The first courtyard, the **Patio de la Montería**, has beautiful arabesques, with lions amid castles for Castile and León; this was the public court of the palace, where visitors were received, corresponding to the Mexuar at the Alhambra. At the far end of the Patio is the lovely **façade** of the interior palace, decorated with inscriptions in Gothic and Arabic scripts.

Much of the best *mudéjar* work can be seen in the adjacent halls and courts; their seemingly haphazard arrangement was in fact a principle of the art, to increase the surprise and delight in passing from one to the next. The **Patio de Yeso** (Court of Plaster) is largely a survival of the Almoravid palace of the 1170s, itself built on the site of a Roman *praetorium*. The **Patio de las Doncellas** (Court of the Maidens), entered through the gate of the palace façade, is the largest of the courtyards, a little more ornate than the rooms of the Alhambra—built at the same time and possibly by some of the same craftsmen.

The Patio de las Doncellas leads to the **Salón de los Embajadores** (Hall of the Ambassadors), a small domed chamber that is the finest in the Alcázar despite jarring additions from the time of Charles V. In Moorish times this was the throne room. Another small court, the **Patio de la Muñecas** (Court of the Dolls) where King Pedro's bodyguards cut down Don Fadrique, takes its name from two tiny faces on medallions at the base of one of the horseshoe arches—a little joke on the part of the Muslim stone-carvers. The columns here come from the ruins of Medinat az-Zahra.

Spanish kings after Pedro couldn't leave the Alcázar alone. Ferdinand and Isabella spoiled a large corner of it for their **Casa de Contratación**, a planning centre for the colonization of the Indies. There's little to see in it: a big conference table, Isabel's bedroom, a model of the *Santa María* in wood and a model of the royal family (Isabel's) in silver. Charles V added a **palace** of his own, as he did in the Alhambra. This contains a spectacular set of **Flemish tapestries** showing finely detailed scenes of Charles's campaigns in Tunisia. Within its walls, the Alcázar has extensive and lovely **gardens**, with reflecting pools, palm trees, avenues of clipped hedges, and lemons and oranges everywhere. The park is deceptively large, but you can't get lost unless you find the little **labyrinth** near the pavilion built for Charles V in the lower gardens. Outside the walls, there are more gardens, a formal promenade called the **Plaza Catalina de Ribera** with two monuments to Columbus, and the **Jardines de Murillo**, small though beautifully landscaped, bordering the northern wall of the Alcázar.

West of the Cathedral

Avenida de la Constitución, passing the façade of the cathedral, is Seville's main street. Between it and the Guadalquivir are mostly quiet neighbourhoods, without the distinction of the Barrio Santa Cruz but still with a charm of their own.

Hospital de la Caridad

Built in 1647 behind a colourful façade on Calle Temprado is the Hospital de la Caridad. The Hospital's original benefactor was a certain Miguel de Mañara, a reformed rake who may have been a prototype for Tirso de Molina's Don Juan. Though it still serves its intended purpose as a charity home for the aged, visitors come to see the art in the hospital chapel. The best is gone, unfortunately—in the lobby they'll show you photographs of the Murillos stolen by Napoleon. Among what remains are three works of art, ghoulish even by Spanish standards. Juan de Valdés Leal (1622–90) was a compe-tent enough painter, but warmed to the task only with such subjects as you see here: a bishop in full regalia decomposing in his coffin, and Death snuffing out your candle while bestriding paintings, church paraphernalia and books. Even better than these is the anonymous, polychrome bloody Jesus, surrounded by smiling baroque *putti*, who carry, instead of harps and bouquets, whips and scourges.

Torre del Oro

The Moorish **tower of gold** stands on the banks of the Guadalquivir. In the days of the explorers, ships were still small enough to make this the maritime centre of the city. With a little imagination you can picture the scene when the annual silver fleet came in: the great, low-riding galleons tossing ropes to stevedores on the quay, the crowds and scram-bling children, the king's officials and their battalions of guards, more than a few Indians probably, and the agents of the Flemish and Italian bankers in the background, smiling bemusedly while mentally plotting the most expeditious means of finessing the booty out of Spain. For over a century the fleet's arrival was the event of the year, the turning-point of an annual feast-or-famine cycle when all debts would be made good, and long-deferred indulgences could finally be had.

The Torre del Oro, built by the Almohads in 1220, was the southernmost point of the city's fortifications, constructed on a now-demolished extension of the walls to guard the river. In times of trouble a chain would be stretched from the tower and across the Guadalquivir. It took its name from the gold and *azulejo* tiles that covered its 12-sided exterior in the days of the Moors. The interior now houses a small **Maritime Museum** (*open daily except Mon, 10–2, Sun 10–1*). On the Guadalquivir, however, there probably won't be a ship in sight, apart from the odd paddle-steamer tourist boat. The water you see, in fact, isn't the Guadalquivir at all; the river has been canalized around the city to the new ports to the south, leaving the old bed a backwater.

La Maestranza Bullring

On the river just north of the tower is another citadel of Sevillan *duende*. La Maestranza bullring, built in 1760, is not as big as Madrid's, but is still a lovely building, and perhaps the most prestigious of all *plazas de toros*. It also carries the third-busiest schedule, after Madrid and Barcelona; if you like to watch as your *cola de toro* is prepared, you may be fortunate enough to see a *corrida* while in town (*see* **Snapshots**, p.67). The bullring's name comes from the big **Maestranza** (naval dockyard) across the street.

Tapas and Gypsy Eggs

 Sevillanos claim that they invented tapas and, though this is probably just another idle boast from a city in love with itself, there is no better place in Spain to enjoy them. Sevillanos spend whole evenings *'El Tapeo'*—moving from bar to bar, sampling *espinacas con garbanzos* (spinach and chick peas), *puntillitas fritas* (deep-fried baby squid), *pincho moruno* (little meat kebabs) and a bewildering number of other snacks.

Tapa literally means top—as in the top of a bottle—called so after the original custom of placing a small plate of food over the top of a glass of beer as a free enticement to drink in a particular bar. You'll be hard pushed to find free tapas in modern Seville and many places overcharge, so don't be fooled by the size of the portion—check the price.

Though tapas bars dominate Seville, the city also has a reputation for *huevos a la flamenca* or gypsy eggs. The eggs are oven-baked with chorizo, ham, tomatoes, potatoes and numerous other vegetables. There are three wine-producing regions in the province of Seville but the favourite tipple is *manzanilla* sherry, which is matured in Sanlúcar de Barrameda in *bodegas* along the coast.

Triana

Across the Guadalquivir from the bullring is the neighbourhood of Triana, an ancient suburb that takes its name from the Emperor Trajan. It has a reputation as the 'cradle of flamenco' and its workmen make all Seville's *azulejo* tiles. Queipo de Llano's troops wrecked a lot of it at the start of the Civil War, but there are still picturesque white streets overlooking the Guadalquivir, and quite a few bars and clubs.

Nights in the Gardens of Spain

 The first proper garden in al-Andalus, according to legend, was planted by the first Caliph himself, Abd ar-Rahman. This refugee from Damascus brought with him fond memories of the famous Rusāfah gardens in that city, and he also brought seeds of the palm tree to plant. As Caliph, he built an aqueduct to Cordoba, partly for the city and partly to furnish his new Rusāfah; his botanists sent away for more palms, and also introduced the peach and the pomegranate into Europe.

Following the Caliph's example, the Arabs of the towns laid out recreational gardens everywhere, particularly along the riverfronts. The widely travelled geographer al-Shaquindi wrote in the 11th century that the Guadalquivir around Cordoba was more beautiful than the Tigris or the Nile, lined with orchards, vines, pleasure gardens, groves of citrus trees and avenues of yews. Every city did its best to make a display, and each had its district of villas and gardens. Seville's was in Triana and on the river islands. Valencia too, which had another copy of the Rusāfah, came to be famous for its gardens; poets called the city 'a maiden in the midst of flowers'.

All this gardening was only part of a truly remarkable passion for everything green. Andalucia's climate and soil made it a paradise for the thirsty Arabs and Berbers, and bringing southern Spain into the wider Islamic world made possible the introduction of new crops and techniques from all over: rice, peppers, sugar, cotton, saffron, oranges (*naranja* in Spanish, from the Persian *nārang*), even bananas. In the 12,000 villages of the Guadalquivir valley, Moorish farmers were wizards they learned how to graft almond branches on to apricot trees, and they refined irrigation and fertilizing to fine arts (one manuscript that survives from the time is a 'catalogue of dung'; pigs and ducks were considered very bad, while the horse was best for almost all fields). Sophisticated techniques of irrigation were practised throughout al-Andalus, and everywhere the rivers turned the wooden water wheels, or *norias* (another Persian word, *nā'urāh*); one in Toledo was almost 200ft tall. No expense was spared in bringing water where it was needed; near Moravilla remains can be seen of a mile-long subterranean aqueduct, 30ft in width. The farmers had other tricks, mostly lost to us; it was claimed they could store grain to last for a century, by spreading it between layers of pomegranate leaves and lime or oak ash.

Flowers were everywhere. On the slopes of Jabal al-Warad, the 'Mountain of the Rose' near Cordoba, vast fields of these were grown for rose water; other blooms widely planted for perfumes and other products included violet, jasmine, gillyflower, narcissus, gentian and tulip. And with all the flowers and gardens came poetry, one of the main preoccupations of life in al-Andalus for prince and peasant alike. When Caliph Abd ar-Rahman saw his palm tree growing, he wrote a lyric in its honour:

> *In the centre of the Rusāfah I saw a palm tree growing,*
> *born in the west, far from the palm's country.*
>
> *I cried: 'Thou art like me, for wandering and peregrination,*
> *and the long separation from family and friends.*
>
> *'May the clouds of morning water thee in thy exile,*
>
> *'May the life-giving rains that the poor implore never*
> *forsake thee.'*

Northwest of the Cathedral

Back across the river, over the Puente de Triana, you'll approach the San Eloy district, full of raucous bars and hotels. On Calle San Pablo is **La Magdalena** (1704), with an eccentric baroque façade decorated with sundials. Among the art inside are two paintings of the *Life of St Dominic* by Zurbarán, and gilded reliefs by Leonardo de Figueroa.

Museo de Bellas Artes

> *Open daily except Wed, Mon–Sat 9–8, Sun 9–3; adm free to EU citizens,*
> *250 pts for others.*

This excellent collection is housed in the **Convento de la Merced** (1612), on Calle San Roque. There are some fine medieval works—sweetly naïve-looking virgins, and an especially expressive triptych by the 'Master of Burgos' from the 13th century. The Italian sculptor Pietro Torregiani (the fellow who broke Michelangelo's nose, and who died in a Seville prison) has left an uncanny barbaric wooden **St Jerome**. This saint, *Jerónimo* in Spanish, is a favourite in Seville, where he is pictured with a rock and a rugged cross instead of his usual lion; as the Doctor of the Church, he helped most to define the concepts of heresy and self-mortification.

The museum has a roomful of Murillos (the painter was Sevillan and is buried in the Barrio Santa Cruz), including an *Immaculate Conception* and many other artful missal-pictures. Much more interesting are the works of Zurbarán, who could express spirituality without the simpering of Murillo or the hysteria of the others. His series of **female saints** is especially good, and the *Miracle of Saint Hugo* is perhaps his most acclaimed work. Occasionally even Zurbarán slips up; you may enjoy the *Eternal Father* with great fat toes and a triangle on his head, a *St Gregory* who looks like the scheming church executive he really was, and the wonderful *Apotheosis of St Thomas Aquinas*, where the great scholastic philosopher rises to his feet as if to say 'I've got it!'. Don't miss El Greco's portrait of his son Jorge. There are also more Valdés Leals—heads on plates, and such—and works by Jan Brueghel, Ribera, Caravaggio, and Mattia Preti.

North of the Cathedral

Seville's business and shopping area has been since Moorish times the patch of narrow streets north of La Giralda. **Calle Sierpes** ('serpent street') is its heart, a sinuous pedestrian lane lined with every sort of old shop. Just to the north, **El Salvador** is a fine baroque church by Leonardo de Figueroa, picturesquely mouldering; the base of its tower was the minaret of an important mosque that once stood here. The plaza in front is a popular hang-out of Seville's youth, as well as their backpacking cousins from northern Europe. On the **Plaza Nueva**, Seville's modern centre, you can see the grimy 1564 **Ayuntamiento**, with a fine, elaborate plateresque façade. From here, Avenida de la Constitución changes its name to Calle Tetuán. Seville has found a hundred ways to use its *azulejos*, but the best has to be in the **billboard** on this street for 1932 Studebaker cars; so pretty that no one's had the heart to take it down.

Macarena

The north end of Seville contains few monuments; most of it is solid, working-class neighbourhoods clustered around baroque parish churches. The **Alameda de Hércules**, a once fashionable promenade adorned with copies of ancient statues, is in the middle of one of the shabbier parts. **Santa Clara** and **San Clemente** are two interesting monasteries in this area: Santa Clara includes a Gothic tower built by Don Fadrique, Pedro the Cruel's brother; its pretty chapel has one of Seville's best *artesonado* ceilings. North of Calle San Luis, some of the city's **Moorish walls** survive, near the **Basilica of La Macarena,** which gives the quarter its name. The Basilica is the home of the most worshipped of Seville's idols, a delicate Virgin with glass tears on her cheeks who always steals the show in the Holy Week parades. Like a film star she makes her admirers gasp and swarm around her, crying '*¡O la hermosa! ¡O la guapa!*' ('O the beautiful! O the handsome!'). The small adjacent **museum** is divided between La Macarena's trinkets and costumes of famous bullfighters.

South from here, along Calle San Luis, you'll pass another baroque extravaganza, Leonardo de Figueroa's **San Luis**, built for the Jesuits (1699–1731), with twisted columns and tons of encrusted ornament. **San Marcos**, down the street, has one of Seville's last surviving *mudéjar* towers.

East of the Cathedral

Barrio Santa Cruz

If Spain envies Seville, Seville envies **Barrio Santa Cruz**, a tiny, exceptionally lovely quarter of narrow streets and whitewashed houses. It is the true homeland of everything *sevillano*, with flower-bedecked patios and iron-bound windows through which the occasional nostalgic young man still manages to get up the nerve to embarrass his sweetheart with a serenade.

Before 1492, this was the Jewish quarter of Seville; today it's the most aristocratic corner of town. In the old days there was a wall around the *barrio*; today you may enter through the Jardines de Murillo, the Calle Mateos Gago behind the cathedral apse, or from the **Patio de las Banderas**, a pretty Plaza Mayor-style square next to the Alcázar. On the eastern edge of the Barrio, **Santa María la Blanca** (on the street of the same name) was a pre-Reconquista church; some ancient details remain, but the whole was rebuilt in the 1660s, with spectacular rococo ornamentation inside and paintings by Murillo.

Casa de Pilatos

Open daily 9–7; adm 1000 pts.

On the eastern fringes of the old town, the Barrio Santa Cruz fades gently into other peaceful pretty areas—less ritzy, though their old streets contain more palaces. One of these, built by the Dukes of Medinaceli (1480–1571), is the **Casa de Pilatos** on Plaza Pilatos. The dukes like to tell people that it is a replica of 'Pontius Pilate's house' in Jerusalem. (Pilate, without whom Holy Week would not be possible, is a popular figure; there's a common belief that he was a Spaniard.) It is a pleasant jumble of *mudéjar* and Renaissance work, with a lovely patio and lots of *azulejos* everywhere.

The entrance, a mock-Roman triumphal arch done in Carrara marble by sculptors from Genoa, leads through a small court into the **Patio Principal**, with 13th-century Granadan decoration, beautiful coloured tiles, and rows of Roman statues and portrait busts—an introduction to the dukes' excellent collections of antique sculpture in the surrounding rooms, including a Roman copy of a Greek *herm* (boundary marker, with the head of the god Hermes), imperial portraits, and a bust of Hadrian's boyfriend, Antinous.

Behind the Casa de Pilatos, **San Esteban**, rebuilt from a former mosque, has an altarpiece by Zurbarán; around the corner on Calle Luis Montoto are remains of an Almoravid **aqueduct**. A few streets away to the northeast, the **Palacio de la Condesa de Lebrija**, is worth a visit for its fine Roman mosaics brought from Itálica. On Calle Águilas, **San Ildefonso** has a pretty yellow and white 18th-century façade. Another post-1492 palace with *mudéjar* decoration, several streets north on Calle Bustos Tavera, is the huge **Palacio de las Dueñas**.

South of the Cathedral

Seville has a building even larger than its cathedral—twice as large, in fact, and probably better known to the outside world. Since the 1950s it has housed parts of the city's **university** and it does have the presence of a college building, but it began its life in the 1750s as the state **Fábrica de Tabacos** (Tobacco Factory). In the 19th century, it employed as many as 12,000 women to roll cigars—as historians note, the biggest female urban proletariat in the world. (One of its workers, of course, was Bizet's Carmen.) These sturdy women, with 'carnations in their hair and daggers in their garters', hung their capes on the altars of the factory chapels each morning, rocked their babies in cradles while they rolled cigars, and took no nonsense from anybody.

Next to the Fábrica, the Hotel Alfonso XIII, built in 1929, is believed to be the only hotel ever commissioned by a reigning monarch—Alfonso literally used it as an annexe to the Alcázar when friends and relations came to stay. This landmark is well worth a visit, if you're not put off by an icy doorman. To the west of the hotel lies the baroque **Palacio de San Telmo**. Originally a naval academy, the palace was the residence of the dukes of Montpensier. It has been a seminary since 1900, and has recently been lavishly restored by the Junta de Andalucía.

THE TOBACCO FACTORY

Parque de María Luisa

For all its old-fashioned grace, Seville has been one of the most forward-looking and progressive cities of Spain in the 20th century. In the 1920s, while they were redirecting the Guadalquivir and building the new port and factories that are the foundation of the city's growth today, the *sevillanos* decided to put on an exhibition. In a tremendous burst of energy, they turned the entire southern end of the city into an expanse of gardens and grand boulevards. The centre of it is **Parque de María Luisa**, a paradisiacal half-mile of palms and orange trees, elms and Mediterranean pines, covered with flower beds and dotted with hidden bowers, ponds and pavilions. Now that the trees and shrubs have reached maturity, the genius of the landscapers can be appreciated—this is one of the loveliest parks in Europe.

Two of the largest pavilions on the **Plaza de América** have been turned into museums. The **Archaeological Museum** (*open Tues 3–8; Wed–Sat 9–8; Sun 9–2.30; EU citizens free, others 250 pts*) has one of the best collections of pre-Roman jewellery and icons, reproductions of the fine goldwork of the 'Treasure of Carambelo', and some tantalizing artefacts from mysterious Tartessos. The Romans are represented, as in every other Mediterranean archaeology museum, with copies of Greek sculpture and oversized statues of emperors, but also with a mosaic of the *Triumph of Bacchus*, another of Hercules, architectural fragments, some fine glass, and finds of all sorts from Itálica and other nearby towns.

Across the plaza, the **Museum of Popular Art and Customs** (*open Tues 3–8; Wed–Sat 9–8; Sun 9–2.30; EU citizens free, others 250 pts*) is Andalucía's attic, with everything from ploughs and saucepans to *azulejo* tiles, flamenco dresses (polka dots weren't always the style), musical instruments, religious bric-a-brac and exhibits for the city's two famous celebrations, Semana Santa and the April Feria.

The Plaza de España

In the 1920s at least, excess was still a way of life in Seville, and to call attention to the *Exposición Iberoamericana* they put up a building even bigger than the Tobacco Factory. With its grand baroque towers (stolen gracefully from Santiago de Compostela), fancy bridges, staircases and immense colonnade, the Plaza de España is World Fair architecture at its grandest and most outrageous. Much of the fanciful neo-Spanish architecture of 1930s Florida and California may well have been inspired by this building. *Sevillanos* gravitate naturally to it at weekends, to row canoes in the Plaza's canals and nibble curious pastries. One of the things Seville is famous for is its painted *azulejo* tiles; they adorn nearly every building in town, but here on the colonnade a few million of them are devoted to maps and historical scenes from every province in Spain.

Cartuja

The island, northwest across the Río Guadalquivir, is currently open Tues–Sun, 11–6.30. For more information, © 95 448 06 11.

The Isla de la Cartuja was part of the Expo '92 site during the World Fair. The theme was the 'Age of Discoveries' and marked the 500th anniversary of the discovery of the New World. More than a hundred countries took part in Expo '92, which had 98 pavilions and attracted 16 million people. Today Cartuja has been repackaged as the 'Park of Discoveries', and includes four of the original Expo pavilions (focusing on Nature, Discovery, Navigation and the Future), a planetarium, a giant Omnimax Cinema and a tacky 17th-century island theme park complete with roller coaster. Everything is overpriced and uninspiring; though it costs just 500 pts to walk around, entry to any of the pavilions is 2000 pts, and the amusement park costs 3500 pts.

More interesting is **Santa Maria de las Cuevas** (*open Tues–Sat 10–9; Sun 10–3; adm 300 pts*), the restored Carthusian monastery where Columbus once stayed while he mulled over his ambitions and geographical theories. Since then, the building has suffered various indignities; the monks were driven out by Marshal Soult who used it as a garrison during the Napoleonic occupation of 1810–12 and is responsible for the damage to the artesonado ceiling in the refectory—his troops used it for target practice. As if this wasn't enough, the city sold it off to wealthy Liverpudlian Charles Pickman, in the 1830s, who had the bright idea of turning it into a ceramics factory.

The brick kilns have been lovingly restored at great expense, presumably as some kind of tribute to the Industrial Age, and stand bizarre and incongruous next to the monastery garden. Now the monastery is the temporary home for the **Andalucían Centre of Contemporary Art**, which mounts obscurely titled exhibitions throughout the year.

Shopping

All the paraphernalia associated with Spanish fantasy, such as *mantillas*, castanets, wrought iron, gypsy dresses and Andalucían dandy suits, *azulejo* tiles and embroidery, is available in Seville. Most of it's made here, and if you're interested in tours or just shopping, ask the tourist information office what's currently available.

There are two branches of **El Corte Inglés**, where the well-heeled *sevillanos* shop, a branch of C&A on Calle Sierpes and a sizeable Marks & Spencer—its food department is the only place we know where you can find Indian food in Seville—on Plaza Duque de la Victoria. **Vértice** is a bookshop on Mateos Gago near the cathedral, with a small selection of English-language literature and local guide-books and history books; but for a pleasant wander head for the pedestrianised Calle Sierpes.

Seville ✉ *41000*   ***Where to Stay***

Not many of Seville's hotels are distinctive in any way, but there are plenty of rooms all over the centre. High season is March and April. During *Semana Santa* and the April *Feria* you should book even for inexpensive *hostales*, preferably a year ahead.

expensive

The ★★★★★**Alfonso XIII**, C/ San Fernando 2, ✆ 95 422 28 50, ✆ 95 421 60 33, was built by King Alfonso for the Exposición Iberoamericana in 1929. The grandest hotel in southern Spain, this huge building, set in landscaped grounds next to the university, attracts heads of state, opera stars and tourists who want a unique experience, albeit at a price. Seville society still meets around its lobby fountain and somewhat dreary bar (*28,000 pts for a low-season single, rising to 56,000 pts for a double during feria*).

The ★★★★★**Hotel Colón**, C/ Canalejas 1, ✆ 95 422 29 00, ✆ 95 422 09 38, is grand and extremely comfortable. It used to be a haunt of bullfighters and their hangers-on (*20,000–38,000 pts*).

By the Macarena walls, the ★★★★**Sol Macarena**, San Juan de Rivera 2, ✆ 95 437 58 00, ✆ 95 438 18 03, is another classy establishment although it's not exactly central; there is a beautiful *azulejo*-tiled fountain, a swimming pool, and views over the city from the roof-top terrace. The service is excellent and rates are very reasonable for this category (*from 14,000 pts*).

Near the Prado de San Sebastián, the ★★★★**Meliá Seville**, Doctor Pedro de Castro 1, ✆ 95 442 15 11, ✆ 95 442 16 08, is a pleasant modern hotel within easy walking distance of the city centre, with some lovely suites (*21,000–29,000 pts*).

The utterly charming ★★★★**Hotel Doña María**, C/ Don Remondo 19, ✆ 95 422 49 90, ✆ 95 421 95 46, is superbly located by the cathedral. Among the mostly antique furniture are some beautifully painted headboards (*13,000–26,000 pts*).

The deliciously appointed **Los Seises**, Segovias s/n in the Barrio, ℰ 95 422 94 95, ✉ 95 422 43 34, offers urban chic on a small scale—only it's well-nigh impossible to find it on your own, so take a cab (*16,000–35,000 pts*).

The **Hotel Taberna de Alabardero**, Zaragoza 20, ℰ 95 456 0637, in a former nobleman's house, has intimate rooms, all charmingly decorated in an individual style. Prices include breakfast in the restaurant which has won numerous awards (*18,000 pts*).

moderate

Las Casas de la Judería, Callejón de Dos Hermanos 7, ℰ 95 441 51 50, ✉ 95 422 2170, is a row of perfectly restored townhouses in the Barrio Santa Cruz, expertly run by the Medina family—well-known and very stylish Seville hoteliers (*10,000–13,000 pts*).

The ★**Hotel Simón**, García de Vinuesa 14, ℰ 95 422 66 60, ✉ 95 456 22 41, in a fine position just off the Avenida de la Constitución by the cathedral, is in a restored 18th-century mansion, spoilt by a Coke machine in the entrance courtyard (*6000–9000 pts*).

The **Hotel Alvarez Quintero**, Alvarez Quintero 12 ℰ 95 422 12 98, has fine views of the cathedral a few streets to the south, air-conditioned rooms *from 14,000 pts*, and a delightful patio.

The ★★**Hostal Atenas**, C/ Caballerizas 1, ℰ 95 421 80 47, is quiet and very nice, in a good location between the Plaza Pilatos and the cathedral. Take a cab, it's hard to find (*8000–13,000 pts*).

The ★**Hostal Plaza Seville**, Canalejas 2, ℰ 95 421 71 49, ✉ 95 421 07 73, has a beautiful neoclassical façade, the work of Aníbal González, architect of the 1929 Exposición, and is ideally placed near the restaurants and bars of St Eloy (*10,000–13,000 pts*).

The ★**Pensión Toledo**, Santa Teresa 15, ℰ 95 421 53 35, is respectable and good value (*5000–7000 pts*) and the **Hotel Europa**, Jimios 5, ℰ 95 421 43 05, ✉ 95 421 00 16, very close to the cathedral, in the Barrio Santa Cruz, has big, quiet rooms, some of which are air-conditioned (*from 7500 pts*).

inexpensive

For inexpensive *hostales*, the Barrio Santa Cruz is surprisingly the best place to look. Even in July and August, you'll be able to find a place on the quiet side streets off C/ Mateos Gago.

The ★**Monreal**, C/ Rodrigo Caro 8, ℰ 95 421 41 66, is closest to the cathedral, a lively place with almost too much character and a good cheap restaurant when it's open (*4000–7000 for a double, singles available at an amazing 2500 pts*).

The ★**Pensión Fabiola**, Fabiola 6, ℰ 95 421 83 46 (*6000–8000 pts*), the **Hostal Javier**, Archeros 16, ℰ 95 441 23 25 (*3500–5000 pts*), and **Pension Archeros**, Archeros 23, ℰ 95 441 84 65 (*3500–6000 pts for a double, 2000 pts for a single*), are quiet, cooler than most in summer and have little patios.

Hostal Círdoba, Farnesio 12, ✆ 95 422 74 98 (*3000–4500 pts*) and the
★Hostal El Buen Dormir, Farnesio 8, ✆ 95 421 74 92 (*3500–4500 pts*) both
offer clean rooms with fans.

Cheapest of the lot are **Huespedes La Montorena**, San Clemente 12, ✆ 95
441 24 07 (*singles for 1500 pts and doubles for 3000 pts*) and **Pension
Cruces El Patio**, Plaza Cruces de las Cruces 10, ✆ 95 422 96 33 (*dormitory
beds for 1200 pts, singles at 2500 pts and doubles from 4500 pts*).

There are some other cheap options outside Barrio Santa Cruz. The family-run
Hostal La Francesa, Juan Rabadan 28, ✆ 95 438 31 07, is in a quiet part of
town, close to the river and San Lorenzo Church with doubles *from 3000 pts*,
and the **Hostal ñ** (*4000–6000 pts*), at Dona Guiomar 1, just off Zaragoza near
the Plaza Nueva, ✆ 95 421 68 40, is spacious, clean and run by a slightly para-
noid old woman who behaves as if she's still living under Franco.

Eating Out

Restaurants here are more expensive than in most of Spain, but even
around the cathedral and the Barrio Santa Cruz, in contrast to
Cordoba, there are few places that can simply be dismissed as tourist
traps. Remember that in the evening the *sevillanos*, even more than
most Andalucíans, enjoy bar-hopping for tapas, rather than sitting
down to one meal; two *sevillanos* in a bar is a party, three is a fiesta.

expensive

A few places have attractions beyond the cuisine: **La Albahaca**, Pza. Santa Cruz
12, ✆ 95 422 07 14, has tables outside, artwork on its crockery and three well-
proportioned dining rooms; it is situated in Santa Cruz on one of Seville's most
delightful small squares. Specialities include scorpion fish with fennel and
peanuts, mushrooms with green asparagus, and partridge with endives. Prices
start at around *5000 pts* per head. *Closed Sun*.

Nearby is **Corral del Agua**, Callejón del Agua 6, ✆ 95 422 07 14; well-seasoned
travellers usually steer clear of cutesy wishing-wells, but the garden in which this
one stands is a haven of peace and shade, a perfect stopping place for a lazy lunch
or unashamedly romantic dinner. The Corral del Agua is next to Washington
Irving's garden.

Splendidly situated on the corner of the Jardines Alcázar, opposite the university,
is one of Seville's best-loved restaurants, the **Egaña-Oriza**, San Fernando 41,
✆ 95 422 72 11. It serves the best of *andaluz* and Basque cuisine. Among its
tempting delights are clams on the half-shell, baked *hongos* mushrooms, and a
kind of *sevillano* jugged hare (*6000 pts minimum with wine*). *Closed Sat lunch,
Sun and Aug*. Attached to it, the restaurant's own tapas bar is chic, bright,
cosmopolitan—and the Basque tapas are sensational.

Northwest of La Giralda, you can dine in one of Seville's most celebrated restaurants, the **Taberna del Alabardero**, Zaragoza 20, ✆ 95 456 06 37. It's Michelin-starred, formerly a nobleman's house, and serves such specialities as aubergine and shrimp in filo, and *urta* (a firm-fleshed, white fish caught locally around Rota) cooked in red wine. There are seven guest rooms available if you over-indulge and can't make it home. The taberna is open daily year-round; its basement café serves an excellent set lunch at *1500 pts*.

By the cathedral, in the narrow Argote de Molina (at No.26), is **Mesón Don Raimundo**, ✆ 95 422 33 55, a restaurant in what was once a convent. No enforced abstinence here, though. You can pig out on the large selection of fish, shellfish, and game dishes amid an eclectic décor of religious artefacts and suits of armour (*3500–4500 pts*). *Closed Sun evening.*

Along the Triana side of the Guadalquivir you can dine with a tremendous view of the Torre del Oro and La Giralda at the restaurant **Río Grande**, C/ Betis s/n, ✆ 95 427 39 56. The kitchen here specializes in regional cuisine (*3500 pts*). The place has a faded Edwardian elegance about it, but the food doesn't quite cut the mustard. Along from here is the unfortunately named **Ox's**, C/ Betis 61, ✆ 95 427 95 85, with Basque novelties—cod-stuffed peppers, fish and steaks (*from 4000 pts*). *Closed Sun night and Aug.*

moderate

Don Raimundo also owns two other restaurants near his Mesón: **La Barca**, Placentines 25, ✆ 95 456 04 91, which specializes in fish and seafood; and **Las Meninas** on Calle Manara. Also serving excellent fish tapas is **Restaurante A Babor**, C/ Teodosio 51. The **Bodegón Torre del Oro**, C/ Santander 15, ✆ 95 421 42 41, specializes in *urta*. There's a three-course meal with wine (*1300 pts*) and the *raciones* are good.

At **Mordisco**, Virgen de la Regla 18, ✆ 95 428 15 94, the home-cooking is distinctly Mediterranean. And in a country where meat and fish reign supreme, it's a nice surprise to find **La Mandrágora**, a very friendly vegetarian restaurant with an interesting menu (*2000 pts*). *Closed Sun.*

A good place for lunch is the **Restaurante San Marco**, Cuna 6, ✆ 95 421 24 40, in the shopping district, no relation of the **Pizzeria San Marco**, Meson del Moro 6–10, ✆ 95 421 43 90, which serves reasonably priced, delicious food.

inexpensive

One particular pleasure, in a city which pursues so many, is to set out on a bar crawl, trying different sherries and tapas. Some will appeal, others will not; you will soon discover a favourite. To start, the lively tapas bar **Bodega La Andana**, C/ Argote de Molina, is where hordes of Seville's *caballeros* and *señoritas* spill out on to the pavement, particularly at weekends, to misspend their youth.

Around the corner you can eat decently at the bar-restaurant **Gonzalo**, on the corner of Alemanes and Argote de Molina, with the Giralda looming overhead.

There's a reasonably priced and varied menu (*around 1200 pts*), but the walls could do with a lick of paint.

Bar Giralda, C/ Mateos Gago, as its name suggests, is closer still and has a good selection of sherries. **Bar Modesto** is a short walk away from the cathedral on Calle Cano y Cueta, serving breakfast, *raciones* and full meals.

Kiosko de las Flores, a little difficult to find but well worth the search, is the best tapas bar in Seville, and the most charming in all of Andalucía, serving light fish lunches of *boquerones*, among other things. The place is an informal café-bar, right by the Puente de Isabel II, and part of it looks over the water. Prices are a little high—a glorified fishy snack with a drink costs 1300 pts.

North of the cathedral, between the church of San Pedro and the convent Espíritu Santo, is **El Rinconcillo**, at C/ Gerona 42, the oldest bar in Seville. The place dates back to 1670 and is decorated in moody brown *azulejos*; here lively *sevillano cognoscenti* gather to dabble at the tasty nibbles, but their real purpose is to model their designer clothes and spend the evening in loud animated high-brow chatter. The staff, oblivious, chalk up the bill on the bar.

cheap

Seville's cheapest restaurants lurk around Calle San Eloy. Some almost give meals away, and they're worth the price. It's better to stick with the tapas and *mariscos* bars here and in the little streets of Calle Tetuán and Calle Sierpes. The **Antigua Bodequita** is a find, a tiny bar opposite the church on Plaza del Salvador, but if you just fancy cakes, coffee or ice cream head for **La Campana** on Calle Sierpes. Established in 1885, it's probably the prettiest pâtisserie around. There are a string of cheap restaurants at the Guadalquivir end of Calle San Jose Santa Maria La Blanca in Santa Cruz. Most offer a three-course set menu including a drink for *800 pts*. The **Il Garibaldi** has good options for breakfast and a delicious range of frozen yogurts.

tapas

The **Bar Manolo**, Plaza de Alfalfa, is the best of a number of tapas bars on the square, and is lively at breakfast time and in the evening. The **Bar Alicantina** nearby, on the Plaza del Salvador, has great *ensalada rusa* and is a favoured hangout of the young and fashionable. The **Becerrita Centro**, near the cathedral on C/Hernando Colon,1, serves some of Seville's most traditional and tastiest tapas whilst the **Bar Giralda**, Mateos Gago 1, in an old Moorish bathhouse, has a great range to choose from and is popular with tourists and locals. Opposite is a more rustic and basic local haunt, the **Bodega de Juan Garcia Aviles**, Mateos Gago 20. In Barrio Santa Cruz, try **Hostaría del Laurel**, Plaza de los Venerables 5, which serves superb tapas in a room filled with hanging *jamon* and beautiful Triana tiles. The **Casa Roman**, next door at Plaza de los Venerables 1, is famous for its ham tapas. In Triana, across the river, the moorish-looking **Bar Anslema**, Pages del Corro 49, has occasional impromptu flamenco. Opposite is **Las Golondrinas**, Antillano Campos 26, which serves great **alcauciles** (artichokes) and tortilla in a charming tiled two-floor bar.

Entertainment and Nightlife

flamenco

If you've been longing to experience **flamenco**, Seville is a good place to do it, though not the best—shows in Granada and Cordoba are more authentic. The most touristy flamenco factories will hit you for *1500 pts* and up per drink. Bars in Triana and other areas do it better for less; Calle Salado and environs in Triana, for example, has some good bars like **La Caseta**, C/Febo 36, which though a long way from either Sevillana dance or pure flamenco, is young, vibrant and popular with locals. The equally youthful and occasionally impromptu **El Simpecao**, Paseo de la O, near the Iglesia de O in Triana, is closer to the real thing. There are more venues across the river in Barrio Santa Cruz. The king of modern flamenco, El Camaron de la Isla, used to play at **La Carboneria**, C/Levies 18, and the bar is still one of the best venues in the city for extemporaneous performances of all styles. Thursday is best for flamenco. If you're looking for *sevillano* dancing (very similar to flamenco though slightly less tortured and frenetic) head for **El Tamboril** on Plaza Santa Cruz, which is as popular with *sevillanos* as it is with tourists. **Los Gallos**, a few doors away, is less spontaneous, with a *3000 pts* entrance charge and *sevillano* and flamenco dancing lit by the flashes of tourist cameras. Even more formal is **El Palacio Andaluz**, Av. Maria Auxiliadora, 18B, a 1½-hour staged show for tourists in an expensive Seville restaurant.

music and theatre

They do play other kinds of music in Seville, and two publications, *El Giraldillo* and *Ocio*, available around town, have listings. For mainstream **drama**, the best-known theatre is the **Teatro Lope de Vega**, Avda. María Luisa, ℗ 95 423 45 46, built for the 1929 exhibition, though a newcomer has recently taken over as principal lead: the **Teatro de Maestranza**, Pso. de Cristíbal Colín, ℗ 95 422 33 44, opened in time for Expo 92, has quickly established itself as one of the top **opera** houses in Europe.

other entertainments

Take a **river cruise** along the Guadalquivir. Three companies do it daily (3.45 and 4.30), all from around the Torre del Oro: Cruceros Turisticos Torre del Oro S.L, Paseo Alcalde Marques del Contadero (℗ 95 421 13 96), Cruseros del Sur, Paseo de Colon, 11 (℗ 95 456 16 72) and Buque El Patio, Paseo de Colon, 11 (℗ 95 421 38 36). See a **bullfight** in the famous Maestranza if you can, but don't just turn up! Get tickets as far ahead as possible; prices at the ring office, ℗ 95 422 45 77, will be cheaper than at the little stands on Calle Sierpes.

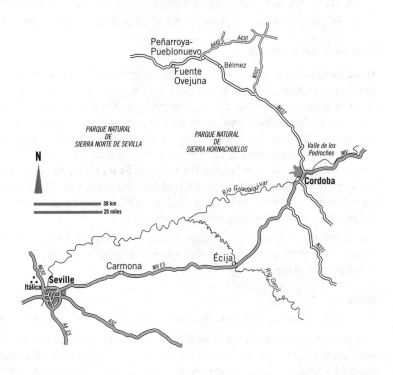

Getting Around

There is no train service for the villages around Seville, but plenty of buses. **Itálica** is on the Ctra. Menda, with local buses leaving every half-hour from the Plaza de Armas, near the Puerto del Cachorro; the main highway east and south is the NIV.

The train from Seville in the Cordoba direction, and many of the direct buses, unfortunately take a rather dull route through the flat lands along the Guadalquivir. The only landmark here is the Spanish-Moorish castle of Almodóvar del Río, perched romantically on a height planted with olive trees, overlooking the river. The southern route (the NIV) from Seville towards Cordoba also follows the Guadalquivir valley, but the scenery is a little more varied, and the road passes through two fine towns, **Carmona** and **Écija**. There are regular buses from Seville to these towns, from where you can easily find connecting buses for Cordoba.

Carmona: Oficina Municipal de Turismo, Arco de la Puerta de Seville, ✆ 95 419 09 55, *carmona@andal.es. Open Mon–Fri 9–2, Sat and Sun 10.30–1.30.* **Écija**: Ayuntamiento, Pza. de España, ✆ 95 590 02 40. *Open Mon–Fri 9–1.*

Villages South of Seville

Alcalá de Guadaira, off the N334 just south of Seville, is jocularly known in Seville as Alcalá de los Panaderos ('of the bakers'), as it used to supply the city with its daily bread. Its **castle** is the best-preserved Almohad fortress in Andalucía. Just outside **Utrera**, the tiny village of **Palmar de Troya** received a visit in 1968 from the Virgin Mary (to little girls, as usual) that has led to the founding of a new church, the 'Orden de la Santa Faz'. They have their own pope in Palmar and include among their saints Franco, José Antonio and Ramon Llull. In **Lebrija**, the church of **Santa María de la Oliva** is really a 12th-century Almohad mosque, with a typical Middle Eastern roof of small domes and a tower that is a miniature version of La Giralda, built by a Basque architect in the 19th century—but Lebrija is better-known for its wine.

Take care before you start any rambles in the countryside; this area south of Seville contains some of the best-known ranches where fighting bulls are bred, and the bulls are always allowed to run free.

Itálica

Open Tues–Sat 9–8; Sun 10–3; adm free for EU citizens, others 250 pts.

Eight kilometres (5 miles) north of the city, in the direction of Mérida, the only significant Roman ruins in Andalucía are at **Itálica**, a city founded in the 3rd century BC by Scipio Africanus as a home for his veterans. Itálica thrived in the imperial age. The Guadalquivir had a reputation for constantly changing its course in the old days, and this may explain the presence of two important cities so close together. Three great emperors, Trajan, Hadrian and Theodosius, were born here. The biggest ruins are an **amphitheatre**, with seating for 40,000, some remains of temples, and a street of villa foundations. Surviving mosaics portray Hercules and Bacchus, a Cretan labyrinth, and a battle between pygmies and cranes.

The village of Santiponce, near the ruins, has a fine Gothic-*mudéjar* monastery built for the Cistercians in 1301: **San Isidoro del Campo**, with another gruesome St Jerome, carved in the 1600s by Juan Martínez Montañés (1566–1649), on the altarpiece.

Northwest Towards Cordoba: Carmona and Écija

Carmona

The first town along the NIV, Carmona, seems a miniature Seville. It is probably much older. Remains of a Neolithic settlement have been found around town; the Phoenician colony that replaced it grew into a city and prospered throughout Roman and Moorish times. Pedro the Cruel favoured it and rebuilt most of its **Alcázar**. Sitting proudly on top of the town, with views over the valley, this fortress is now a national *parador*.

Carmona is well worth a day's exploration. Its walls, mostly Moorish fortifications built over Roman foundations, are still standing, including a grand gateway on the road from Seville, the **Puerta de Seville**. Continue through the arch and up to the palm-decked Plaza de San Fernando, where the under-16s and over-60s gather; the Ayuntamiento here has a Roman mosaic of Medusa in its courtyard. Next, take Calle Martín López up to the lofty 15th-century church of **Santa María**, built on the site of an old mosque (*open daily 9–12 and 6–9*). The old quarters of town have an ensemble of fine palaces, and *mudéjar* and Renaissance churches. On one of these, **San Pedro** (1466), you'll see another imitation of La Giralda, *La Giraldilla*—though not as fussily ornate as her big sister, she has a cleaner exterior. Carmona's prime attraction is the **Roman necropolis**, a series of rock-cut tombs off the Avenida Jorge Bonsor (*open June–Sept, Tues–Fri 9–2; Oct–May, Tues–Fri 10–2; Sat and Sun all year round 10–2; adm free to EU citizens, 250 pts for others; © 95 414 08 11*). Some, like the 'Tomb of Servilia', are elaborate creations with subterranean chambers and vestibules, pillars, domed ceilings and carved reliefs. Near the entrance to the site are remains of the Roman amphitheatre, forlorn and unexcavated.

Écija

Écija makes much of one of its nicknames, the 'city of towers' and tries to play down the other—the 'frying pan of Andalucía', which isn't exactly fair. Any Andalucían town can overheat you thoroughly on a typical summer's day and, if Écija is a degree hotter and a little less breezy than most, only a born Andalucían could tell the difference. Ask one and you'll soon learn that the Andalucíans are the only people yet discovered who talk about the weather more than the English.

Don't be put off by the clinical outskirts of the town, nor by the ill-concealed gas-holders; all is forgiven when you reach the **Plaza de España**, one of the loveliest in Andalucía, charmingly framed by tall palms with an exquisite fountain at its centre. The façade of the 18th-century **Santa María** wouldn't look out of place in a Sergio Leone movie. The atmosphere here is laid-back, and once you've finished rubbernecking the steeples, choose your favourite corner of the plaza and do what the locals do—sit and watch. Most of the **towers** are sumptuously ornate, rebuilt after the great earthquake of 1755—the one that flattened Lisbon. Santa María has one, along with **San Juan Bautista**, gaily decorated in coloured tiles, and **San Gil**. This last is the highest of the towers, and within are paintings by Alejo Fernández and Villegas Marmolejo.

Écija also has a set of Renaissance and baroque palaces second in Andalucía only to those in Úbeda; most of these showy façades can be seen on or near the **Calle de los Caballeros**. Worth visiting is the **Mudéjar Palace**, dating from the 14th century, where you can find some interesting archaeological remains, part *mudéjar,* part baroque, some Roman mosaics, and various reliefs, coins and glass.

There's a museum in the **Peñaflor Palace** on Calle de Castellar, with exhibitions of 18th-century art and sculpture, contemporary art and local traditional costumes. The palace itself (1728), with its grandiose façade and lovely patio, is one of the outstanding works of Andalucían baroque. In the evening the town buzzes. After the big-city crush of Seville, you might find that this is the perfect place to spend day—busy enough to be interesting, but not too frantic.

Eating Out

Carmona ✉ 39554

The restaurant **San Fernando**, Pza. San Fernando, has the best reputation in town, although Carmona is not known for culinary excellence. The five-course set menu is *5000 pts. Closed Sun eve, Mon and Aug*. Fish features largely on the menu at the **Parador**, where prices are more reasonable, and at **El Ancla**, Bonifacio 4, ✆ 95 414 15 18, where a full fish meal with wine will set you back a moderate *3000–3500 pts. Closed Mon and Sun nights*. **Mesón de la Reja** is on the main street as you enter from Seville. With a cool *azulejo* interior, it's a good place to try *cola de toro* and down a beer (*about 1000 pts*), while keeping an eye on the bus departures opposite. (Incidentally, if you need bus information, don't ask the drivers—the only person who knows for sure is the man behind the bar at the bus stop.)

Écija ✉ 41400

The best place to eat in town is the stylish **Bodegón del Gallego**, C/ A. Aparicio 3, ✆ 95 483 26 18, which concentrates on *andaluz* dishes (*3500 pts*). Also in the heart of town, the **Pasareli**, Pasaje Virgen del Rocío, ✆ 95 483 20 24, looks like any modern cafeteria, but there's a surprisingly efficient little restaurant tucked away in the corner, where you can eat well from a large selection of meat and fish for *under 2000 pts*.

Cordoba

There are a few spots around the Mediterranean where the presence of past glories becomes almost tangible, a mixture of mythic antiquity, lost power and dissipated energy that broods over a place like a ghost. In Istanbul you can find it, in Rome, or among the monuments of Egypt, and also here on the banks of the Guadalquivir at Cordoba's southern gate. Looking around, you can see reminders of three defunct empires: a Roman bridge, a triumphal arch built for Felipe II and Cordoba's Great Mosque, more than a thousand years old. The first reminds us of the city's beginnings, the second of its decline; the last one scarcely seems credible, as it speaks of an age when Cordoba was one of the most brilliant metropolises of all Europe, city of half a million souls, a place faraway storytellers would use to enthral audiences in the rude halls of the Saxons and Franks. The little plaza by the bridge concentrates melancholy like a magnet; there isn't much left for the rest of the town. Cordoba's recent growth has allowed it a chance to renovate its sparkling old quarters and monuments. With the new prosperity has come a contentment the city probably hasn't known since the Reconquista.

Everyone who visits Cordoba comes for the Great Mosque, but you should spare some time to explore the city itself. Old Cordoba is one of the largest medieval quarters of any European city, and certainly the biggest in Spain. More than Seville, it retains its Moorish character, in a maze of whitewashed alleys opening into the loveliest patios in all Andalucía.

History

Roman *Corduba*, built on a prehistoric site, was almost from the start the leading city of interior Spain, capital of the province of *Hispania Ulterior*, and later of the reorganized province of Bætica. Cordoba had a reputation as the garden spot of Hispania; it gave Roman letters Lucan and both Senecas among others, testimony to its prominence as a city of learning. Cordoba became Christianized at an early date. Ironically, the True Faith got its come-uppance here in 572, when the Arian Visigoths under Leovigild captured the city from Byzantine rule. When the Arabs conquered, they found it an important town still, and it became the capital of al-Andalus when Abd ar-Rahman established the Umayyad

MAIMONIDES

emirate in 756. For 300 years, Cordoba enjoyed the position of unqualified leader of al-Andalus. It is impossible to take the chronicles at face value—3000 mosques and 80,000 shops, a library of 400,000 volumes, in a city stretching for 16km (10 miles) along the banks of the Guadalquivir. We could settle for half these totals, and still be impressed. Beyond doubt, Cordoba was a city without equal in the West as a centre of learning; it would be enough to mention two 12th-century contemporaries, **Averroës**, the Muslim scientist and Aristotelian philosopher who contributed so much to the rebirth of classical learning in Europe, and **Moses Maimonides**, the Jewish philosopher (and later personal physician to Saladin in Palestine) whose reconciliation of faith and reason were assumed into Christianity by Thomas Aquinas. Medieval Cordoba was a great trading centre, and its luxury goods were coveted throughout western Europe; the old word *cordwainer* is a memory of Cordoba's skill in leatherwork. At its height, picture Cordoba as a city of bustling international markets, great palaces, schools, baths and mosques, with 28 suburbs and the first street lighting in Europe. Its population, largely Spanish, Moorish and Arab, included students and merchants from all over Europe, Africa and Asia, and an army and palace secretariat made up largely of slaves and black Africans. In it Muslims, Christians and Jews lived in harmony, at least until the coming of the fanatical Almoravids and Almohads. We can sense a certain decadence; street riots in Cordoba were an immediate cause of the break-up of the caliphate in 1031, but here, as in Seville, the coming of the Reconquista was an unparalleled catastrophe.

When Fernando III 'the Saint' captured the city in 1236, much of the population chose flight over putting themselves at the mercy of the priests, although history records that he was unusually tolerant of the Jews. It did not last. Three centuries of Castilian rule sufficed to rob Cordoba of all its glories and turn it into a depressed backwater. Only in the last hundred years has it begun to recover; today Cordoba has also become an industrial city, though you wouldn't guess it from its sympathetically restored centre. It is the third city of Andalucía, and the first and only big town since Franco's death to have elected a communist mayor and council.

History Down the Hatch

 Cordoban cuisine reflects its history—many local dishes maintain Arab and Jewish traditions. There are casseroles with chick peas, chard and spinach, and *rabos de toro* (oxtail stew) is popular. So is *picadillo*—the finely chopped peppers, tomatoes and onions often used as an accompaniment. The surrounding olive groves provide oil for the basis of Cordoban cooking such as an orange salad with oil, cod and green peppers. El Valle de los Pedroches used to be known as 'the valley of granite' by the Moors and its Iberian pig hams are as renowned as those from Huelva. Ham occasionally finds its way into Cordoba's famous desserts, such as *pastel cordobés*, which is otherwise made of puff pastry and angel's hair.

AV. MEDINA AZAHARA

ANTONIO MAURA

AV. REPÚBLICA ARGENTINA

PASEO DE LA VICTORIA

CONCEPCIÓN

San Nicolás

Almodóvar Gate

F. RUANO

BUEN PASTOR

C. SEVILLA

BARROSA

BLANCO

Casa del Indiano

Synagogue (ruin)

ALMANZOR

CALLE DE LAS FLORES

Plaza Benavente

AV. DEL CONDE VELLELLANO

AV. DR. FLEMING

Municipal Museum

Plaza Judá Leví

La Mezquita

C. TORRIJOS

C. REY HEREDIO CARDENEROS

Alcázar de los Reyes Christiános

AMADORDE LOS RÍOS

CARDENAL GONZÁLEZ

Moorish Walls (ruins)

Triunfo

Puerta del Puente

AV. CORREGIDOR

Waterwheel

AVENIDA DEL ALCÁZAR

PUENTE ROMANO

Zoo

PUENTE DE SAN RAFAEL

Calahorra Tower

AVENIDA CONFEDERACIÓN

N

Estación

AVENIDA DE AMÉRICA

Convento
de Merced

Torre de
Malmuerta

Plaza
de
Colón

RONDA DE LOS TEJARES

AV. DE GRAN CAPITÁN

C. GONDOMAR

CALLE CRUZ CONDE

C. CONDE TORRES CABRERA

Cristo de
los Faroles

Santa
Marina

ALFAROS

Moorish Walls
(ruins)

RONDA DEL MARRUBIAL

BELMONTE JESÚS MARÍA

Plaza
Tendillas

Roman Temple
(ruin)

C. CLAUDIO MARCELO

San
Lorenzo

SAN PABLO REALEJO

San
Pablo

San
Andrés

STA. MARÍA DE GRACIA

MARÍA AUXILIADORA

Santa
Victoria

PEDRO LÓPEZ

Plaza de la
Corredera

GUTIÉRREZ DE LOS RÍOS

AVENIDA BARCELONA

National
Archaeological
Museum

MAESE LUIS

SAN FERNANDO

Plaza del
Potro

CARLOS RUBIO

San Pedro

ALFONSO XII.

PUERTA
NUEVA

Museo de
Bellas Artes

RONDA DE ISASA

PASEO DE LA RIBERA

CAMPO MADRE DE DIOS

RÍO GUADALQUIVIR

RONDA MÁRTIRES

0   1/2 kms

0   1/4 miles

Cordoba

135

Getting Around

by train

Cordoba is on the major Madrid–Seville rail line, so there are about 12 trains a day in both directions by AVE, with a journey time of 43 minutes from Seville and 1 hour 40 mins from Madrid. There are aslo frequent AVE/Talgo services to Málaga (about 2 hours 15 mins). There is also one Talgo daily to Cadiz, Valencia and Barcelona, and regular trains to Huelva, Algeciras and Alicante. Trains for Granada and Algeciras pass through Bobadilla Junction, and may require a change. Cordoba's station is off the Avenida de América, 1.6km (1 mile) north of La Mezquita, © 95 749 02 02, and there is a ticket office in town at Ronda de los Tejares 10.

by bus

Buses for Seville (at least three daily), Granada, Cadiz and Malaga and most nearby towns leave from the Alsina Graells terminal on Avenida Medina Azahara 29, © 95 723 64 74. Buses for Madrid (one daily), Valencia (three daily) and Barcelona (two a day), leave from the Ureña office on Avenida de Cervantes 22, © 95 747 23 52. Other firms do go to Seville—but the train's a better bet for that city and for Malaga.

The Cordoba bus network is complicated and it's always best to check with tourist information as to times and departure points. If you want to go to Medinat az-Zahra, take bus no.01 for Villarubia or Veredón (from Republica Argentina at Azahara); it will drop you off short of the site, and you will have to walk about 2km (1.3 miles).

Tourist Information

The very helpful regional tourist office is on C/ Torrijos 10 next to the Mezquita, © 95 747 12 35. The municipal office is in the Judería on Plaza Judá Levi, © 95 720 05 22. It's definitely worth a visit to either to get a detailed map, for Cordoba has the biggest and most labyrinthine old quarter in Spain. To arrange personal guides to the mosque and other sights, © 95 748 69 97, ask at the tourist offices, or turn up at the mosque itself.

La Mezquita

Open Mon—Sat 10–7, Sun 1.30–7 in summer; 10–5.30 in winter; adm 750 pts.

La Mezquita is the local name for Abd ar-Rahman's Great Mosque. Mezquita means 'mosque' and even though the building has officially been a cathedral for more than 750 years, no one could ever mistake its origins. Abd ar-Rahman I, founder of a new state, felt it necessary to construct a great religious monument for his capital. As part of his plan, he also wished to make it a centre of pilgrimage to increase the sense of divorce from eastern Islam; Mecca was at the time held by his Abbasid enemies. Islam was never entirely immune to the exaltation of holy relics, and there is a story that Abd ar-Rahman had an arm of Muhammad to legitimize his mosque as a pilgrimage site. The site, at the centre of the city, had originally held a Roman temple of Janus, and later a Visigothic church. Only about one-third of the mosque belongs to the original. Successive enlargements were made by Abd ar-Rahman II, al-Hakim, and al-Mansur. Expansion was easy; the plan of the mosque is a simple rectangle divided into aisles by rows of columns, and its size was increased to serve a growing population simply by adding more aisles. The result was one of the largest of all mosques, exceeded only by the one in Mecca. After 1236, it was converted to use as a cathedral without any major changes. In the 1520s, however, the city's clerics succeeded in convincing the Royal Council, over the opposition of the Cordoba city government, to allow the construction of a choir and high altar, enclosed structures typical of Spanish cathedrals. Charles V, who had also opposed the project, strongly reproached them for the desecration when he saw the finished work—though he himself had done even worse to the Alhambra and Seville's Alcázar.

Most people come away from a visit to La Mezquita somewhat confused. The endless rows of columns and red and white striped arches make a picture familiar to most of us, but actually to see them in this gloomy old hall does not increase one's understanding of the work. They make a pretty pattern, but what does it mean? It's worth going into some detail, for learning to see La Mezquita the way its builders did is the best key we have to understanding the refined world of al-Andalus.

Before entering, take a few minutes to circumnavigate this massive, somewhat forbidding pile of bricks. Spaced around its 685m of wall are the original entrances and windows, excellent examples of Moorish art. Those on the western side are the best, from the time of al-Mansur: interlaced Visigothic horseshoe arches, floral decorations in the Roman tradition, and Islamic calligraphy and patterns, a lesson in the varied sources of this art.

The only entrance to the mosque today is the **Puerta del Perdón**, a fine *mudéjar* gateway added in 1377, opening to the **Patio de los Naranjos**, the original mosque courtyard, planted with orange trees, where the old Moorish fountain can still be seen. Built into the wall of the courtyard, over the gate, the original minaret—a legendary tower said to be the model for all the others in al-Andalus—has been replaced by an ill-proportioned 16th-century bell tower. From the courtyard, the mosque is entered through a little door, the **Puerta de las Palmas**, where they'll sell you a ticket and tell you to take off your hat. Inside, it's as chilly as Seville Cathedral.

Now here is the first surprise. The building is gloomy only because the Spanish clerics wanted it that way. Originally there was no wall separating the mosque from the courtyard, and that side of the mosque was entirely open. In the courtyard, trees were planted to continue the rows of columns, translating inside to outside in a remarkable tour-de-force that has rarely been equalled in architecture. To add to the effect, the entrances along the other three walls would have been open to the surrounding busy markets and streets. It isn't just a trick of architecture, but a way of relating a holy building to the life of the city around it. In the Middle East, there are many medieval mosques built on the same plan as this one; the pattern originated with the first Arabian mosques, and later in the Umayyad Mosque of Damascus, one of the first great shrines of Islam. In Turkey they call them 'forest' mosques, and the townspeople use them like indoor parks, places to sit and reflect or talk over everyday affairs. In medieval Christian cathedrals, whose doors were always open, it was much the same. The sacred and the secular become blurred, or rather the latter is elevated to a higher plane. In Cordoba, this principle is perfected.

In the aesthetics of this mosque, too, there is more than meets the eye. Many European writers have seen it as devoid of spirituality, a plain prayer-hall with pretty arches. To the Christian mind it is difficult to comprehend. Christian churches are modelled after the Roman basilica, a government hall, a seat of authority with a long central aisle designed to humble the suppliant as he approaches the praetor's throne (altar). Mosques are designed with great care to free the mind from such behaviour patterns. In this one, the guiding principle is a rarefied abstraction—the same kind of abstraction that governs Islamic geometric decoration. The repetition of columns is like a meditation in stone, a mirror of Creation where unity and harmony radiate from innumerable centres. Another contrast with Christian churches can be found in an obscure matter—the distribution of weight. The Gothic masters of the Middle Ages learned to pile stone upwards from great piers and buttresses to amazing heights, to build an edifice that aspires upwards to heaven. Cordoba's architects amplified the height of their mosque only modestly by a daring invention—adding a second tier of arches on top of the first. They had to, constrained as they were by the short columns they were recycling from Roman buildings, but the result was to make an 'upside-down' building, where weight increases the higher it goes, a play of balance and equilibrium that adds much to the mosque's effect. There are about 580 of these columns, mostly from Roman ruins and Visigothic churches the Muslims pulled down; originally, legend credits La Mezquita with a thousand. Some came from as far as Constantinople, a present from the emperors. The same variety can be seen in the capitals—Roman, Visigothic, Moorish and a few mysteries.

The surviving jewel of the mosque is its *mihrab*, added in the 10th century under al-Hakim II, an octagonal chamber set into the wall and covered by a beautiful dome of interlocking arches. A Byzantine emperor, Nikephoras Phokas, sent artists to help with its mosaic decoration, and a few tons of enamel chips and coloured glass cubes for them to work with. That these two states should have had such warm relations isn't that surprising; in those days, any enemy of the Pope and the western Christian states was a friend of Constantinople. Though the *mihrab* is no longer at the centre of La Mezquita, it was at the time of al-Hakim II; the aisle extending from it was the axis of the original mosque.

Looking back from the *mihrab*, you will see what once was the exterior wall, built in Abd ar-Rahman II's extension, from the year 848. Its gates, protected indoors, are as good as those on the west façade, and better preserved. Near the *mihrab* is the **Capilla de Villaviciosa**, a Christian addition of 1377 with fancy convoluted *mudéjar* arches that almost succeed in upstaging the Moorish work. Behind it is a small chapel, usually closed off. Fortunately, you can see most of the **Capilla Real** above the barriers; its exuberant stucco and *azulejo* decoration are among the greatest works of *mudéjar* art. Built in the 14th century as a funeral chapel for Fernando IV and Alfonso XI of Castile, it is contemporary with the Alhambra and shows some influence of the styles developing in Granada. Far more serious intrusions are the 16th-century **Coro** (choir) and **Capilla Mayor** (high altar). Not unlovely in themselves, they would not offend anywhere but here. Fortunately, La Mezquita is so large that from many parts of it you won't even notice them. Begun in 1523, the Plateresque Coro was substantially altered in the 18th century, with additional stucco decoration, as well as a set of baroque choir stalls by Pedro Duque Cornejo. Between the Coro and Capilla Mayor is the tomb of Leopold of Austria, Bishop of Cordoba at the time the works were completed (and, interestingly, Charles V's uncle). For the rest of the Christian contribution, dozens of locked, mouldering chapels line the outer walls of the mosque. Never comfortable as a Christian building, today the cathedral seems to be hardly used at all, and regular Sunday masses are generally relegated to a small corner of the building.

Around La Mezquita

The masses of tatty souvenir stands and third-rate cafés that surround La Mezquita on its busiest days unwittingly do their best to re-create the atmosphere of the Moorish *souks* that once thrived here, but walk a block in any direction and you'll enter the essential Cordoba—brilliant whitewashed lanes with glimpses into dreamily beautiful patios, each one a floral extravaganza. One of the best is a famous little alley called **Calle de las Flores** ('street of the flowers') just a block northeast of La Mezquita, although sadly its charms are diminished by the hordes of tourists who flock to see it.

Below La Mezquita, along the Guadalquivir, the melancholic plaza called **Puerta del Puente** marks the site of Cordoba's southern gate with a decorative **arch** put up in 1571, celebrating the reign of Felipe II. The very curious Churrigueresque monument next to it, with a statue of San Rafael (the Archangel Raphael), is called the **Triunfo** (1651). Wild baroque confections such as this are common in Naples and southern Italy (under Spanish rule at the time); there they are called *guglie*. Behind the plaza, standing across from La Mezquita, is the **Archbishop's Palace**, built on the site of the original Alcázar, the palace of Abd ar-Rahman.

The **Roman bridge** over the Guadalquivir probably isn't Roman at all any more; it has been patched and repaired so often that practically nothing remains of the Roman work. Another statue of Raphael can be seen in the middle—probably replacing an old Roman image of Jupiter or Mercury. The stern-looking **Calahorra Tower**, © 95 729 39 29, built in 1369 over Moorish foundations, once guarded the southern approaches of the bridge and has been in its time a girls' school and a prison; now it contains a small **museum** of Cordoba's history (*open daily 10.30–6*), with old views and plans of the city, and the armour of Gonzalo Fernández de Cordoba, the 'Gran Capitán' who won much of Italy for Ferdinand and Isabella. It also has an historical multivision spectacle, which is probably only of interest to the dedicated tourist.

Just to the west, along the river, Cordoba's **Alcázar de los Reyes Cristianos**, © 95 747 20 00 ext. 210, was rebuilt in the 14th century and used for 300 years by the offi-cers of the Inquisition. There's little to see, but a good view of La Mezquita and the town from the belvedere atop the walls. The **gardens** (*open daily 9.30–7*) are peaceful and lovely, an Andalucían amenity much like those in Seville's Alcázar. The gigantic stone figures of Columbus and the Catholic Kings are impressive. On the river's edge you'll see an ancient **waterwheel**. At least some of the Moors' talent for putting water to good use was retained for a while after the Reconquista. This mill disturbed Isabel's dreams when she stayed at the Alcázar; it was rebuilt only in the early 1900s. If you continue walking along the Guadalquivir, after about a kilometre you'll come to Parque Cruz Conde and the new **Cordoba zoo**, currently being renovated. When it reopens (*check with the tourist office*) you'll be able to see a rare black lion, who probably doesn't enjoy being called 'Chico'.

The Judería

How lovely is Thy dwelling-place O Lord of Hosts!
My soul grows weak and longs for Thy courtyards.

Hebrew inscription on synagogue wall

As in Seville, Cordoba's ancient Jewish quarter has recently become a fashionable area, a nest of tiny streets between La Mezquita and Avenida Dr Fleming. Part of the Moorish walls can be seen along this street, and the northern entrance of the Judería is the old **Almodóvar gate**. The streets are tricky, and it will take some effort to find Calle Maimonides and the 14th-century **synagogue** (*open daily except Mon, 10–2; 3.30–5.30; adm free for EU citizens, others 1000 pts*), after which you will find your-self repeatedly back at this spot, whether or not you want to be here.

The diminutive Cordoban synagogue is one of the two oldest and most interesting Jewish monuments in Spain (the other is the Tránsito in Toledo). Set back from the street in a tiny courtyard, it was built in the Granadine style of the early 14th century and, according to Amador de los Rios, dates from 1315. After the expulsion, it was used as a hospital for hydrophobes, and later became the headquarters of the cobblers' guild. There is an interesting plasterwork frieze of Alhambra-style arabesques and Hebrew inscriptions. The recess for the Ark (which contained the holy scrolls) is clearly visible, and the women's gallery still intact. Despite few obvious signs of the synagogue's orig-inal function, its atmosphere is still charged; it is somehow easy to imagine this small sanctum as a focus of medieval Jewry's Golden Age, a centre of prayer and scholarship spreading religious and moral enlightenment. While modern Cordoba has no active Jewish community, several *marrano* families live in the city and can trace their ancestry to the pre-expulsion age. Some have opened shops in the *Judería* selling 'Judaica', which ranges from tacky tourist trinkets and tapes of Israeli folk song, to beautiful Jewish artefacts worked from Cordoban silver.

On Calle Ruano Torres, the 15th-century **Casa del Indiano** is a palace with an eccentric façade. On Plaza Maimonides is the **Museo Municipal de Arte Cordobés y Taurino** (*open Tues–Sat 10–2 and 6–8, Sun 9.30–3; adm 450 pts, free on Tues*) with its beautiful courtyard—not surprisingly, it's a museum dedicated to the bullfights. Manolete and El Cordobés are the city's two recent contributions to Spanish culture; here you can see a replica of Manolete's sarcophagus, the furniture from his home and the hide of Islero, the bull that did him in, along with more bullfight memorabilia than you ever thought existed. The turn-of-the-century Art Nouveau posters are beautiful, and among the old prints you can pay homage to the memory of the famous taurine malcontent Moñudo, who ignored the *toreros* and went up into the stands after the audience.

White Neighbourhoods

From the mosque you can walk eastwards through well over a mile of twisting white alleys, a place where the best map in the world wouldn't keep you from getting lost and staying lost. Though it all looks much the same, it's never monotonous. Every little square, fountain or church stands out boldly, and forces you to look at it in a way different from how you would look at a modern city—another lesson in the Moorish aesthetic. These streets have probably changed little since 1236, but their best buildings are a series of **Gothic churches** built soon after the Reconquista. Though small and plain, most are exquisite in a quiet way. Few have any of the usual Gothic sculptural work on their façades, to avoid offending a people accustomed to Islam's prohibition of images. The lack of decoration somehow adds to their charm. There are a score of these around Cordoba, and nothing like them elsewhere in the south of Spain. **San Lorenzo**, on Calle María Auxiliadora, is perhaps the best, with a rose window designed in a common Moorish motif of interlocking circles. Some 15th-century frescoes survive around the altar and on the apse. **San Pablo** (1241), on the street of the same name, is early Gothic (5 years after the Christian conquest) but contains a fine *mudéjar* dome and ceiling. **San Andrés**, on Calle Varela, two streets east of San Pablo, **Santa Marina** on Calle Morales, and the **Cristo de los Faroles** on Calle Alfaros are some of the others. Have a look inside any you find open; most have some Moorish decoration or sculptural work in their interiors, and many of their towers (like San Lorenzo's) were originally minarets. **San Pedro**, off Calle Alfonso XII, was the Christian cathedral under Moorish rule, though largely rebuilt in the 1500s.

The neighbourhoods have other surprises, if you have the persistence to find them. **Santa Victoria** is a huge austere baroque church on Calle Juan Valera, modelled after the Roman Pantheon. Nearby, on Plaza Jerónimo Páez, a fine 16th-century palace houses the **National Archaeological Museum**, © 95 747 10 76 (*open Tues–Sun 10–1.30 and 6–8; adm 500 pts, free for EU citizens*), the largest in Andalucía, with Roman mosaics, a two-faced idol of Janus that probably came from the temple under La Mezquita, and an unusual icon of the Persian *torero*-god Mithras; also some Moorish-looking early Christian art, and early funeral steles with odd hieroglyphs. The large collection of Moorish art includes some of the best work from the age of the caliphate, including finds from Medinat az-Zahra.

East of the Calle San Fernando, the wide street that bisects the old quarter, the houses are not as pristinely whitewashed as those around La Mezquita. Many parts are a bit run down, which does not detract from their charm. In the approximate centre of the city is the **Plaza de la Corredera**, which is an enclosed '*Plaza Mayor*', like the famous ones in Madrid and Salamanca (*see* p.60). This ambitious project, surrounded by uniform blank façades (an echo of the *estilo desornamentado*) was never completed. Now neglected and a bit eerie, the city is apparently being rehabilitated a little at a time.Continuing south, the **Museo de Bellas Artes**, © 95 747 33 45 (*open Tues–Sat 10–2 and 5–7; Sun 10–1.30; adm 250 pts, free for EU citizens*) is on the lovely Plaza del Potro (mentioned by Cervantes, along with the little *posada* that still survives on it); its collections include works of Valdés Leal, Ribera, Murillo and Zurbarán, two royal portraits by Goya, and works by Cordoban artists of the 15th and 16th centuries. Beware the 'museum' across the plaza, dedicated exclusively to the works of a local named Julio Romero de Torres, the Spanish Bouguereau. Much prized by the Cordobans, this turn-of-the-century artist's *œuvre* consists almost entirely of naked ladies. Eastwards from here, the crooked whitewashed alleys continue for almost a mile, as far as the surviving stretch of **Moorish walls** along Ronda del Marrubial.

Plaza de las Tendillas

The centre of Roman *Corduba* has, by chance, become the centre of the modern city. Cordoba is probably the slickest and most up-to-date city in Andalucía (Seville would beg to differ), and it shows in this busy district of crowded pavements, modern shops, cafés and wayward youth. The contrast with the old neighbourhoods is startling, but just a block off the plaza on Calle Gondomar the beautiful 15th-century **Church of San Nicolás** will remind you that you're still in Cordoba.

In the other direction, well-preserved remains of a collapsed **Roman temple**, one of the most complete Roman monuments in Spain, have been discovered on the Calle Nueva near the Ayuntamiento. The city has been at work reassembling the walls and columns and already the front pediment is partially complete, though its setting, in the middle of what looks like an abandoned building site, makes it a far from captivating sight.

Next to the **Plaza de Colón**, a park a few blocks north of the Plaza de las Tendillas, the **Torre de Malmuerta** ('Bad Death') takes its name from a commander of this part of the old fortifications who murdered his wife in a fit of passion; it became the subject of a well-known play by Lope de Vega, *Los Comendadores de Cordoba*.

Across the plaza is a real surprise, the rococo **Convento de Merced** (1745), an enormous building that has recently been restored to house the provincial government and often hosts cultural exhibitions on various subjects. Don't miss it. The façade has been redone in its original painted *esgrafiado*, almost decadently colourful in pink and green, and the courtyards and grand staircases inside are incredible—more a palace than a monastery.

Medinat az-Zahra

Open Tues–Sat 10–1.30 and 6–8.30, Sun 10–1.30, ✆ 95 723 4025. (Check winter hours with the tourist office.)

Eight kilometres (5 miles) northwest of the centre of Cordoba, Caliph Abd ar-Rahman III began to build a palace in the year 936. The undertaking soon got out of hand and, with the almost infinite resources of the caliphate to play with, he and his successors turned Medinat az-Zahra ('city of the Flower', so named after one of Abd ar-Rahman's wives) into a city in itself, with a market, mosques, schools and gardens, a place where the last caliphs could live in isolation from the world, safe from the turbulent street politics of their capital. Hisham II was kept a virtual prisoner here by his able vizier, al-Mansur.

The scale of it is pure *Arabian Nights*. One chronicler records an ambassador, being taken from Cordoba to the palace, finding his path carpeted the entire 8km (5-mile) route and lined from end to end with maidens to hold parasols and refreshments for him.

Stories were told of the palace's African menageries, its interior pillars and domes of crystal, and curtains of falling water for walls; another fountain was filled with flowing mercury. Such carrying-on must have aroused a good deal of resentment; in the disturbances that put an end to the caliphate, Medinat az-Zahra was sacked and razed by Berber troops in 1013.

After having served as a quarry for 900 years it's surprising anything is left at all; even under Muslim rule, columns from the palace were being carted away as far as Marrakesh. But in 1944 the royal apartments were discovered, with enough fragments to permit a restoration of a few arches with floral decorations. One hall has a roof on, and more work is under way, but as yet the rest is only foundations.

Shopping

Cordoba is famous for its **silverwork**—try the shops in C/ José Cruz Grande, where you'll get better quality than in the old quarter round the mosque. Handmade **crafts** are made on the premises at Meryan, C/ de las Flores 2, ✆ 95 747 59 02, where they specialize in embossed wood and leather furniture. For **antiques**, there's one shop with a very good selection of Spanish art and furniture in Plaza San Nicolás, and they'll arrange packing and shipment. High-quality ladies' and gents' suede and **leather goods** are sold at Sera, on the corner of Rondo de los Teares and Cruz Conde. The mainstream shopping areas are along Calle Conde de Gondomar and Calle Claudio Marcelo on either side of the Plaza de las Tendillas (also *see* p.156).

Cordoba ✉ *14000*   **Where to Stay**

Near La Mezquita, of course. Even during big tourist assaults the advantages outweigh the liabilities. However, if this area is full, or if you have a car and do not care to brave the old town's narrow streets and lack of parking, there are a few hotels in the new town and on the periphery worth trying.

moderate

The best bet is the newly opened ★★★★**NH Amistad Cordoba**, Pza. de Maimónides 3, ✆ 95 742 03 35, ✉ 95 742 03 65. It has been sensitively converted from an old *palacio*, the main entrance fronting the Plaza de Maimónides, with a back entrance neatly built into the old wall of the Judería. Thoughtful management makes it a comfortable and extremely convenient place to stay. The double-room price of *15,000 pts* includes an excellent breakfast buffet. Underground parking is available for a small supplement.

The ★★★★**Meliá Cordoba**, ✆ 95 729 80 66, ✉ 95 729 81 47, is a big modern hotel right in the middle of the Jardines de la Victoria, on the edge of the Judería. It has every conceivable luxury the chain is known for, including a pool and TV. A double room will set you back *15,600 pts*—worth it for the car park alone, some would consider.

The recently refurbished ★★★★**El Conqistador**, C/ Magistral González Francés 15, ✆ 95 748 11 02, has rooms that look out on to the floodlit walls of La Mezquita, literally just a few metres from your balcony. The breakfasts are somewhat meagre, though, and service is old-fashioned in the worst sense; but there is an underground car park (*13,500 pts*).

Also next to the mosque is the slightly gloomy ★★★**Maimónides**, Torrijos 4, ✆ 95 747 15 00, ✉ 95 748 38 03, very much catering to the package tour market though again with underground parking and similar prices (*12,000–15,000 pts*).

Five minutes north of the train station is ★★★★**Las Adelfas**, Avda. de la Arruzafa s/n, ✆ 95 727 74 20, ✉ 95 727 27 94, a modern hotel set in spacious gardens with a pool and beautiful views over Cordoba, definitely worth considering if you visit in summer, and a bargain at present for its rates at *16,000 pts*.

On the outskirts of town, service at the ★★★★**Parador de la Arruzafa**, Avda. de la Arruzafa, ✆ 95 727 59 00, ✉ 95 728 04 09, in common with much of the chain, seems to be improving. It isn't in a historic building (it was built in the 1960s), but offers a pool, tennis courts and air-conditioned rooms and a view (*15,500 pts*).

A bargain in this category is the **Al-Mihrab**, Avda. del Brillante, Km 5, ✆ 95 727 21 98. Situated just 5km from the centre of town, this agreeable hotel, which is a listed building, offers peace and a view of the Sierra Morena (*7500 pts*).

In the Judería, near La Mezquita, is the attractive, affordable and immaculate ★★**Albucasis**, C/ Buen Pastor 11, ✆/🖷 95 747 86 25, a former silversmith's with a charming flower-filled courtyard; it's one of the prettiest hotels in Cordoba (*8500 pts*). *Closed Jan–mid-Feb.*

The ★★**Marisa**, C/ Cardinal Herrero 6, ✆ 95 747 31 42, is a simple but well-run establishment opposite the Patio de los Naranjos. The location is the only real amenity, but it will just do for the price (*9000 pts*). The ★★**Hotel González** is on the edge of the Judería, ✆ 95 747 98 19, 🖷 95 748 61 87 (*10,000 pts*). Rooms contain family antiques and the arabesque patio houses a popular restaurant.

The ★**Hostal Seneca**, C/ Conde y Luque 5, ✆ 95 747 32 34, just north of La Mezquita, is the real find among the inexpensive *hostales*, with a beautiful patio full of flowers, nice rooms and sympathetic management. Not surprisingly, it's hard to get a room (*5500 pts with breakfast included*).

Plenty of other inexpensive *fondas* can be found in the area east of La Mezquita, especially on and around Calle Rey Heredia—which is also known as the street with five names so don't be thrown by the number of different signs.

The **Fonda Agustina** on nearby Calle Zapatería Vieja, ✆ 95 747 08 72, is clean and central (*2500 pts*).

Off the Plaza de las Tendillas, the ★**Boston**, C/ Málaga 2, ✆ 95 747 41 76, has modern clean rooms that are air-conditioned at night and popular with a young American crowd (*4900 pts*).

The ★★**Hostal Las Tendillas**, C/ Jesús y María 1, ✆ 95 722 30 29, has simple and unpretentious doubles for *2900 pts*, while the **Hostal La Magdalena**, ✆ 95 748 37 53, is good for those who don't mind a 10-minute walk through the picturesque backstreets into town. It's in a quiet location, there's no trouble parking (*doubles around 3600 pts*).

The Hostal Maestre, C/ Romero Barros 16 & 18, ✆ 95 747 53 95, is popular with backpackers (so make a reservation), and has a range of rooms from doubles for *6000 pts* to small apartments for *6500 pts*; all have private bathrooms and those in the hotel have a/c.

Next door is **Hostal Los Arcos**, C/ Romero Barros 14, ✆ 95 748 56 43, 🖷 95 748 60 11 (3500–4500 pts). The cheapest place in town is the **Hostal Martínez Rücker**, C/ Martínez Rücker 14, ✆ 95 47 25 62, which has tiny box-like rooms around a pleasant Moorish courtyard (*1500–3500 pts*).

Don't forget that Cordoba is the heart of a wine-growing region; there are a few *bodegas* in town that appreciate visitors, including **Bodega Campos**, C/ Colonel Cascajo; and **Bodega Doña Antonia**, Avda. Virgen Milagrosa 5, really a small restaurant serving its own wines.

expensive

Sitting in the heart of the old Jewish quarter, **El Churrasco**, C/ Romero 16, ✆ 95 729 08 19, is Cordoba's best-loved restaurant, located in an old town house. For food and atmosphere it is perhaps the finest restaurant in southern Spain—but it's not a grand restaurant, actually rather small, very intimate, and just a little bit cliquey. It specializes in grilled meats—*churrasco* is the name of the grill the meat is cooked on, and by extension the piece of grilled meat itself—and unless you're vegetarian or a mad fish-lover, a *churrasco* is your obvious choice here. In winter braziers are put under tables making it possible to dine on the patio all year round, and there's even valet parking if you need it. Additionally, El Churrasco has the best cellar in Andalucía, now so large it is housed in a separate building along the street—ask at the restaurant if you would like to visit. Relatively speaking, El Churrasco is not expensive—count on *4000–5000 pts. Closed Aug.*

Another of Cordoba's best-known restaurants is **El Caballo Rojo**, Cardenal Herrero 28, ✆ 95 747 53 75. Its menu is supposed to be based on traditional *andaluz* cooking and old Arab recipes—*salmorejo* with cured ham, artichokes in Montilla wine, Mozarabic angler fish—but it has rather lost its way. Dreary-looking tourists sporting bumbags have hardly a word to say to each other and the restaurant is ugly and modern (*2500–4000 pts*).

The **Almudaina**, Jardines de los Santos Mártires 1, ✆ 95 747 43 42, is in an attractive old house dating from the 16th century, and would be a sophisticated spot to eat, but it has sold out to coachloads of Japanese. Its menu varies from day to day, depending on market availability, and special attention is paid to local produce. Look out for *ensalada de pimientos*, *alcachofas a la Cordobés*, and *lomo relleno a la Pedrocheña*, which are above average (*menú del día 3350–4050 pts, à la carte 4000 pts and up*). *Closed Sun from Jun to Sept, and Sun evening the rest of the year.*

More easygoing than the above is **Oscar's**, Pza. de Chirinos 6, ✆ 95 747 75 17, where the emphasis is on fish—*ensalada de salmón marinado, lubina al vino oloroso de Montilla, lomos de merluza con langostinos en salsa de ajo* (*3500–4500 pts*). *Closed Sun and Aug.*

moderate

Adjoining El Caballo Rojo is **El Burlaero**, C/ La Hoguera 5, ✆ 95 747 27 19, inevitably trippery but with the advantage of a courtyard. Specialities include run-of-the-mill *rabo de toro, Paloma Torcaz, perdiz, jabalí* (*3500 pts with wine*).

Rincón de Carmen, C/ Romero 4, ℅ 95 729 10 55, is family-run, noisy and full of atmosphere. The local dishes are prepared as well as at any establishment in the city, and the prices are low (*3000 pts*).

cheap

Just around the corner from La Mezquita, **El Tablón**, Cardenal González 75, ℅ 95 747 60 61, is a restaurant with character, offering one of the best bargains in the city, with a choice of *menús del día* (*1350 pts*) or *platos combinados* at *around 1500 pts*, glass of wine included.

On Calle Cardenal Herrero, there are some good options, the best of which is the above-average **Los Patios** at No.18.

On the corner of Calle Deanes and Buen Pastor is the take-it-or-leave-it **Bodegón Rafaé**, with true *bodega* atmosphere and food. Sausages drape from barrels, religious figurines hang next to fake bulls' heads, the radio and TV are on simultaneously; *cola de toro* with a glass of wine at one of the vinyl-topped tables will cost you an exorbitant *700 pts*.

For the young, or young at heart, a lively spot is **El Campeón**, C/ Munda 8, ℅ 95 747 02 07, near Plaza de las Tendillas in one of those narrow streets. Here students gather amid the dotty décor to order enormous glass tankards of beer and *sangría*, and enjoy the loud music and snack food in one of the half-dozen tiny rooms with wooden benches.

Bar Sociedad de Plateros, C/ San Francisco 6, is another popular place with good tapas and cheap wine.

Entertainment and Nightlife

flamenco

Cordoba is the birthplace of Paco Peña—one of Spain's most famous modern flamenco maestros. His flamenco academy is still based in Cordoba and offers a range of guitar and dance courses; contact them at Compania de Paco Peña, Plaza del Potro 15, Cordoba 14002. Paco Peña is part of a long tradition of Cordoba flamenco and the city is a good place to catch some great players and dancers in more authentic venues than, say, Seville.

If you love flamenco, June is the best time to visit the city, during the guitar festival, when flourishes and trills drift out of every other room in Cordoba's White Neighbourhood and there are several concerts every night (check with the Spanish tourist office for details). At other times, wait until midnight and then head for one of the secluded little flamenco bars tucked away throughout the city. These include the **Peña Flamenca Fostorito** on C/Ocaña 4, near the Plaza de San Agustín or the **Peña Flamenca Las Orejas Negras**, on Av. Carlos III 18, in Fatima Barrio, in the Cordoba suburbs. You could also try the shows at **Tablao Cardenal**, C/Torrijos 10, strategically positioned next to the tourist office, or **La Buleria**, on C/Pedro Lopez 3, though don't be deluded into thinking that either is much more than a tourist spectacle.

tapas bars

Though flamenco may be more authentic in Cordoba than in Seville, the bar nightlife is less lively. The most popular bars with locals are the street bars (*terrazas*) in Barrio Jardín, northwest of the Jardínes de la Vitoria, on the Avenida de Republica end of Camino de los Sastrés. **El Loro Verde** and the **Albaicín** are two of the busiest. **Barrio El Brillante**, northwest of the Plaza Colon is full of upper-middle class Spanish in the summer, particularly the night-clubs and bars around Plaza El Tablero. The **Taberna San Miguel**, by the Iglesia de San Miguel off Calle Cruz Conde to the east, is an authentic old tapas bar worth a visit, or try **Casa Elisa**, C/ Almanzor.

Day Trips from Cordoba

Villages of the Sierra Morena

Getting Around

Although **buses** do run from Cordoba up into the Sierra and villages of Los Pedroches, they are infrequent and very time-consuming. To explore the best parts, you really need a car.

The N432 out of Cordoba leads north to the Sierra Morena, the string of hills that curtain the western part of Andalucía from Extremadura, Castilla and La Mancha. This area is the **Valle de los Pedroches**, fertile grazing lands for the pigs, sheep and goats and an important hunting area for deer and wild boar—though it's a sad fact that most Spaniards are still irresponsible sportsmen and the Andalucían hunter, a mild-mannered plumber or tobacconist during the week, will take a gun in his hand on Sunday and kill anything that moves. Thousands of these animals are stalked and shot in the numerous annual hunts, or *monterías*. It's also healthy hiking territory, but keep yourself visible at all times—you don't want to be mistaken for someone's supper.

A road winds 73km (46 miles) up to **Belmez**, with its Moorish castle perilously perched on a rock, from which there are panoramic views over the surrounding arid countryside. **Peñarroya-Pueblonuevo** is a dull industrial town that has fallen into decline, but is useful here as a reference point. Sixteen kilometres (10 miles) west on the N432, the village of **Fuente Ovejuna** is best remembered for the 1476 uprising of its villagers, who dragged their tyrannical lord from his palace and treated him to a spectacularly brutal and bloody end. The event is the subject of the drama *Fuente Ovejuna* by Lope de Vega. The village also has some excavations of Roman silver mines.

Forty-four kilometres (27½ miles) east of Peñarroya (take the C421, then the C420) is the village of **Pozoblanco**, famous for the last *corrida* of the renowned bullfighter Francisco Rivera, better known as Paquirri. Gored, he died in the ambulance on the way to Cordoba; presumably, bouncing around on those roads didn't help. Paquirri's widow, the singer Isabel Pantoja, soared to even greater heights of popularity on his death, with the Spanish public obsessed as ever by the drama of life and mortality.

Pedroche, 10km (6 miles) away, is a sleepy little village with a fine 16th-century Gothic church with a proud, lofty spire, and a Roman bridge. This place too has had its fair share of drama—in 1936 Communist forces shot nearly a hundred of the menfolk. Beyond the villages of **Villanueva de Cordoba** and **Cardeña** to the east is the **Parque Natural de Sierra Cardeña**—rolling hills forested in oak, more stag-hunting grounds and ideal rambling terrain.

Eating Out

This area is famed throughout Andalucía for its supreme quality *jamón ibérico* (locally cured ham) and sucking pig, the excellent *salchichón* from Pozoblanco, and the strong, spicy cheese made from ewes' milk. Sadly it is often difficult for visitors to the region to sample them.

There are no outstanding restaurants around, and even indifferent ones are pretty thin on the ground, so finding a good roadside *venta* such as the **Huerta de San Rafael** at Luque, Ctra. Badajoz–Granada, ✆ 95 766 74 97, is a real boon. Driving off into the countryside in search of gastronomic delight can be a risky business. And, though it's true that it occasionally pays rich dividends, to be sure of eating really well you should head for the tapas bars in the villages or, better still, grab some goodies from a supermarket and have a picnic out on the slopes.

East Towards Úbeda

In this section of the Guadalquivir valley the river rises into the heights of the Sierra Morena; endless rolling hills covered with neat rows of olive trees and small farms make a memorable Andalucían landscape. The three large towns along the way, **Andújar**, **Bailén** and **Linares**, are much alike, amiable industrial towns still painted a gleaming white.

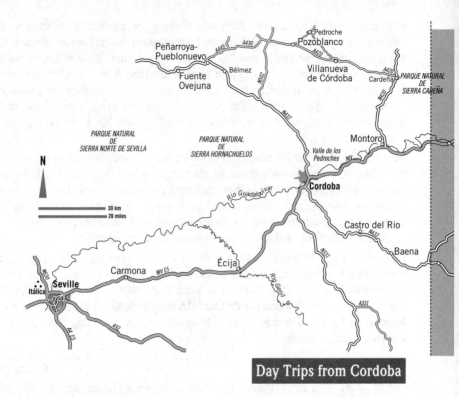

The Gateway to Andalucía

This area is Andalucía's front door. The roads and railways from Madrid branch off here for Seville and Granada. Many important battles were fought nearby, including Las Navas de Tolosa near La Carolina, in 1212, which opened the way for the conquest of al-Andalus; and Bailén, in 1808, where a Spanish-English force gave Napoleon's boys a sound thrashing and built up Spanish morale for what they call their War of Independence.

Montoro

The NIV snakes along the Guadalquivir valley, and 42km (26 miles) east of Cordoba it brings you to the delightfully placed town of **Montoro**, sitting on a bend in the river. The facetious-looking tower that rises above the whitewashed houses belongs to the Gothic church of **San Bartolomé** in Plaza de España. Also in the square is the 16th-century **Ducal Palace**, with a plateresque façade. The beautiful 15th-century bridge that connects Montoro to its suburb, Retamar, is known as the Puente de Las Doñadas, a tribute to the women of the village who sacrificed their jewellery to help finance its construction. Seek out the kitsch **Casa de las Conchas**, a house and courtyard done out in sea shells.

Andújar

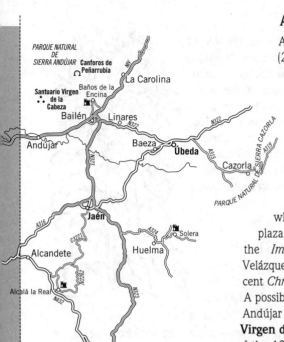

Approaching **Andújar**, a further 35km (22 miles) down the NIV, you'll find the countryside dominated by huge, blue sunflower-oil refineries like fallen space stations. Sunflowers, like olives, are a big crop in the region and much in evidence in late summer. Nothing remains of Andújar's Moorish castle, but there are a couple of surprises in this town which might tempt you to linger a while. The church of **Santa María**, in the plaza of the same name, has in one chapel the *Immaculate Conception* by Pacheco, Velázquez's teacher, and in another the magnificent *Christ in the Garden of Olives*, by El Greco. A possible diversion, 30km (19 miles) north of Andújar on the J501, is the **Santuario de la Virgen de la Cabeza**. Although very little is left of the 13th-century sanctuary, and the present one is disappointing, it's worth packing a picnic and enjoying the drive; when you get there you'll be rewarded with panoramic views. One of southern Spain's biggest fiestas is the annual *romería* to the sanctuary on the last Sunday in April, when a quarter of a million pilgrims trek up on foot, horseback, carts and donkeys. The day before there's a competition for the best-decorated carriage.

Bailén

Twenty-seven kilometres (17 miles) further east on the NIV is the modern, unprepossessing town of **Bailén**. The tomb of the Spanish general Francisco Javier Castaños (1756–1852), who so cleverly whipped the French troops and sent Napoleon back to the drawing board, is in the Gothic parish church of the **Encarnación**, which also has a sculpture by Alonso Cano. But don't dally here—the real treat is to be found 11km (7 miles) to the north on the NIV at **Baños de la Encina**, where the 10th-century oval Moorish castle is one of the best preserved in all Andalucía. Dominating the town, the castle has 14 sturdy, square towers and a double-horseshoe gateway, scarcely touched by time, and from the walls you get a sweeping vista of the olive groves and distant peaks beyond Úbeda. An hour's trek from Baños, through difficult, hilly terrain, lies the natural refuge of **Canforos de Peñarrubia**, with its remarkably preserved Bronze Age paintings of deer and scenes of animal-taming. Serious hikers should ask for a guide at the Ayuntamiento in the town, © 95 361 30 04.

La Carolina

Twenty kilometres (12½ miles) north of here on the NIV is **La Carolina**, a model of 18th-century grid planning. The village owes its existence to forward-thinking Carlos III, who imported a few thousand German artisans in the late 1700s and set them to work excavating the lead and copper mines, tilling the fields and herding sheep. A side effect of this colonization was supposed to be the decline of banditry in the then wild and unpopulated hills. But within two generations almost all the Germans had died off or fled. The town and surrounding area are best known now as a large game-hunting reserve.

Linares

From Bailén the N322 heads eastward to the mining town of **Linares**, birthplace of the guitarist Andrés Segovia, who later moved on; others weren't so lucky—in 1947 the great bullfighter Manolete had an off day and met his end on the horns of a bull in the ring here.

If things had gone well for him, he might have gone to view the finds from the Roman settlement of nearby Castulo, housed in the town's **archaeology museum**, but unfortunately the last thing he probably saw was the ornate baroque portal of the hospital **San Juan de Dios**. From Linares it's a 27km (17 mile) run to Úbeda; a little more than halfway you'll pass an elegant castle at **Canena**.

Eating Out

In Andújar is the **★★Don Pedro**, C/ Gabriel Zamora 5, ✆ 95 350 12 74, 🖅 95 350 47 85, in the centre of town, with pleasant rooms for 5500 pts, and a tavern-style restaurant that specializes in game dishes; a meal with wine is about *3300 pts*. There's a modern **★★★Parador**, Ctra. NIV, Km 296, ✆ 95 367 01 00, 🖅 95 367 25 30, just outside Bailén, which houses a restaurant and tapas bar.

In Linares **Mesón Castellano**, C/ Puente 5, ✆ 95 369 00 09, is the place to go (*3500 pts*). *Closed Sun, July and Aug*. In La Carolina the hotel **★★★★Perdiz**, Ctra. NIV, Km 268, ✆ 95 366 03 00, 🖅 95 368 13 62, is a classic stopover for travellers between Andalucía and northern Spain and has an appealing, coaching-inn ambience. It's got a pretty good restaurant too and, as its name ('partridge') implies, it has seasonal game dishes (*3000 pts*). Baños de la Encina has a reliable restaurant, the **Mesón Buenos Aires**, Cateyana, ✆ 95 361 32 11, with good country cooking, including wild boar and venison in season.

Baeza

Campo de Baeza, soñaré contigo cuando no te vea
(Fields of Baeza, I will dream of you when I can no longer see you)

Antonio Machado (1875–1939)

Sometimes history offers its recompense. The 13th-century Reconquista was especially brutal here; nearly the entire population fled, many of them moving to Granada, where they settled the Albaicín. The 16th century, however, when the wool trade was booming in this corner of Andalucía, was good to Baeza, leaving it a distinguished little town of neatly clipped trees and tan stone buildings, with a beautiful ensemble of monuments in styles from Romanesque to Renaissance. It seems a happy place, serene and quiet as the olive groves that surround it.

Getting There

Come to Baeza by **train** at your own risk. The nearest station, officially named Linares-Baeza, is far off in the open countryside, 14km away. A bus to Baeza usually meets the train, but if you turn up at night or on a Sunday you may be stranded. Baeza's **bus** station, ✆ 95 74 04 68, is a little way from the centre on Av. Alcalde Puche Pardo. Baeza is a stop on the Cordoba–Úbeda bus route,.

Tourist Information

Pza. del Pópulo (also known as the Plaza de los Leones), ✆ 95 374 04 44. *Open Mon–Fri 9–2, Sat 10–12.30.*

The prettiest corner of the town is the small square, the **Plaza del Pópulo**, which houses the tourist office. It is enclosed by decorative pointed arches and Renaissance buildings, and contains a fountain with four half-effaced lions; the fountain was patched together with the help of pieces taken from the Roman remains at Castulo, and the centrepiece, the fearless lady on the pedestal, is traditionally considered to be Imilce, the wife of Hannibal. In Plaza Cardinal Benavides, the façade of the **Ayuntamiento** (1599) is a classic example of Andalucían plateresque, and one of the last.

Heading north on the Cuesta de San Felipe, which can be reached by the steps leading off the Plaza del Pópulo, you pass the 15th-century **Palacio de Jabalquinto**, with an eccentric façade covered with coats of arms and pyramidal stone studs (a Spanish fancy of that age; you can see others like it in Guadalajara and Salamanca). The *palacio* was built in the 15th century by the Benavides family, and is now a seminary. Its patio is open to the public (*open Mon–Fri 9–2*) and boasts a beautiful two-tiered arcade around a central fountain, as well as a fine carved baroque staircase. Adjoining the *palacio*, the 16th-century **Antigua Universidad** was a renowned centre of learning for three hundred years, until its charter was withdrawn during the reign of Fernando VII. It has since been used as a school; its indoor patio, like that of the Jabalquinto, is open to the public (*officially open Mon–Fri 9–2, but times vary according to the school timetable*).

The school has found latter-day fame through Antonio Machado (Juan de Mairena), the *sevilleno* poet who taught there (1913–19). His most famous prose work, *Sentencias, donaires, apuntes y recuerdos* (1936), follows the career of a fictional schoolmaster and draws heavily on his experiences in Baeza.

A right turn at the next corner leads to the 16th-century **cathedral** on Plaza Santa María, a work of Andrés de Vandelvira. This replaced a 13th-century Gothic church (the chancel and portal survive), which in turn took the place of a mosque; a colonnade from this can be seen in the cloister. For the best show in town, drop a coin in the box marked *custodia* in one of the side chapels; this will reveal, with a noisy dose of mechanical *duende*, a rich and ornate 18th-century silver tabernacle. The fountain in front of the cathedral, the **Fuente de Santa María**, with a little triumphal arch at its centre (1564), is Baeza's landmark and symbol. Behind it is the Isabelline Gothic **Casas Consistoriales**, formerly the town hall, while opposite stands the 16th-century seminary of **San Felipe Neri**, its walls adorned with student graffiti—recording their names and dates in bull's blood. It's curiously reminiscent of the rowing eights' hieroglyphics which cover the quadrangle walls of the sportier Oxford and Cambridge colleges.

The Paseo de la Constitución, at the bottom of the hill, is Baeza's main, albeit quiet, thoroughfare, an elegant rectangle lined with crumbling shops and bars. Two buildings are especially worthy of note: **La Alhóndiga**, the 16th-century, porticoed Corn Exchange and, almost opposite, on the west side of the Paseo, the **Casa Consistorial**, the 18th-century town hall. At the end northern end of the Paseo, the inelegant Plaza de España marks the northern boundary of historic Baeza and houses yet more bars.

Baeza ✉ *23440*   ***Eating Out***

 The restaurant of the **Juanito** is Michelin-listed. You can also try regional specialities at **Andrés de Vandelvira**, C/ San Francisco 14, ✆ 95 374 43 61. The restaurant is inside the San Francisco convent with tables filling the arched quadrangle; for more intimacy, dine upstairs (*around 5000 pts*). *Closed Sun afternoons.*

Úbeda

Even with Baeza for an introduction, the presence of this nearly perfect little city comes as a surprise. If the 16th century did well by Baeza, it was a golden age here, leaving Úbeda a 'town built for gentlemen' as the Spanish used to say, endowed with one of the finest collections of Renaissance architecture in all of Spain. Two men can take much of the credit: Andrés de Vandelvira, an Andalucían architect who created most of Úbeda's best buildings, and Francisco de los Cobos, imperial secretary to Charles V, who paid for them. Cobos is a forgotten hero of Spanish history. While Charles was off campaigning in Germany, Cobos had the job of running Castile. By the most delicate management, he kept the kingdom afloat while meeting Charles's ever more exorbitant demands for money and men. He could postpone the inevitable disaster, but not prevent it. Like most public officials in the Spanish Age of Rapacity, though, he also managed to salt away a few hundred thousand ducats for himself, and he spent most of them embellishing his hometown.

Like Baeza, Úbeda is a peaceful and happy place; it wears its Renaissance heritage gracefully, and is always glad to have visitors. Slowly, it's gearing up for them. Tourism is less of a novelty here than it was even a couple of years ago, and a tour bus of camera-wielding Japanese trying to negotiate the delicate Renaissance *plazas* is not an uncommon sight. But it's still easy to understand the Spanish expression '*irse por los cerros de Úbeda*' ('take the Úbeda hill routes'). It basically equates to getting off the subject or wasting time and arose many years ago after Úbeda gradually lost traffic to more commercial routes. Legend has it that a Christian knight fell in love with a Moorish girl and was reproached for his absence by King Fernando III. When questioned about his whereabouts during the battle the knight idly replied, 'Lost in those hills, sire.'

Getting There

Úbeda's **bus** station, C/ San José, © 95 375 21 57, is at the western end of town, and various lines connect the city directly to Baeza, (16 daily, 20mins), Cordoba (3 daily, 2½hrs), Seville (3 daily), and Granada (2 daily, 2½hrs).

Tourist Information

The office is currently in Hospital de Santiago, © 95 3 75 08 97, and is due to move in late 1999 to the Palacio Marques de Contadero in C/ Baja de Marques. *Open Mon–Fri 9–2.30; Sat 11–1.30.*

Úbeda today leaves no doubt how its local politics are going. In the **Plaza de Andalucía**, joining the old and new districts, there is an old metal statue of a fascist civil war general named Sero glaring down from his pedestal. The townspeople have put so many bullets into it, it looks like a Swiss cheese. They've left it here as a joke, and have merrily renamed another square, from Plaza del Generallísimo to Plaza 1 de Mayo.

The **Torre de Reloj**, in the Plaza de Andalucía, is a 14th-century defensive tower now adorned with a clock. The plaque near the base, under a painting of the Virgin, records a visit of Charles V. From here, Calle Real takes you into the heart of the old town. Nearly every corner has at least one lovely palace or church on it. Two of the best can be seen on this street: the early 17th-century **Palacio de Condé Guadiana** has an ornate tower and distinctive windows cut out of the corners of the building, a common conceit in Úbeda's palaces. Two blocks down, the **Palacio Vela de los Cobos** (*open 10–2 and 6–8*) is in the same style, with a loggia on the top storey. Northeast of here, on C/ Cervantes, lies a small **museum** (*open Tues–Sun 11–12.45; 5–6.30*) with the tiny monastic cell where San Juan de la Cruz (St John of the Cross) died of cancer and ulceration of the flesh in 1591. Friar John, much persecuted in his lifetime because of his unorthodox teachings, is one of Spain's most illustrious poets and mystics. The home of Francisco de los Cobos's nephew, another royal counsellor, was the great **Palacio de**

Úbeda's Pottery

 Traditional dark green pottery, fired in kilns over wood and olive stones, is literally Úbeda's trademark. You'll see it all over town—try to pick up some authentic pieces before they become available in Habitat. **Tito**, on the Plaza Ayuntamiento, is a class establishment that produces and fires pieces on the premises. The designs are exquisite and are packed and shipped all over the world.

Highly recommended is a visit to the potters' quarter around the **Calle Valencía**, a 15-minute stroll from the Plaza Ayuntamiento. Heading northeast to the Plaza 1 de Mayo, cross the square diagonally and leave again by the northeast corner, along the Calle Losal to the Puerta de Losal, a 13th-century *mudéjar* gate. Continue downhill along the Calle de Merced, passing the Plaza Olleros on your left, and you come to Calle Valencia. Nearly every house is a potter's workshop; all are open to the public and you will soon find your own favourite. Ours is at no.36, where **Juan José Almarza** runs his family business, handed down through several generations. Juan spent two years in Edinburgh and is possibly the only potter in the province of Jaén with a Scottish accent.

las Cadenas, now serving as Úbeda's Ayuntamiento, on a quiet plaza at the end of Calle Real. The side facing the plaza is simple and dignified but the main façade, facing the **Plaza Vázquez de Molina**, is a stately Renaissance creation, the work of Vandelvira.

Plaza Vázquez de Molina

This is the only place in Andalucía where you can look around and not regret the passing of the Moors, for it is the only truly beautiful thing in all this great region that was not built either by the Moors or under their influence. The Renaissance buildings around the Palacio de las Cadenas make a wonderful ensemble, and the austere landscaping, old cobbles and plain six-sided fountain create the same effect of contemplative serendipity as any chamber of the Alhambra. Buildings on the plaza include the church of **Santa María de los Reales Alcázares** (which is currently being restored); a Renaissance façade on an older building with a fine Gothic cloister around the back; the *parador*; two sedate palaces, both from the 16th century; and Vandelvira's **Sacra Capilla del Salvador**, begun in 1540, the finest of Úbeda's churches, where Cobos is buried.

All the sculpture on the façades of Úbeda is first-class, especially the west front of the Salvador. This is a monument of the time when Spain was in the mainstream of Renaissance ideas, and humanist classicism was still respectable. Note the mythological subjects on the west front and inside the church, and be sure to look under the arch of the main door. Instead of Biblical scenes, it has carved panels of the ancient gods representing the five planets; Phoebus and Diana with the sun and moon; and Hercules, Aeolus, Vulcan and Neptune to represent the four elements. The interior, with its great dome, is worth a look despite a thorough sacking in 1936 (the sacristan lives on the first door on the left of Calle Francisco Cobos, on the north side of the church). Behind El Salvador, the **Hospital de los Honrados** has a delightful open patio—but only because the other half of the building was never completed. South of the plaza, the end of town is only a few blocks away, encompassed by a street called the **Redonda de Miradores**, a quiet spot favoured by small children and goats, with remnants of Úbeda's wall and exceptional views over the Sierra de Cazorla to the east.

Beyond Plaza Vázquez de Molina

Calle Montiel, north of El Salvador, has a few more fine palaces. At the foot of the street, on Plaza 1 de Mayo, is the 13th-century **San Pablo** church, much renovated in the 16th century; inside is an elegant chapel of 1536, the Capilla del Camarero Vago. **San Nicolás de Bari**, further north, was originally a synagogue, though nothing now bears witness to this. It was confiscated in 1492, which has left it with one Gothic door and the other by Vandelvira, who oversaw the reconstruction. On the western outskirts of town, near the bus station on Calle Nueva is Vandelvira's most remarkable building, the **Hospital de Santiago** (*open 9–3 and 4–9*). This huge edifice, recently restored, has been called the 'Escorial of Andalucía'. Both have the same plan, a grid of quadrangles with a church inside. Oddly, both were begun at about the same time, though this one seems to have been started a year earlier, in 1568. Both are supreme examples of the *estilo desornamentado*. The façade here is not as plain as Herrera's; its quirky decoration and clean, angular lines are unique, more like a product of the 20th century than the 16th.

Eating Out

The **★★★★Parador Condestable Dávalos**, Pza. Vázquez de Molina 1, © 95 375 03 45, ✆ 95 375 12 59, in a 16th-century palace with a glassed-in courtyard, is one of the loveliest and most popular of the chain (*16,000 pts for a big double room*). All the beamed ceilings and fireplaces have been preserved and the restaurant is the best in town (which isn't saying a lot), featuring local specialities for around *3500 pts* for a full dinner. Ask to see the ancient wine cellar.

Apart from the Parador, there are few good restaurants in Úbeda. The best is **Cuzco**, Parque Vandelvira 8, © 95 375 34 13, which has local dishes and standard *andaluz* fish and meat menus. It has a *750 pts* menu of the day which includes two courses and wine. Near the Plaza Ayuntamiento, **El Seco**, C/ Corazón de Jesús 8, © 95 379 14 52, is a small dining-room with reasonable food if little atmosphere. There are plenty of characters at the bar in **El**

Gallorojo, C/ Estrella, at the top of Calle Trinidad, during the day and it's a lively place in the evening with excellent tapas and restaurant (*1000–2000 pts*). Also good for tapas and light meals is **Mesón Gabino**, Fuente Seca s/n, ✆ 95 375 42 07.

A smattering of unremarkable places are around Calle Ramón y Cajal. **El Olivo**, Avda. Ramón y Cajal 6, ✆ 95 375 20 92, has average fare at average prices (1500–2000 pts). The restaurant at the **Hostal Seville**, Avda. Ramón y Cajal 20, ✆ 95 375 0612, is good value, and for pre-dinner drinks try the **Bar Palacio** in the courtyard of the Palacio de los Bussianos on Calle Trinidad. The bar scene is fairly advanced in Úbeda. Try **Lupo**, in Plaza de San Pedro with its state-of-the-art interior, or the Gothic **Siglo XV**, which used to be a brothel, on Calle de Muñoz García, Úbeda's liveliest street after dark.

Castellano, as Spanish is properly called, was the first modern language to have a grammar written for it. When a copy was presented to Queen Isabel in 1492, she understandably asked what it was for. 'Your majesty', replied a perceptive bishop, 'language is the perfect instrument of empire'. In the centuries to come, this concise, flexible and expressive language would prove just that: an instrument that would contribute more to Spanish unity than any laws or institutions, while spreading itself effortlessly over much of the New World.

Among other European languages, Spanish is closest to Portuguese and Italian—and of course, Catalan and Gallego. Spanish, however, may have the simplest grammar of any Romance language, and if you know a little of any one of these, you will find much of the vocabulary looks familiar. It's quite easy to pick up a working knowledge of Spanish; but Spaniards speak colloquially and fast, and in Andalucía they do it with a pronounced accent, leaving out half the consonants and adding some

Language

strange sounds all their own. Expressing yourself may prove a little easier than understanding the replies. Spaniards will appreciate your efforts, and when they correct you, they aren't being snooty; they simply feel it's their duty to help you learn. There are dozens of language books and tapes on the market; one particularly good one is *Teach Yourself Spanish*, by Juan Kattán-Ibarra (Hodder & Stoughton, 1984). If you already speak Spanish, note that the Spaniards increasingly use the familiar *tú* instead of *usted* when addressing even complete strangers.

Pronunciation

Pronunciation is phonetic but somewhat difficult for English speakers.

Vowels

a	short *a* as in 'pat'	u	silent after *q* and gue- and gui-;
e	short *e* as in 'set'		otherwise long *u* as in 'flute'
i	as *e* in 'be'	ü	*w* sound, as in 'dwell'
o	between long *o* of 'note' and short *o* of 'hot'	y	at end of word or meaning *and*, as **i**

Dipthongs

ai, ay	as *i* in 'side'	**ei, ey**	as *ey* in 'they'
au	as *ou* in 'sound'	**oi, oy**	as *oy* of 'boy'

Consonants

c	before the vowels *i* and *e*, it's a *castellano* tradition to pronounce it as *th*; many Spaniards and all Latin Americans pronounce it in this case as an *s*
ch	like *ch* in 'church'
d	often becomes *th*, or is almost silent, at end of word
g	before *i* or *e*, pronounced as **j** (*see below*)
h	silent
j	the *ch* in loch—a guttural, throat-clearing *h*
ll	*y* or *ly* as in million
ñ	*ny* as in canyon (the ~ is called a tilde)
q	*k*
r	usually rolled, which takes practice
v	often pronounced as *b*
z	*th*, but *s* in parts of Andalucía

Stress is on the penultimate syllable if the word ends in a vowel, an *n* or an *s*, and on the last syllable if the word ends in any other consonant; exceptions are marked with an accent.

If all this seems difficult, consider that English pronunciation is even worse for Spaniards. Young people in Spain seem to be all madly learning English these days; if your Spanish friends giggle at your pronunciation, get them to try to say *squirrel*.

Practise on some of the place names:

Madrid	ma-DREED	**Trujillo**	troo-HEE-oh
León	lay-OHN	**Jerez**	her-ETH
Sevilla	se-BEE-ah	**Badajóz**	ba-da-HOTH
Cáceres	CAH-ther-es	**Málaga**	MAHL-ah-gah
Cuenca	KWAYN-ka	**Alcázar**	ahl-CATH-ar
Jaén	ha-AIN	**Valladolid**	ba-yah-dol-EED
Sigüenza	sig-WAYN-thah	**Arévalo**	ahr-EB-bah-lo

yes	*sí*	Goodbye	*Adios/*
no	*no*		*Hasta luego*
I don't know	*No sé*	Good morning	*Buenos días*
I don't understand	*No entiendo*	Good afternoon	*Buenas tardes*
Spanish	*español*	Good evening	*Buenas noches*
Do you speak English?	*¿Habla uste*	What is that?	*¿Qué es eso?*
	inglés?	What ...?	*¿Qué ...?*
Does someone here	*¿Hay alguien que*	Who ...?	*¿Quién ...?*
speak English?	*hable inglés?*	Where ...?	*¿Dónde ...?*
Speak slowly	*Hable despacio*	When ...?	*¿Cuándo ...?*
Can you help me?	*¿Puede usted*	Why ...?	*¿Por qué ...?*
	ayudarme?	How ...?	*¿Cómo ...?*
Help!	*¡Socorro!*	How much?	*¿Cuánto/Cuánta?*
please	*por favor*	How many?	*¿Cuántos/*
thank you (very much)	*(muchas) gracias*		*Cuántas?*
you're welcome	*de nada*		
It doesn't matter	*No importa*	I am lost	*Me he perdido*
	Es igual	I am hungry	*Tengo hambre*
all right	*está bien*	I am thirsty	*Tengo sed*
OK	*vale*	I am sorry	*Lo siento*
excuse me	*perdóneme*	I am tired	*Estoy*
Be careful!	*¡Tenga cuidado!*	(man/woman)	*cansado/a*
maybe	*quizá(s)*	I am sleepy	*Tengo sueño*
nothing	*nada*	I am ill	*No siento bien*
It is urgent!	*¡Es urgente!*	Leave me alone	*Déjeme en paz*
How do you do?	*¿Cómo está*	good	*bueno/buena*
	usted?	bad	*malo/mala*
or more familiarly	*¿Cómo estás?*	slow	*despacio*
	¿Qué tal?	fast	*rápido/rápida*
Well, and you?	*¿Bien, y usted?*	big	*grande*
or more familiarly	*¿Bien, y tú?*	small	*pequeño/*
What is your name?	*¿Cómo se llama?*		*pequeña*
or more familiarly	*¿Cómo te llamas?*	hot	*caliente*
My name is ...	*Me llamo...*	cold	*frío/fría*
My number is ...	*Mi nombre es...*		
Hello	*¡Hola!*		

Numbers

one	uno/una	twenty-one	veintiuno
two	dos	thirty	treinta
three	tres	thirty-one	treinta y uno
four	cuatro	forty	cuarenta
five	cinco	forty-one	cuarenta y uno
six	seis	fifty	cincuenta
seven	siete	sixty	sesenta
eight	ocho	seventy	setenta
nine	nueve	eighty	ochenta
ten	diez	ninety	noventa
eleven	once	one hundred	cien
twelve	doce	one hundred and one	ciento-uno
thirteen	trece	five hundred	quinientos
fourteen	catorce	one thousand	mil
fifteen	quince	first	primero
sixteen	dieciséis	second	segundo
seventeen	diecisiete	third	tercero
eighteen	dieciocho	fourth	cuarto
nineteen	diecinueve	fifth	quinto
twenty	veinte	tenth	décimo

Time

What time is it?	¿Qué hora es?	morning	mañana
It is 2 o'clock	Son las dos	afternoon	tarde
… half past 2	… las dos y media	evening	noche
… a quarter past 2	… las dos y cuarto	today	hoy
… a quarter to 3	… las tres menos cuarto	yesterday	ayer
		soon	pronto
noon	mediodía	tomorrow	mañana
midnight	medianoche	now	ahora
month	mes	later	después
week	semana	it is early	está temprano
day	día	it is late	está tarde

Days

Monday	lunes	Friday	viernes
Tuesday	martes	Saturday	sábado
Wednesday	miércoles	Sunday	domingo
Thursday	jueves		

Months

January	*enero*	July	*julio*
February	*febrero*	August	*agosto*
March	*marzo*	September	*septiembre*
April	*abril*	October	*octubre*
May	*mayo*	November	*noviembre*
June	*junio*	December	*diciembre*

Shopping and Sightseeing

I would like...	*Quisiera...*	police station	*comisaría*
Where is/are...?	*¿Dónde está/están...?*	policeman	*policía*
How much is it?	*¿Cuánto vale eso?*	post office	*correos*
open	*abierto*	postage stamp	*sello*
closed	*cerrado*	sea	*mar*
cheap/expensive	*barato/caro*	shop	*tienda*
bank	*banco*	Do you have any change?	*¿Tiene cambio?*
beach	*playa*		
booking/box office	*taquilla*	telephone	*teléfono*
church	*iglesia*	telephone call	*conferencia*
hospital	*hospital*	tobacco shop	*el estanco*
money	*dinero*	supermarket	*supermercado*
museum	*museo*	toilet/toilets	*servicios/aseos*
theatre	*teatro*	men	*señores/ hombres/caballeros*
newspaper (**foreign**)	*periódico (extranjero)*	women	*señoras/damas*
pharmacy	*farmacía*		

Accommodation

Where is the ... hotel?	*¿Dónde está el ... hotel?*	... with 2 beds	*con dos camas*
Do you have a room?	*¿Tiene usted una habitación?*	... with double bed	*con una cama grande*
Can I look at the room?	*¿Podría ver la habitación?*	... with a shower/ bath	*con ducha/baño*
How much is the room per day/ week?	*¿Cuánto cuesta la habitación por día/ semana?*	... for one person/ two people	*para una persona/ dos personas*
		... for one night/ one week	*una noche/ una semana*

Driving

rent	*alquiler*	driver	*conductor, chófer*
car	*coche*	speed	*velocidad*
motorbike/moped	*moto/ciclomotor*	exit	*salida*
bicycle	*bicicleta*	entrance	*entrada*
petrol	*gasolina*	danger	*peligro*
garage	*garaje*	dangerous	*peligroso*
This doesn't work	*Este no funciona*	no parking	*estacionamento prohibido*
road	*carretera*		
motorway	*autopista*	narrow	*estrecha*
Is the road good?	*¿Es buena la carretera?*	give way/yield	*ceda el paso*
		road works	*obras*
breakdown	*avería*		
(international) driving licence	*carnet de conducir (internacional)*		

Note: Most road signs will be in international pictographs

Transport

aeroplane	*avión*	platform	*andén*
airport	*aeropuerto*	port	*puerto*
bus/coach	*autobús/autocar*	seat	*asiento*
bus/railway station	*estación*	ship	*buque/barco/embarcadero*
bus stop	*parada*		
car/automobile	*coche*	ticket	*billete*
customs	*aduana*	train	*tren*

Directions

I want to go to...	*Deseo ir a...*	I want a (return) ticket to...	*Quiero un billete (de ida y vuelta) a*
How can I get to...?	*¿Cómo puedo llegar a...?*		
Where is...?	*¿Dónde está...?*	How much is the fare?	*¿Cuánto cuesta el billete?*
When is the next...?	*¿Cuándo sale el próximo...?*		
		Have a good trip!	*¡Buen viaje!*
What time does it leave (arrive)?	*¿Parte (llega) a qué hora?*	here	*aquí*
		there	*allí*
From where does it leave?	*¿De dónde sale?*	close	*cerca*
		far	*lejos*
Do you stop at ...?	*¿Para en...?*	left	*izquierda*
How long does the trip take?	*¿Cuánto tiempo dura el viaje?*	right	*derecha*
		straight on	*todo recto*

Directions (*cont'd*)

forwards	*adelante*	**south** (n./adj.)	*sur/meridional*
backwards	*hacia atrás*	**east** (n./adj.)	*este/oriental*
up	*arriba*	**west** (n./adj.)	*oeste/occidental*
down	*abajo*	**corner**	*esquina*
north (n./adj.)	*norte/septentri*	**square**	*plaza*
	onal	**street**	*calle*

Eating Out

Hors d'œuvres & Eggs (*Entremeses y Huevos*)

aceitunas	**olives**	*sopa de ajo*	**garlic soup**
alcachofas con	**artichokes with**	*sopa de arroz*	**rice soup**
mahonesa	**mayonnaise**	*sopa de espárragos*	**asparagus soup**
ancas de rana	**frog's legs**	*sopa de fideos*	**noodle soup**
caldo	**broth**	*sopa de garbanzos*	**chickpea soup**
entremeses	**assorted hors**	*sopa de lentejas*	**lentil soup**
variados	**d'œuvres**	*sopa de verduras*	**vegetable soup**
huevos de	**baked eggs in**	*tortilla*	**Spanish**
flamenco	**tomato sauce**		**omelette,**
gambas pil pil	**shrimp in hot**		**with potatoes**
	garlic sauce	*tortilla a la*	**French omelette**
gazpacho	**cold soup**	*francesa*	
huevos al plato	**fried eggs**		
huevos revueltos	**scrambled eggs**		

Fish (*Pescados*)

acedías	**small plaice**	*boquerones*	**anchovies**
adobo	**fish marinated**	*caballa*	**mackerel**
	in white wine	*calamares*	**squid**
almejas	**clams**	*cangrejo*	**crab**
anchoas	**anchovies**	*centollo*	**spider crab**
anguilas	**eels**	*chanquetes*	**whitebait**
angulas	**baby eels**	*chipirones*	**cuttlefish**
ástaco	**crayfish**	*... en su tinta*	**... in its own ink**
atún	**tuna fish**	*chirlas*	**baby clams**
bacalao	**codfish (usually**	*dorado, lubina*	**sea bass**
	dried)	*escabeche*	**pickled or**
besugo	**sea bream**		**marinated fish**
bogavante	**lobster**	*gambas*	**prawns**
bonito	**tunny**	*langosta*	**lobster**

Fish (*cont'd*)

langostinos	giant prawns	platija	plaice
lenguado	sole	pulpo	octopus
mariscos	shellfish	rape	anglerfish
mejillones	mussels	raya	skate
merluza	hake	rodaballo	turbot
mero	grouper	salmón	salmon
navajas	razor-shell clams	salmonete	red mullet
ostras	oysters	sardinas	sardines
pejesapo	monkfish	trucha	trout
percebes	barnacles	veneras	scallops
pescadilla	whiting	zarzuela	fish stew
pez espada	swordfish		

Meat and Fowl (*Carnes y Aves*)

albóndigas	meatballs	lomo	pork loin
asado	roast	morcilla	blood sausage
bistec	beefsteak	paloma	pigeon
buey	ox	pato	duck
callos	tripe	pavo	turkey
cerdo	pork	perdiz	partridge
chorizo	spiced sausage	pinchitos	spicy mini-kebabs
chuletas	chops		
cochinillo	sucking pig	pollo	chicken
conejo	rabbit	rabo/cola de toro	bull's tail cooked with onions and tomatoes
corazón	heart		
cordero	lamb		
faisán	pheasant	riñones	kidneys
fiambres	cold meats	salchicha	sausage
filete	fillet	salchichón	salami
hígado	liver	sesos	brains
jabalí	wild boar	solomillo	sirloin steak
jamón de York	raw cured ham	ternera	veal
jamón serrano	baked ham		
lengua	tongue		

Note: *potajes, cocidos, guisados, estofados, fabadas* and *cazuelas* are various kinds of stew.

Vegetables (*Verduras y Legumbres*)

alcachofas	artichokes	arroz marinera	rice with saffron and seafood
apio	celery		
arroz	rice	berenjena	aubergine (eggplant)

Vegetables (*cont'd*)

cebolla	onion	lentejas	lentils
champiñones	mushrooms	patatas	potatoes
col, repollo	cabbage	(fritas/salteadas)	(fried/sautéed)
coliflor	cauliflower	(al horno)	(baked)
endibias	endives	pepino	cucumber
ensalada	salad	pimiento	pepper
espárragos	asparagus	puerros	leeks
espinacas	spinach	remolachas	beetroots (beets)
garbanzos	chickpeas	setas	Spanish
guisantes	peas		mushrooms
judías (verdes)	French beans	zanahorias	carrots
lechuga	lettuce		

Fruits (*Frutas*)

albaricoque	apricot	manzana	apple
almendras	almonds	melocotón	peach
cerezas	cherries	melón	melon
ciruelas	plums	naranja	orange
ciruela pasa	prune	pera	pear
frambuesas	raspberries	piña	pineapple
fresas	strawberries	plátano	banana
(con nata)	(with cream)	pomelo	grapefruit
higos	figs	sandía	watermelon
limón	lemon	uvas	grapes

Desserts (*Postres*)

arroz con leche	rice pudding	pajama	flan with ice
bizcocho/pastel/torta	cake		cream
blanco y negro	ice cream and	pasteles	pastries
	coffee float	queso	cheese
flan	crème caramel	requesón	cottage cheese
galletas	biscuits (cookies)	tarta de frutas	fruit pie
helados	ice creams	turrón	nougat

Drinks (*Bebidas*)

agua con hielo	water with ice	café (con leche)	coffee (with milk)
agua mineral	mineral water	cava	Spanish champagne
(sin/con gas)	(without/with fizz)	cerveza	beer
batido de leche	milkshake	chocolate	chocolate

Drinks (*cont'd*)

jerez	**sherry**	*vino (tinto, rosado blanco)*	**wine (red, rosé, , white)**
granizado	**slush, iced squash**		
leche	**milk**	*zumo de naranja*	**orange juice**
té (con limón)	**tea (with lemon)**		

Other Words

(olive) oil	*aceite (de oliva)*	**sandwich (made from English-type bread)**	*sandwich*
marinade	*adobo*	**toast**	*tostada*
garlic	*ajo*	**vinegar**	*vinagre*
sugar	*azúcar*		
sandwich (made from French-type bread)	*bocadillo*	**breakfast**	*desayuno*
savoury pie	*empanada*	**lunch**	*almuerzo/comida*
ice	*hielo*	**dinner**	*cena*
butter	*mantequilla*	**knife**	*cuchillo*
marmalade	*mermelada*	**fork**	*tenedor*
honey	*miel*	**spoon**	*cuchara*
bread	*pan*	**cup**	*taza*
roll	*panecillo*	**plate**	*plato*
ground pepper	*pimienta*	**glass**	*vaso*
(without) salt	*(sin) sal*	**napkin**	*servilleta*
sauce	*salsa*	**table**	*mesa*

Restaurant Vocabulary

menu	*carta/menú*	**Can I see the menu, please?**	*Déme el menú, por favor*
bill/check	*cuenta*		
change	*cambio*	**Do you have a wine list?**	*¿Hay una lista de vinos?*
set meal	*menú del día*		
waiter/waitress	*camarero/a*	**Can I have the bill (check), please?**	*La cuenta, por favor*
Do you have a table?	*¿Tiene una mesa?*		
... for one/two?	*¿... para uno/dos?*	**Can I pay by credit card?**	*¿Puedo pagar con tarjeta de crédito?*

ajaracas	trellis work brick design, often decorating *mudéjar* apses
ajmez	in Moorish architecture, an arched double window
alameda	tree-lined promenade
albarrani	projected tower joined to a main wall by a bridge
alcazaba	Moorish fortress
alcázar	Moorish fortified palace
Almohads	people of Berber origin and Islamic faith, who ruled Spain from about 1147 to 1213
Almoravids	people of Berber origin and Islamic faith, who founded an empire in North Africa that spread over much of Spain in the 11th century
arabesque	decoration in the form of scrolling or interlacing flowers and leaves
arrabal	quarter of a Moorish city
artesonado	*mudéjar*-style carved wooden ceilings, panels or screens
ayuntamiento	city hall
azulejo	painted glazed tiles, popular in *mudéjar* work and later architecture (from the Arabic *az-zulaiy*, a piece of terracotta)
banderillero	bullfighter's assistant who plants *banderillas* (sharp darts) into the base of the bull's neck in order to weaken the animal
barrio	city quarter or neighbourhood
bodega	wine bar, cellar or warehouse
bóveda	vault
calle	street
capilla mayor	seat of the high altar in a cathedral
capilla real	royal chapel
Carmen	Carmelite convent, or *morisco* villas with pleasure gardens outside Granada
carretera	main road
cartuja	Carthusian monastery
castillo	castle
castrum	Roman military camp
Churrigueresque	florid baroque style of the late 17th and early 18th centuries in the style of José Churriguera (1665–1725), Spanish architect and sculptor
ciudad	town or city
ciudadela	citadel

Glossary

converso	Jews who converted to Christianity
coro	the walled-in choir in a Spanish cathedral
coro alto	raised choir
corregidor	chief magistrate
corrida de troos	bullfight
cortijo	Andalucían country house

cúpula	cupola; dome or rounded vault forming a roof or ceiling
custodia	tabernacle, where sacramental vessels are kept
diputación	seat of provincial government
embalse	reservoir
ermita	hermitage
esgrafiado	style of painting, or etching designs in stucco, on a façade
estilo desornamentado	austere, heavy Renaissance style inaugurated by Felipe II's architect, Juan de Herrera; sometimes described as Herreran
fandango	traditional dance and song, greatly influenced by the gypsies of Andalucía
feria	major festival or market, often an occasion for bullfights
finca	farm, country house or estate
fonda	modest hotel, from the Arabic *funduq*, or inn
fuero	exemption or privilege of a town or region under medieval Spanish law
grandee	select member of Spain's highest nobility
hammam	Moorish bath
Herreran	see *estilo desornamentado*
hidalgo	literally 'son of somebody'—the lowest level of the nobility, just good enough for a coat of arms
homage tower	the tallest tower of fortification, sometimes detached from the wall
humilladero	calvary, or stations of the Cross along a road outside of town
Isabelline Gothic	late 15th-century style, roughly corresponding to English perpendicular
Judería	Jewish quarter
junta	council, or specifically, the regional government
khan	inn for merchants
Kufic	angular style of Arabic calligraphy originating in the city of Kufa in Mesopotamia, often used as architectural ornamentation
lonja	merchants' exchange
madrasa	Muslim theological school, usually located near a mosque
majolica	type of porous pottery glazed with bright metallic oxides
mantilla	silk or lace scarf or shawl, worn by women to cover their head and shoulders
maqsura	elevated platform usually with grills
matador	the principal bullfighter, who finally kills the bull
medina	walled centre of a Moorish city
mercado	market
mezquita	mosque
mihrab	prayer niche facing Mecca, often elaborately decorated in a mosque
mirador	scenic viewpoint or belvedere
monterías	hunting scenes (in art)
moriscos	Muslims who submitted to Christianization to remain in al-Andalus after the Reconquista

mozárabes	Christians under Muslim rule in Moorish Spain
mudéjar	Moorish-influenced architecture, characterized by decorative use of bricks and ceramics; Spain's 'national style' in 12th–16th centuries
moufflon	wild, short-fleeced mountain sheep.
muqarnas	hanging masonry effect created through multiple use of support elements
ogival	pointed (arches)
parador	state-owned hotel, often a converted historic building
paseo	promenade, or an evening walk along a promenade
patio	central courtyard of a house or public building
picador	bullfighter on horseback, who goads and wounds the bull with a pica or short lance in the early stages of a bullfight in order to weaken the animal
plateresque	heavily ornamented 16th-century Gothic style
plaza	town square
plaza de toros	bullring
plaza mayor	main square at the centre of many Spanish cities, often almost totally enclosed and arcaded
posada	inn or lodging house
pronunciamiento	military coup
pueblo	village
puente	bridge
puerta	gate or portal
Reconquista	the Christian Reconquest of Moorish Spain beginning in 718 and completed in 1492 by the Catholic Kings
reja	iron grille, either decorative in a church or covering the exterior window of a building
retablo	carved or painted altarpiece
Los Reyes Católicos	The Catholic Kings, Isabella (Isabel) and Ferdinand (Fernando)
romería	pilgrimage, usually on a saint's feast day
sagrario	reliquary chapel
sala capitular	chapterhouse
sillería	choir stall
souk	open-air marketplace in Muslim countries
stele	stone slab marking a grave or displaying an inscription
taifa	small Moorish kingdom; especially one of the so-called Party Kingdoms which sprang up in Spain following the 1031 fall of the caliph of Córdoba
taracea	inlaid wood in geometric patterns
torero	bullfighter, especially one on foot
torre	tower
vega	cultivated plain or fertile river valley

General and Travel

Baird, David, *Inside Andalusia* (Lookout Publications). Background reading. Glossy, full of history and anecdote.

Brenan, Gerald, *The Face of Spain* (Penguin, 1987). An account of his journey through central and southern Spain in the spring of 1949.

Chetwode, Penelope, *Two Middle-Aged Ladies in Andalusia*. A delightful bosom-heaving burro-back look at the region.

Elms, Robert, *Spain A Portrait After the General* (Heinemann, 1992). Incisive, witty, honest look at the new Spain from one of Britain's foremost young travel writers.

Ford, Richard, *Gatherings from Spain* (Everyman). A boiled-down version of the all-time classic travel book *A Handbook for Travellers in Spain*, written in 1845. Hard to find but worth the trouble.

Hooper, John, *The Spaniards* (Penguin, 1987). A comprehensive account of contemporary Spanish life and politics. Well done.

Jacobs, Michael, *A Guide to Andalusia* (Viking). Informative and well-researched volume on history, culture and sights.

Lee, Laurie, *As I Walked Out One Midsummer Morning* and *A Rose for Winter*. Very well written adventures of a young man in Spain in 1936, and his return 20 years later.

History

Brenan, Gerald, *The Spanish Labyrinth* (Cambridge, 1943). Origins of the Civil War.

Castro, Américo, *The Structure of Spanish History* (E L King, 1954). A remarkable interpretation of Spain's history, published in exile during the Franco years.

Elliott, J H, *Imperial Spain 1469–1714* (Pelican, 1983). Elegant proof that much of the best writing these days is in the field of history.

Gibson, Ian, *The Assassination of Federico García Lorca* (Penguin, 1983).

Mitchell, David, *The Spanish Civil War* (Granada, 1982). Anecdotal; wonderful photographs.

O'Callaghan, J F, *History of Medieval Spain* (Cornell University, 1983).

Thomas, Hugh, *The Spanish Civil War* (Penguin, 1977). The best general work.

Watt, W H, and Cachia, P, *A History of Islamic Spain* (Edinburgh University Press, 1977).

Art and Literature

Brenan, Gerald, *The Literature of the Spanish People* (Cambridge, 1951).

Burckhardt, Titus, *Moorish Culture in Spain* (Allen and Unwin). Indispensable for understanding the world of al-Andalus.

Further Reading

García Lorca, Federico, *Three Tragedies* and *Five Plays Comedies and Tragi-comedies* (Penguin).

Goodwin, Godfrey, *Islamic Spain* (Penguin, 1991). From the informative 'Architectural Guides for Travellers' series.

Irving, Washington, *Tales of the Alhambra* and *The Conquest of Granada* (London, 1986).

BC

*c.*50,000	Earliest traces of man in Andalucía.
*c.*25,000	Palaeolithic Proto-Spaniards occupy and decorate region's caves.
*c.*7000	Arrival of Iberians, probably from North Africa.
*c.*2300	Bronze-Age settlement at Los Millares, largest in Europe.
*c.*1100	**Phoenicians** found Cádiz.
*c.*800	Celts from over the Pyrenees join the Iberians; period of the kingdom of **Tartessos** in Andalucía.
*c.*636	**Greeks** found trading colony near Málaga.
*c.*500	**Carthage** conquers Tartessos.
241	Carthage loses **First Punic War** to Rome.
227	Rome and Carthage sign treaty, assigning lands south of the Ebro to Carthage.
219	**Second Punic War** breaks out when Hannibal besieges Roman ally Sagonte.
218	Hannibal takes his elephants and the war to Italy.
211–206	**Romans** under Proconsul Scipio Africanus take the war back to Spain, defeating Carthage.
206	Founding of Itálica, a Roman veterans' colony, near Seville.
55	The elder Seneca born in Cordoba.
46	During the ups and downs of the wars and colonizations of Spain, Caesar intervenes, riding from Rome to Obulco (60km from Cordoba) in 27 days; founds veterans' colony at Osuna.
27	Octavian divides Iberian peninsula into Interior Spain, Lusitania (Portugal) and Further Spain, soon better known as Bætica (Andalucía).

AD

39	Roman poet Lucan born in Cordoba.
50	All of Spain finally conquered by Romans, who lay out the first road network.
54	Trajan, future Roman emperor, born at Itálica.
70	Romans under Titus destroy the Temple in Jerusalem; in the subsequent diaspora thousands of Jews end up in Spain.
76	Hadrian, Trajan's successor in 117, born at Itálica.
306	Council of Iliberis (Elvira, near Granada) consolidates the Christianization of Spain, votes for the celibacy of priests and also bans Christians from marrying pagans.
409–28	**Vandals** vandalize Bætica and (probably) change its name to Vandalusia.
478	**Visigoths**, followers of the Arian heresy, control most of Spain, including Andalucía.
554	Byzantine Emperor Justinian sends troops to take sides in Visigoth civil war, and overstays his welcome.

Chronology

573	King Leovigild of the Visigoths chases the Greeks out of their last footholds in Andalucía.
589	Leovigild's son, Reccared, converts to Catholicism.
602–35	Writings of St Isidore, Bishop of Seville, which provide main link between the ancient and medieval worlds.
711	**Arabs** and **Berbers** under Tariq ibn-Ziyad defeat Roderick, the last Visigoth king.
718	Pelayo, in Asturias, defeats Muslims at Covadonga, marking the official beginning of the Reconquista.
756	**Abd ar-Rahman**, of the Ummayyad dynasty, first emir of al-Andalus begins the Great Mosque of Cordoba.
844	**Abd ar-Rahman II** begins the Alcázar in Seville.
880–917	Revolt against the Ummayyads by Ibn-Hafsun, at Bobastro.
912–76	**Abd ar-Rahman III** declares himself caliph of Cordoba and begins the magnificent palace-city of Madinat az-Zahra.
977	Last enlargements of the Great Mosque by al-Mansur.
994	Birth of Ibn-Hazm of Cordoba (Abernhazam; d. 1064), greatest scholar of century and author of the famous treatise on love, *The Ring of the Dove*.
1003	Birth of the love poet Ibn-Zaydun in Cordoba (d. 1070).
1008	Caliphate starts to unravel.
1013	Berbers destroy Madinat az-Zahra.
1031	Caliphate abolished as al-Andalus dissolves into factions of the Party Kings.
1085	**Alfonso VI** of Castile and El Cid capture Toledo from the Muslims.
1086	*Taifa* kings summon aid of the Berber Almoravids.
1105	Birth of philosopher Ibn-Tufayl (Abubacer) in Guadix, author of the charming narrative romance *Hayy ibn-Yaqzan* (The Awakening of the Soul), one of the masterworks of al-Andalus.
1110	**Almoravids** gobble up the *taifa* kingdoms.
1126	Birth of Ibn-Rushd in Cordoba, philosopher and commentator on Aristotle, better known in the west as Averroës (d. 1198).
1135	**Alfonso VII** of Castile and León takes the title of Emperor of Spain.
1145	Uprisings against the Almoravids.
1172	**Almohads** conquer Seville, rounding off the defeat of the Almoravids.
1195	Completion of La Giralda in Seville.
1212	Alfonso VII's victory at Las Navas de Tolosa opens the gate to al-Andalus.
1231	Muhammad ibn-Yusuf ibn-Nasr carves out a small realm around Jaén.
1236	**Fernando III** ('the Saint') captures Cordoba.
1238	Muhammad ibn-Yusuf ibn-Nasr takes Granada, founding the Nasrid dynasty, and begins construction of the Alhambra.
1248	Fernando III takes Seville with the help of his vassal, Muhammad ibn-Yusef ibn-Nasr.
1262	**Alfonso X** ('the Wise') picks up Cádiz.
1292	**Sancho IV** takes Tarifa.

1309	Guzmán el Bueno seizes Gibraltar.
1333	**Alfonso XI** loses Gibraltar to the king of Granada.
1350–69	Reign of **Pedro the Cruel** of Castile.
1415	Ceuta is captured by Portuguese, though it remains in Spanish hands after the division of the two kingdoms.
1462	**Enrico IV** gets Gibraltar back for Castile.
1479	**Isabella** and **Ferdinand** (Isabel and fernando) unite their kingdoms of Castile and Aragon.
1480	Spanish Inquisition sets up a branch office in Seville.
1492	Ferdinand and Isabella complete the Reconquista with the capture of Granada and expel Jews from Spain; Columbus sets off from Seville to discover the New World.
1500	First Revolt of the Alpujarras.
1516	Birth of lyric poet Luis de Góngora in Cordoba.
1516–56	Isabella and Ferdinand's grandson becomes King **Carlos I**.
1519	Carlos is promoted and becomes Holy Roman Emperor **Charles V**.
1528	Sculptor Pietro Torrigiano dies in the Inquisition's prison in Seville.
1556–98	Reign of Carlos's bureaucratic son, **Felipe II**.
1568	Felipe II's intolerance leads to the Second Revolt of the Alpujarras.
1580	Seville largest city in Spain, with population of 85,000.
1578–1621	Reign of Felipe's rapacious son, **Felipe III**.
1599	Diego Velázquez born in Seville (d. 1660).
1609–14	Felipe III forces half a million Muslims to move to North Africa.
1617	Murillo born in Seville (d. 1682).
1621–65	Reign of **Felipe IV**, chiefly remembered through Velázquez's portraits.
1627	Birth of Sevillen libertine Don Miguel de Mañara, believed to be the original Don Juan Tenorio of Tirso de Molina (the Don Giovanni of Mozart).
1630	Madrid becomes the largest city in Spain.
1649	Plague leaves one out of three people dead in Seville.
1665–1700	Reign of the weak and deformed **Carlos II**, last of the Spanish Habsburgs.
1700–46	Louis XIV exports his brand of Bourbon to Spain, in the form of his grandson **Felipe V**. The danger of Spain and France becoming united under a single ruler leads to the **War of the Spanish Succession**.
1704	Anglo-Dutch fleet, under the auspices of Charles of Austria, captures Gibraltar.
1713	The Spanish cede Gibraltar to Britain under the Treaty of Utrecht.
1726	Spain tries in vain to regain the Rock.
1746–59	Reign of **Fernando VI**.
1757	Completion of Seville's tobacco factory, where Carmen would work.
1759–88	Reign of **Carlos III**.
1779–83	The Great Seige of Gibraltar.
1783	Treaty of Versailles confirms British possession of Gibraltar.
1788–1808	Reign of the pathetic **Carlos IV**, caricatured by Goya.

1808–13	The installation by Napoleon of his brother, Joseph Bonaparte, as king leads to war with France.
1814–33	End of Peninsula War and reinstatement of the Bourbon king, **Fernando VII**; his repeal of the Salic law and the succession of his daughter as **Isabel II** (1833–70) leads to the Carlist wars during her troubled reign.
1830	So many English winter in Málaga that they need their own cemetery.
1832	Washington Irving publishes *Tales of the Alhambra*.
1870–85	Reign of **Alfonso XII**.
1876	Manuel de Falla born in Cádiz (d. 1946).
1881	Pablo Picasso born in Málaga; Nobel-prize winning poet Juan Ramón Jiménez born in Moguer de la Frontera (d. 1958).
1886–1931	Reign of **Alfonso XIII**, who abdicated in favour of a successor who was to become king 'when Spain judges it opportune'.
1893	Andrea Segovia born near Jaén.
1898	Birth of Federico Garcia Lorca near Granada (d. 1936).
1920	Ibero-American Exposition in Seville gets a disappointing turnout.
1936–9	**Civil War**.
1940	Hitler tries to get Spain to join Axis by promising to help Spain conquer Gibraltar, but **Franco** says no.
1953	First economic–military cooperation between Spain and the USA.
1956	Spain ends its protectorate in Morocco, but keeps Ceuta and Melilla.
1962	Franco's Minister of Tourism gives go ahead for development of the Costa del Sol.
1966	An American bomber over Palomares collides with another plane and drops four nuclear bombs.
1975	Death of Franco; **Juan Carlos**, grandson of Alfonso XIII crowned king of Spain.
1982	Felipe González of Seville elected prime minister.
1983	Andalucía becomes an autonomous province.
1985	Frontier between Gibraltar and Spain opens.
1986	Spain and Portugal join the EC.
1992	International Exposition in Seville to commemorate the 500th anniversary of Columbus's departure from Huelva to the New World.
1997	The political troubles of the north reach southern Spain, with a car bomb in Granada, blamed on the Basque Eta group.
1998	In January, a councillor and his wife are shot dead in Seville. Five Eta members are arrested in Seville in March in a safe house where 600kg of explosives are also found.

Note: Page numbers in **bold** indicate main references to subject

Page numbers in *italics* refer to maps

Index

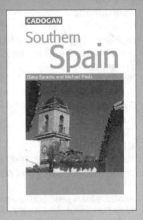

Also Available from Cadogan Guides...

Country Guides

Antarctica
Belize
Central Asia
China: The Silk Routes
Egypt
France: Southwest France;
  Dordogne, Lot & Bordeaux
France: Southwest France;
  Gascony & the Pyrenees
France: Brittany
France: The Loire
France: The South of France
France: Provence
France: the Côte d'Azur
Germany: Bavaria
India
India: South India
India: Goa
Ireland
Ireland: Southwest Ireland
Ireland: Northern Ireland
Italy
Italy: The Bay of Naples and Southern Italy
Italy: Lombardy, Milan and the Italian Lakes
Italy: Venetia and the Dolomites
Italy: Tuscany and Umbria
Japan
Morocco
Portugal
Portugal: The Algarve
Scotland
Scotland's Highlands and Islands
South Africa, Swaziland and Lesotho
Spain
Spain: Southern Spain
Spain: Northern Spain
Syria & Lebanon
Tunisia
Turkey
Western Turkey
Yucatán and Southern Mexico
Zimbabwe, Botswana and Namibia

City Guides

Amsterdam
Brussels, Bruges, Ghent & Antwerp
Edinburgh
Florence, Siena, Pisa & Lucca
Italy: Three Cities—Rome, Florence, Venice
Italy: Three Cities—Rome, Naples, Capri
Italy: Three Cities—Venice, Padua, Verona
Spain: Three Cities—Granada, Seville,
  Cordoba
London
Madrid
Manhattan
Moscow & St Petersburg
Paris
Prague
Rome
Venice

Island Guides

Caribbean and Bahamas
NE Caribbean; The Leeward Is.
SE Caribbean; The Windward Is.
Jamaica & the Caymans

Greek Islands
Crete
Mykonos, Santorini & the Cyclades
Rhodes & the Dodecanese
Corfu & the Ionian Islands

Madeira & Porto Santo
Malta
Sicily

Plus...

Southern Africa on the Wild Side
Bugs, Bites & Bowels
Travel by Cargo Ship
London Markets

Available from good bookshops or via, in the UK, **Grantham Book Services**, Isaac Newton Way, Alma Park Industrial Estate, Grantham NG31 9SD, ✆ (01476) 541 080, ✉ 541 061; and in North America from **The Globe Pequot Press**, 6, Business Park Road, Old Saybrook, Connecticut 06475-0833, ✆ (800) 243 0495, ✉ 820 2329.